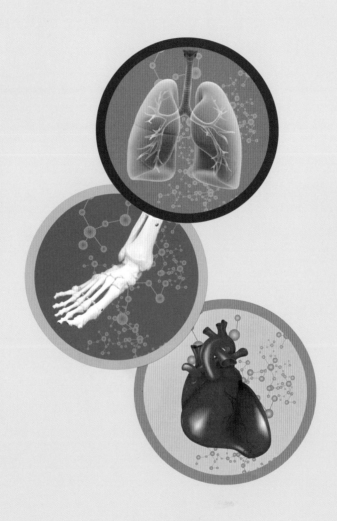

NATIONAL GEOGRAPHIC KiDS

ULTIMATE BODY-PEDIA

AN **AMAZING** INSIDE-OUT TOUR OF THE HUMAN BODY

CHRISTINA WILSDON,
PATRICIA DANIELS,
AND JEN AGRESTA

SELECT MEDICAL ILLUSTRATIONS
BY CYNTHIA TURNER

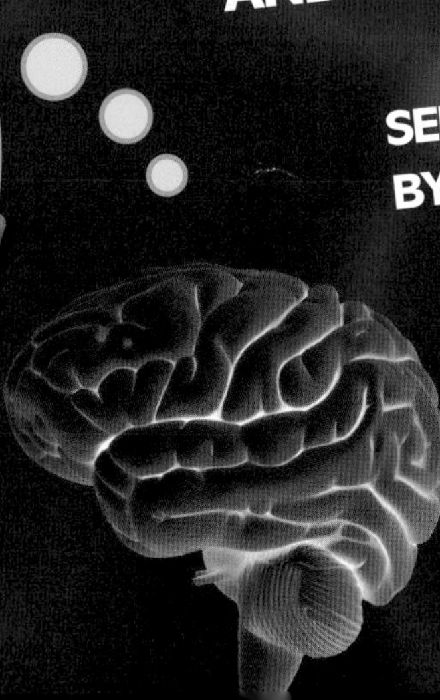

NATIONAL GEOGRAPHIC
Washington, D.C.

CONTENTS

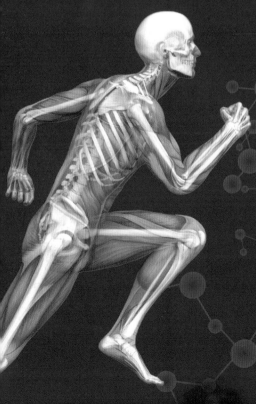

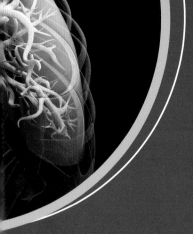

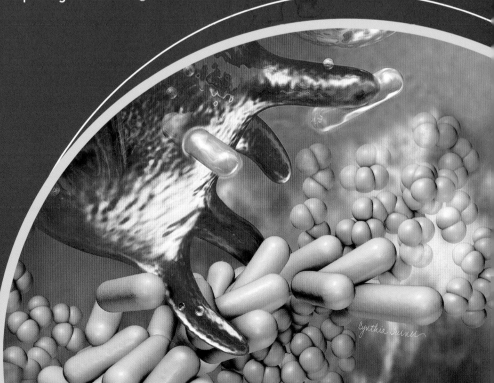

INTRODUCTION

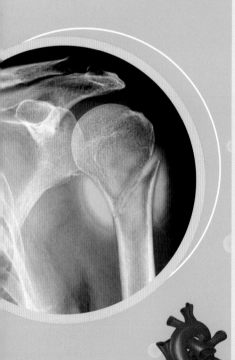

***Ultimate Bodypedia* is all about the amazing, fascinating HUMAN BODY!** It's easy to forget just how incredible the body is, because after all we hang out with our own bodies all the time—so we tend to take them for granted. But if you stop and think about everything your body does, you just might consider how great it is (and you are). For starters, isn't it amazing that you can read this book? It's also amazing that people invented words and ink, paper and cameras, and all the other things that went into making *Ultimate Bodypedia*. All these inventions were devised by the human brain. Your brain, the control center of your body, also enables you to move your body so you can throw a ball, ride a bike, draw a picture, climb a tree, or sing "Happy Birthday." All the while, your body's doing a million things that you're not even aware of—like digesting breakfast, growing new skin, and carrying oxygen to cells from head to toe and ear to ear!

Researching this book was like traveling through a different country, stopping to marvel at new sights and look at old ones with fresh eyes. For instance, as a science writer, I already knew many things about bones, but I didn't know that a young boy who washed ashore after a shipwreck in the mid-1700s helped discover better ways to set broken bones when he grew up. (You can read more about this boy, Evan Thomas, on page 58.) I also learned that today's researchers are experimenting with using 3-D printers to make materials that can be put into damaged joints to help them grow and heal!

As an adult, I'm lucky to blend my love of science with my love of reading and research, which has led me to writing such books as this one. I hope you will enjoy exploring the marvels and mysteries of the human body. Maybe someday you will discover something new and important about how the body functions—and even how to fix it when something goes amiss. There is a world of discovery waiting inside you as well as all around you!

—Christina Wilsdon
Science writer and
co-author of *Ultimate Bodypedia*

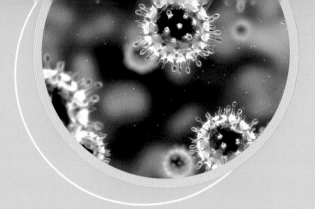
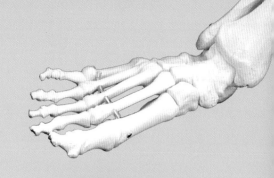

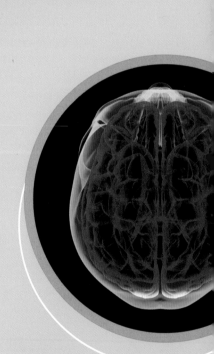

Since I can remember I've been fascinated by how our bodies respond to the world around us. I was always curious why people had different color eyes or why my sister and I had the exact same laugh.

From the moment we wake up in the morning and even while we are asleep, our body and brain are working to make sure we have what we need to be healthy and happy. You may think the newest cell phone that lets you text your friends while playing your favorite music is all that (and it is), but the human body is one of the most amazing and complicated machines on the planet. While technology can do really cool things, the human body and brain are what invented and built those amazing technologies through the centuries, including cell phones.

I was one of those kids who loved learning about how things worked or why things worked a certain way. That passion and curiosity led me to the field of teaching so I could share the hows and whys that I've learned with others. I love teaching anatomy and physiology because it allows me to share the enthusiasm I have for biology with hundreds of college students every year. A lot of my students started out as curious kids, too. It's always exciting for me to see my students go on to work in research in fields like genetics (studying our DNA and one day possibly fixing broken genes), neurophysiology (studying our brain and neurons and possibly curing spinal cord injuries), and many other exciting areas of science.

I had a wonderful time reviewing *Ultimate Bodypedia*! It is such a great book because it tells all about how the human body works with vivid photos and illustrations that really help answer a lot of questions I would have asked as a curious kid—and that you will likely want answered, too. There is so much for you to discover, and I hope you enjoy learning about your awesome body, and finding out, at the same time, what makes you so special.

—Tammatha O'Brien, Ph.D.
Human Biology lecturer
University of Maryland, College Park

Did you know the **human brain** is **wrinkly**?

Did you know your **foot** contains **26 bones?**

Did you know you have **trillions** of cells in your body?

8

Did you know you can get **sunburn** in the **winter,** not just the summer?

Did you know that one lung is **smaller** than the other?

Did you know your heart beats about **100,000 times** a day?

9

HOORAY FOR HUMANS!

CHAPTER

1

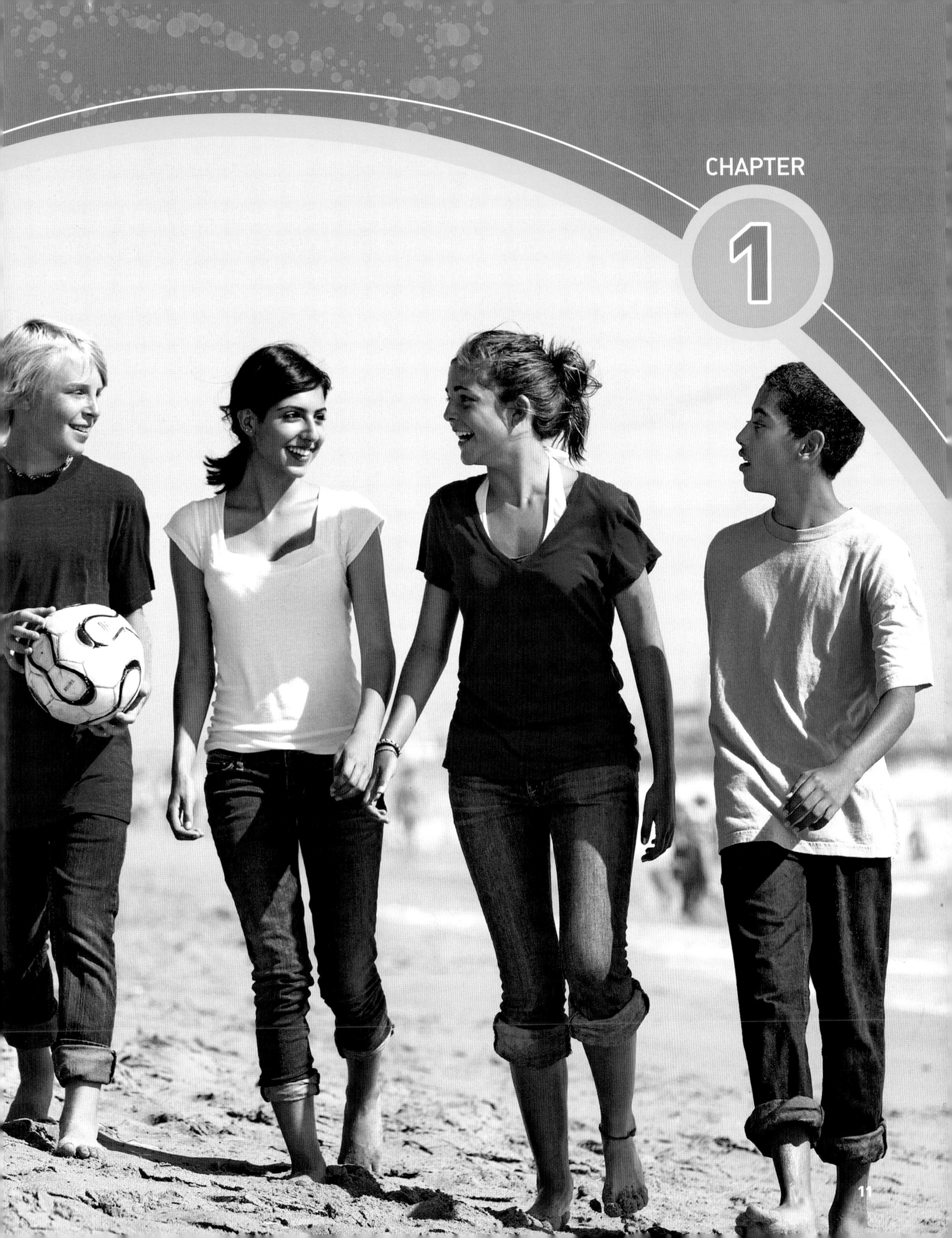

INTRODUCING
AMAZING YOU!

You are one of a kind—a truly special and unique being. Nobody else in the world is exactly like you!

You also belong to a one-of-a-kind species, or type of living thing. All species are wonderful in some way—think of an elephant, a dog, a duck, a honeybee—but no other species can do all the complex things that humans can.

Humans can invent and build an enormous variety of things, from mousetraps and matches to submarines and computers. We have also invented languages and alphabets so we can share information with each other—even across continents and centuries.

Long ago, our curiosity and ability to invent things helped us figure out how to use fire, grow food, and travel far, across lands and oceans. Today, those same traits help us explore our world, our universe, and ourselves. And we couldn't do any of it without the human body.

MARVELOUS MAMMALS

Scientists place living things into different categories. This organizing system is called "classification." Humans are classified as mammals, which are animals that make milk for their young. Mammals are also the only animals that grow hair. Humans additionally are in a mammal group known as the primates—a group that includes gorillas, orangutans, gibbons, and chimpanzees.

Bet you didn't know

A chimpanzee is more closely related to a human than it is to a gorilla. Humans and chimps share more than 96 percent of the same genes.

Standing shoulder-to-shoulder, the entire world's **population** could fit within the 500 square miles (1,300 sq km) of Los Angeles, California, U.S.A.!

13

ADD IT UP

WORLD POPULATION

YEARS		
1960	🧍🧍🧍	3 billion
2000	🧍🧍🧍🧍🧍🧍	6 billion
2050	🧍🧍🧍🧍🧍🧍🧍🧍🧍	9 billion

🧍 = 1 BILLION

In 1960, the human population was about 3 billion. By 2000, it was about 6 billion—twice as many people! The current human population is about 7 billion. It's expected to climb above 9 billion by 2050.

PEOPLE POWER

Can you leap like a deer? Climb like a monkey? Dive as deep as a whale or run as fast as a cheetah? Not likely! These animals have bodies specially formed, or adapted, to leaping, climbing, diving, and running. Many animals can perform amazing physical feats that we can't.

And yet—the human body is still pretty awesome. Your hands and fingers, for example, are just right for holding and using tools. Think of all the things you do with your hands in just one day! You also stand up straight and walk on two legs. That leaves your hands and arms free to carry objects and build things. On top of that upright body of yours is the amazing, thinking, creative human brain.

Thanks to that brain, humans—who are not as strong or as fast as many other animals—have been able to create machines that make us stronger and faster than any other living creature. Unlike many animals, we are also able to make clothes, tools, and other things that help us live in a wide variety of places, from hot and wet rain forests to cold and dry polar lands.

Your **brain** uses just as much power as a ten-watt **lightbulb.**

MIND OVER MATTER

Your brain and nerves use electrical signals to send messages throughout your body so that you can move, think, and feel. Scientists are now researching ways to tap into those electrical signals to help people who can't move their arms or legs due to an illness or injury—a condition known as paralysis. This technology is called a brain-computer interface (BCI for short). It allows people to make robotic devices move, with a computer's help, simply by thinking about the motions involved.

Someday, it may become common for people to use their brainpower alone to direct a computer to perform.

SEEING INSIDE

It's simple to study your outside. You can easily see most of yourself just by looking at your body, and you can see your face by looking in a mirror. If you have two mirrors, you can also study the back of your head. But seeing *inside* your body? That's not easy at all!

For thousands of years, people have wondered about the body parts, called organs, inside them. They studied the bodies of people who died and tried to figure out what different organs did. Ancient Egyptians, for example, studied the lungs and liver as they prepared the dead for burial in tombs.

We've come a long way since then, as you can see on the time line below. We now use technology to see inside the body without operating on it (or without waiting for someone to die).

- **LATE 1800s:** Discovery of x-rays, which were soon used to take pictures of bones
- **1950s:** Invention of ultrasound machines, which use sound waves to see organs
- **1970s:** Invention of computed tomography (CT) scanning, which uses special x-rays and computers to see organs and bones
- **1980s:** Invention of magnetic resonance imaging (MRI), which uses radio waves and magnets to see organs and other soft body parts

EDIBLE ENDOSCOPES

An endoscope is a tube with a light on it that is used to look inside the body. It enters the body through an opening, such as the mouth.

The endoscope lets a doctor look closely at organs, such as the stomach, to find out what might be wrong inside without doing major surgery. It can be used to take pictures and to operate.

There's even an endoscope so small it can be swallowed! It's used to explore the digestive system. This "capsule endoscope" is a camera about the size of a big pill. After the camera is swallowed, it travels through the body, sending images to a recording device. When its job is done, the tiny camera is pooped out and flushed away!

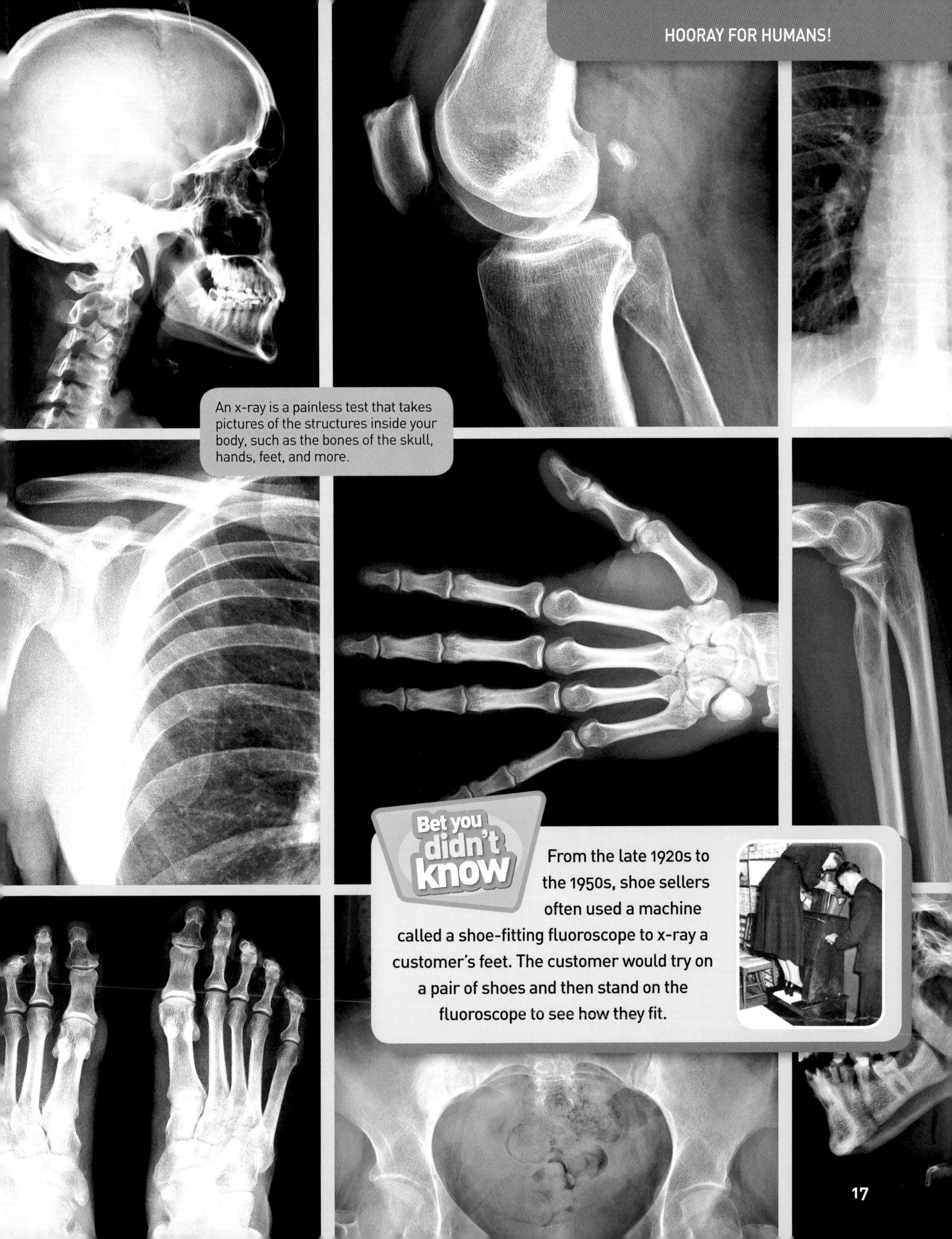

An x-ray is a painless test that takes pictures of the structures inside your body, such as the bones of the skull, hands, feet, and more.

Bet you didn't **know**

From the late 1920s to the 1950s, shoe sellers often used a machine called a shoe-fitting fluoroscope to x-ray a customer's feet. The customer would try on a pair of shoes and then stand on the fluoroscope to see how they fit.

17

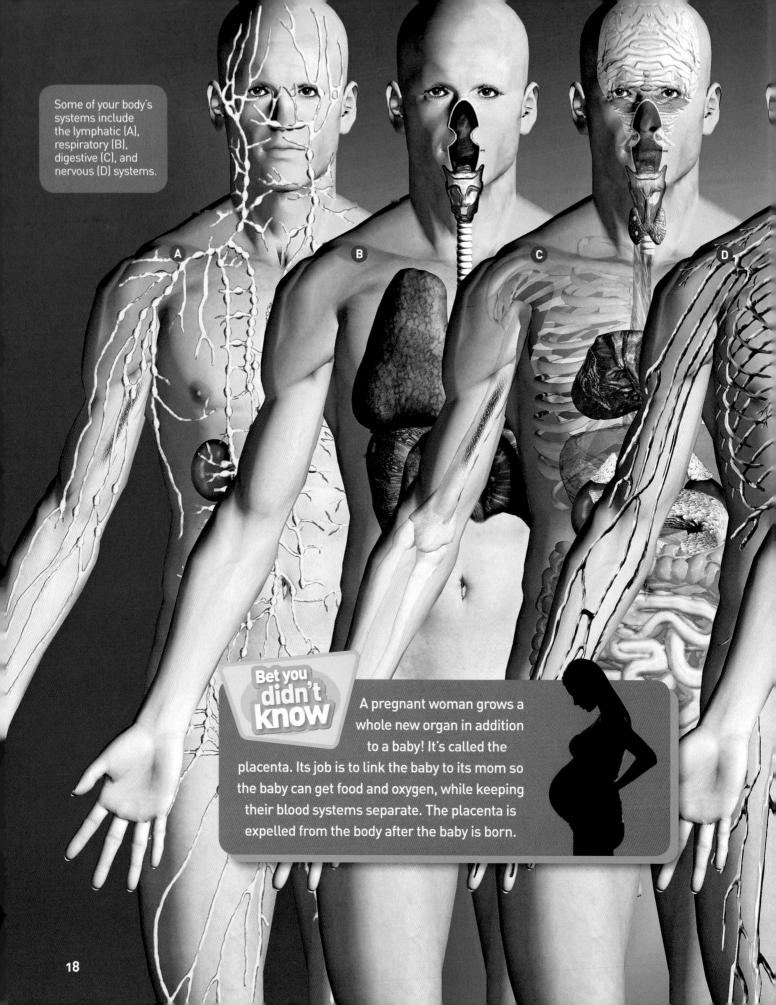

Some of your body's systems include the lymphatic (A), respiratory (B), digestive (C), and nervous (D) systems.

Bet you didn't know

A pregnant woman grows a whole new organ in addition to a baby! It's called the placenta. Its job is to link the baby to its mom so the baby can get food and oxygen, while keeping their blood systems separate. The placenta is expelled from the body after the baby is born.

ALL SYSTEMS ARE GO!

You know *who* you are. You are a unique person with hobbies and interests, talents and skills, and a personality all your own.

What you are, however, is an organism—a living thing—made up of body parts working together to keep you alive. These body parts include your organs, such as your stomach and your heart.

Your entire body is a set of systems. Your muscle-and-bone system moves your body. Your lungs, heart, and blood system brings oxygen-containing air into your body and carries it to all the other organs, along with nutrients from food. That food is processed by your digestive system, which includes your stomach, mouth, and intestines.

Your systems are coordinated and controlled, in part, by your nervous system—your brain and a body-wide web of nerves. The brain constantly gets reports from your body parts and sends messages to them. These messages take the form of electrical and chemical signals that travel along the nerves. Your nervous system also enables you to see, hear, smell, feel, and taste.

Your brain also works closely with your endocrine system. This system produces chemicals, called hormones, that control body functions such as growth, digestion, and sleep.

Luckily, your nervous and endocrine systems keep you running without you having to think about it. Imagine if you had to think about digesting your food or making your heart beat!

THE HUMAN RECIPE

You are much more than the sum of your parts. But it's still cool to know what you're made of—right down to the basic ingredients you share with all other living things as well as air, rocks, and planets!

For example, about 60 percent of your body is made up of water. Water is used in many ways in your body. Nutrients and other chemicals are dissolved in the water in your cells. Water in your blood helps it flow. Water in your urine washes waste products out of your body.

You also contain carbon, the same substance that forms coal. Carbon is found in the proteins that form body parts, the carbohydrates that give you energy.

You're also made up of a few other substances, too, such as nitrogen, which forms most of the air we breathe. In your body, it's an important ingredient in muscles. You also contain calcium and phosphorus, especially in your bones and teeth.

GOT GUTS?

Your body parts are made up of a material called tissue. This tissue is a living fabric, with different ones making up different body parts. Muscle tissue, for example, lets you move. Nerve tissue carries messages back and forth between your brain and body parts. Tough connective tissues hold you together. Covering your outside and parts of your insides is epithelial tissue.

The tissues in your body can do something amazing: They come together to form organs. Your organs are all those mysterious, squishy things inside you—the stuff sometimes called "guts." Some organs, like your heart, brain, and stomach, are ones you know. Other organs may be ones you've never heard of.

An organ is made up of two or more kinds of tissue. Your stomach, for example, has muscle tissue that lets it squish and scrunch food. Its lining is made of epithelial tissue, which protects its walls and also oozes fluids that break down food. Connective tissue supports it in your body.

Each organ has its own special job to do. The stomach stores food and mixes it up. Your heart pumps blood. Your ears hear sounds. Many organs have more than one job. The pancreas, for instance, makes juices that help digest food. It also makes a substance that controls sugar levels in your blood.

BOTTLED BODY PARTS

The ancient Egyptians, who lived more than 3,000 years ago, believed a person needed some of his or her organs after death. Keeping these organs safe was considered especially important for Egyptian kings, called pharaohs.

When a pharaoh died, many of the body's organs were removed. Four of them were treated with special care: the liver, lungs, stomach, and intestines. They were washed, wrapped in cloth, and put into special containers, called canopic jars, that were then stored inside the pharaoh's tomb.

The heart, however, was left inside the body. It was believed to hold the person's intelligence and feelings. But the brain was thrown away!

The word "organ" comes from an old Greek word, *organon*, which meant "tool" or "instrument."

Bet you didn't know

One of the smallest organs in the human body is the pineal gland, which is in the brain. It's no bigger than a grain of rice. It produces substances that play a role in your growth and in your daily sleeping-and-waking cycle.

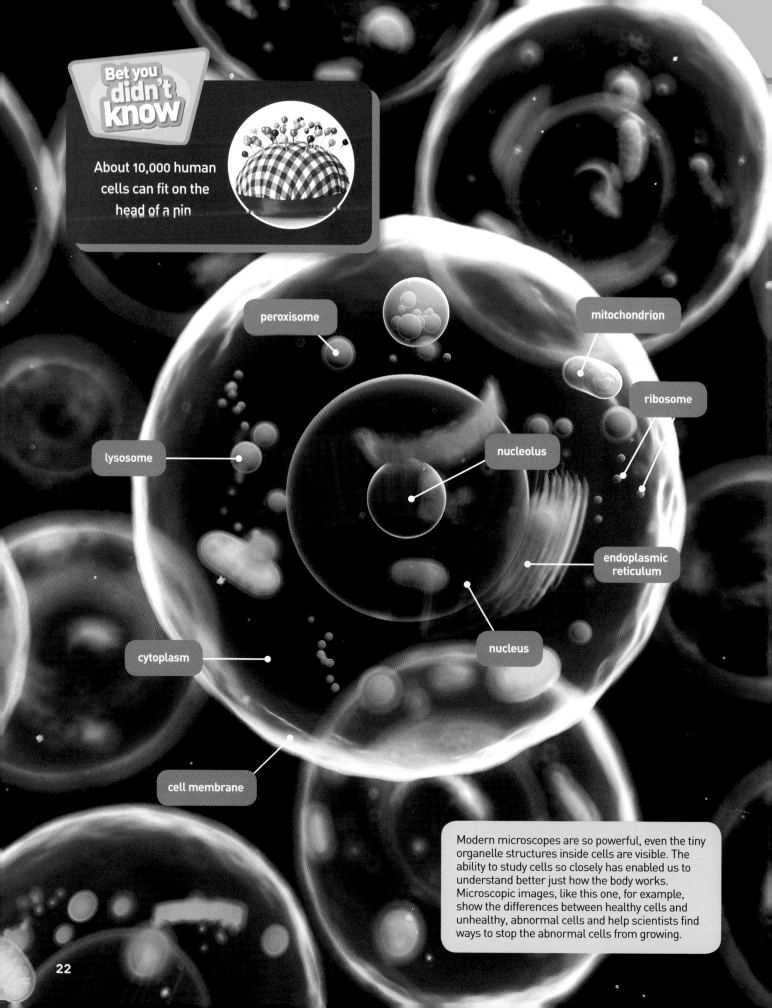

peroxisome

mitochondrion

ribosome

lysosome

nucleolus

nucleus

endoplasmic reticulum

cytoplasm

cell membrane

Modern microscopes are so powerful, even the tiny organelle structures inside cells are visible. The ability to study cells so closely has enabled us to understand better just how the body works. Microscopic images, like this one, for example, show the differences between healthy cells and unhealthy, abnormal cells and help scientists find ways to stop the abnormal cells from growing.

YOU AND YOUR CELLS

Your body is made up of microscopically tiny structures called cells—many trillions of them!

Every living thing—from the tiniest bug to the biggest tree—is made up of cells too. Cells are the smallest building blocks of life. Some living things, such as an amoeba, are made up of just one cell. Other living things contain many more. Estimates for an adult human, for example, range from 10 trillion to 100 trillion cells!

An animal cell is a bit like the world's tiniest water balloon. It's a jellylike blob surrounded by an oily "skin" called a cell membrane. The membrane works to let some chemicals into the cell and keep others out. The "jelly" on the inside is called cytoplasm. It's speckled with tiny cell parts, called organelles. Some organelles make energy. Others take apart and put together various chemicals, which become ingredients for different body functions such as growth and movement.

There are so many nerve cells in your brain that it would take almost 3,000 years to count all of them.

SEEING CELLS

The first microscope that clearly showed anything smaller than a flea was invented in the late 1500s. Later, people tinkered with microscopes and lenses to make them even more powerful. One of these people was the English scientist Robert Hooke.

Hooke designed a microscope of his own and drew detailed pictures of what he saw. In 1665, he published his illustrations in a book called *Micrographia*, which means "little pictures." One picture shows boxy spaces in a slice of cork from a tree. Hooke called the spaces "cells" because they looked like little rooms. It would be another 200 years before scientists realized that cells make up all living things.

DIFFERENT CELLS, DIFFERENT JOBS

Not only do you have loads of cells, you also have many kinds. More than 200 different types of cells form your body parts and do the jobs necessary to keep you alive.

Spiky-looking bone cells support your bones. Long, skinny nerve cells carry electrical signals throughout your body. Blobby fat cells store fuel. Stringy muscle cells form your muscles. And skin cells cover your body like jigsaw pieces.

Your body also contains special cells called stem cells, which don't have a specific job to do at first. Instead, stem cells wait patiently in certain parts of your body, such as your heart, liver, brain, skin, and teeth, ready to make new cells for those body parts when you need them.

Stem cells in your skin, for example, grow new skin cells to heal a cut. Stem cells in your bone marrow make new red blood cells to replace worn-out ones. In your intestines, stem cells make new cells to replace its lining. Stem cells in the earliest days of a baby are even more amazing: All of them can turn into any kind of tissue.

SUPERHERO CELLS

Scientists are trying to find out ways of using stem cells to fight diseases.

Leukemia, for example, is a cancer that harms a person's blood or bone marrow (a jellylike substance inside bones that makes blood cells). Replacing bone marrow is one way to fight the disease. The patient's bone marrow is replaced with new bone marrow that is donated by a healthy person. The new marrow's stem cells produce fresh blood cells for the patient's body.

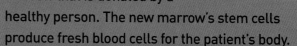

It is not easy, however, to remove adult stem cells from other parts of the body. So scientists hope to discover just how stem cells work so they can find ways to make other body cells work like stem cells. These artificial stem cells could be used to grow new tissues and help cure illnesses such as heart disease.

A: Fat cell B: T cell C: Epidermis (skin cells) D: Stem cell E: Activated T cell F: Nerve cell neuron G: Smooth muscle cell H: B cell I: Embryonic stem cell J: Red blood cells K: Platelet L: Cell division

YOUR AMAZING EXTERIOR

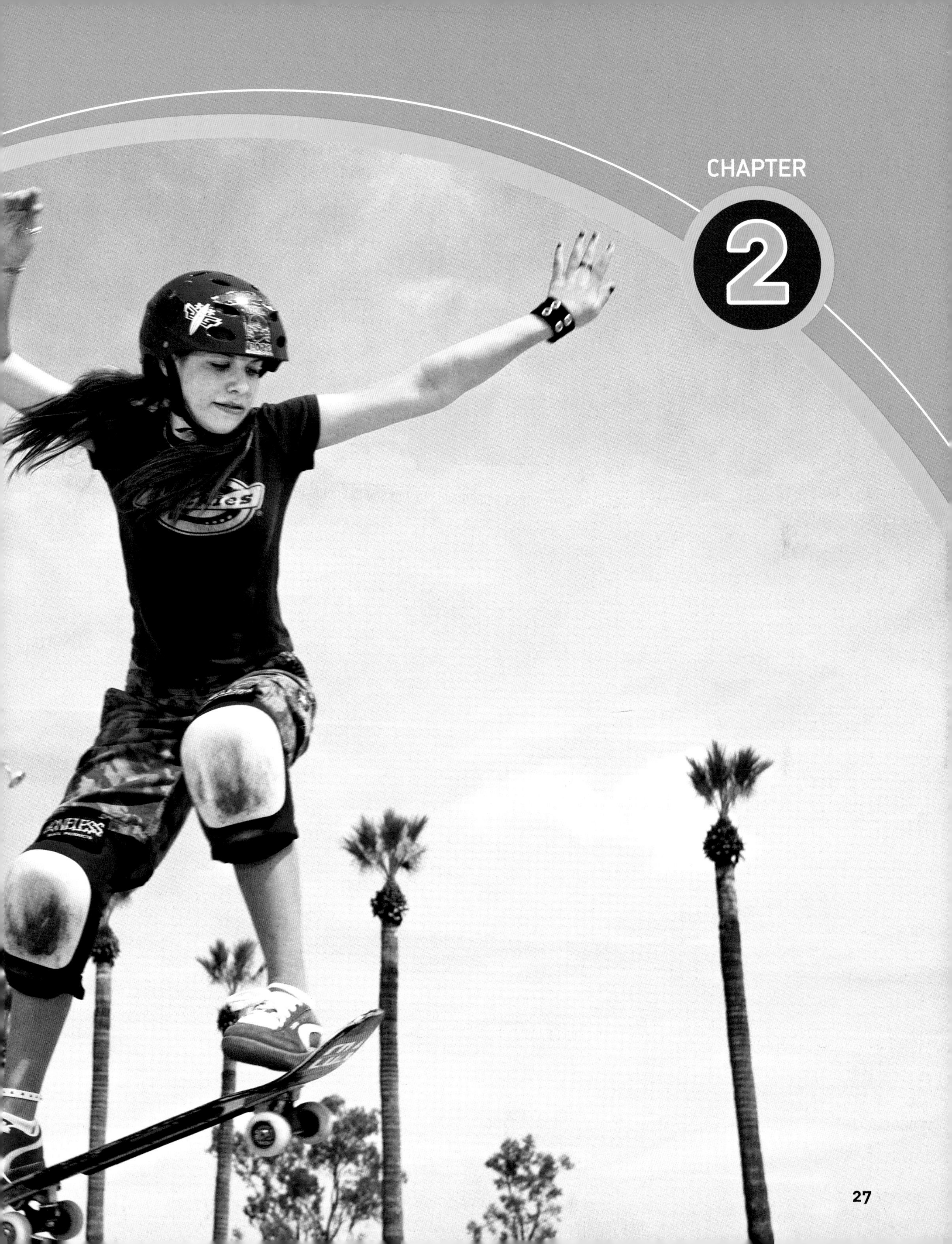

CHAPTER

2

THE SKIN YOU'RE IN

Your body's biggest organ isn't hidden inside you. It's your skin—a head-to-toe wrap that keeps your insides in and the outside out.

But your skin is much more than a built-in pair of footie pajamas. It's a flexible, tough barrier that stops germs from entering your body. Your skin also makes oil that contains germ-fighting substances. The oil helps make your skin waterproof, too. Germs get past this barrier only if your skin is broken by a scratch, sting, bite, cut, or puncture.

Your skin also protects you from the sun's burning rays. At the same time, it uses sunlight to make the vitamin D your body needs to function properly. As if that's not enough, your skin helps regulate your body temperature, too. It teams up with your brain and blood vessels to keep you from overheating or getting too cold.

Your skin isn't the same thickness all over your body. It's **thinnest** on your eyelids and **thickest** on your heels and palms.

STUCK ON YOU

Your skin isn't one-size-fits-all. It fits you perfectly because it grows as you grow. You can't outgrow it the way you outgrow clothing! It's also stuck on tightly. You don't merely move around inside your skin—it's actually attached to your muscles and  bones. The tissues that attach it are loose enough to let your skin slide around, like a comfortable shirt, so you can move freely. Want to see skin moving in a way that matches muscle motion underneath it? Just make faces at yourself in a mirror: Your facial muscles are attached directly to your skin.

ADD IT UP

An adult's skin weighs from 8 to 11 pounds (3.6 to 5 kg). Its surface area—the amount of flat space it would cover if spread out—is about 18 to 22 square feet (1.7 to 2 sq m)! That's about the size of the floor in a one-person tent.

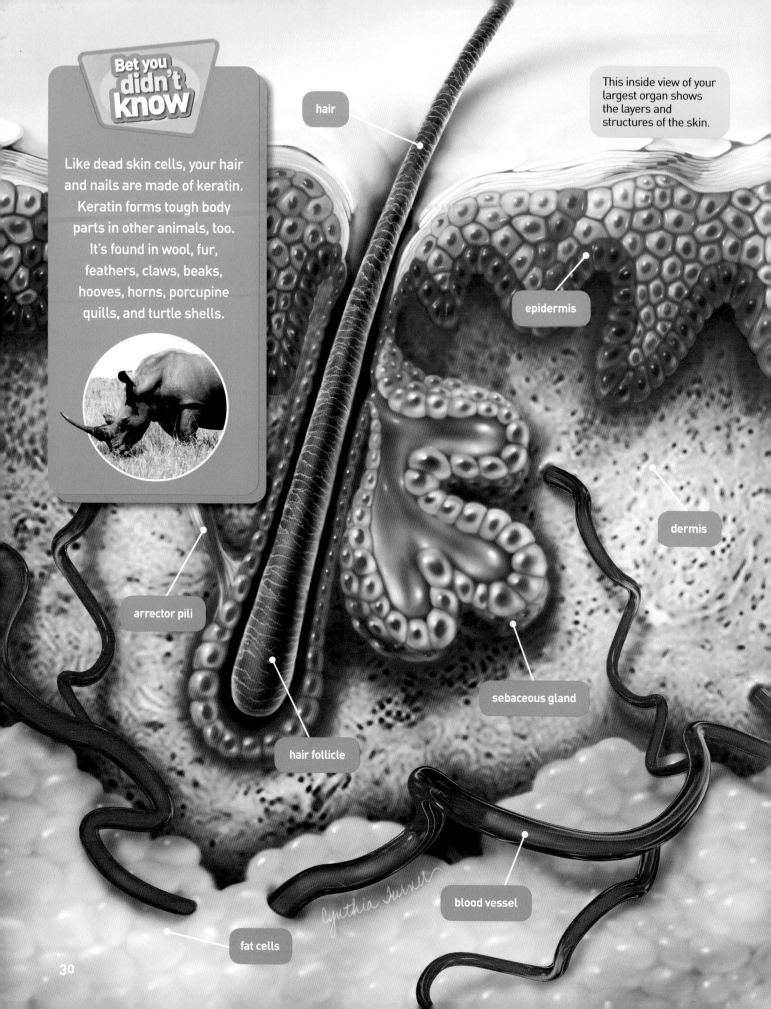

Bet you didn't know

Like dead skin cells, your hair and nails are made of keratin. Keratin forms tough body parts in other animals, too. It's found in wool, fur, feathers, claws, beaks, hooves, horns, porcupine quills, and turtle shells.

This inside view of your largest organ shows the layers and structures of the skin.

hair

epidermis

dermis

arrector pili

sebaceous gland

hair follicle

blood vessel

fat cells

LAYER IT

Your skin is not just "skin deep." It's actually made up of layers: the epidermis and the dermis, which sit on a fatty layer of subcutaneous tissue. When you look at your skin, what you see is the first, outermost layer—the epidermis. "Epi" means "on," and "dermis" means "skin."

Have you ever scratched your epidermis and seen tiny white flakes fall off? These flakes are dead skin cells. They were once living cells in the epidermis's lowest layer, where millions of new skin cells are made every day.

As new cells are made, older ones drift upward. They fill up with a tough protein called keratin. By the time they reach the skin's surface, they are dead cells. Millions of these dead cells fall off you each day.

Below the epidermis is the second layer, the dermis. The dermis contains strands of stretchy material that make it springy and flexible. It also contains blood vessels and nerves. Hair and sweat are produced in the dermis.

Beneath the dermis is a layer of subcutaneous tissue ("sub" means "under" and "cutaneous" means "skin"). It is made mostly of fat. This fat keeps you warm, stores extra fuel for your body, and protects your insides from bumps and bangs.

You may not realize it, but you lose about **nine pounds (5 kg)** of skin cells every year.

MAKE YOUR MARK

Your fingertips are covered with tiny ridges. These ridges improve your sense of touch. But they're probably best known for making fingerprints. Every person has his or her own one-of-a-kind set of fingerprints. If you injure a fingertip, your fingerprint pattern will grow right back.

What do your fingerprints look like? Check them out by pressing your fingers onto an ink pad, then pressing them on a piece of paper. Can you see whorls, loops, and arches? Collect some fingerprints from your family and friends. Compare them to see how similar or different they are from yours and from each other.

DRIP, DROP!
SWEATING IT OUT

Sweating isn't a sign that your skin has sprung a leak. Sweat is actually produced by glands in the dermis. You have about 2.6 million of these sweat glands.

A typical drop of sweat is made of water with small amounts of salts and other substances mixed in. It flows out of the sweat gland through a tube that leads to a tiny hole, or pore, in the skin. The sweat trickles out of this pore. This watery sweat is made by eccrine sweat glands, which are dotted over most of the body. Humans also make a thicker, fatty sweat once they enter the teenage years. It's produced by sweat glands called apocrine glands, which are crowded into just a few areas of the body, such as the armpits.

You sweat nearly all the time, even when you're not aware of it. When you're as cool and calm as a cucumber, your body absorbs most of the sweat before it ever reaches your skin's surface. But when you're hot or exercising, sweat production increases. Then you notice sweat as it pours from your pores!

Sweating helps balance body temperature because the water in sweat evaporates into the air. As the water evaporates, it takes heat away from your body. This makes you feel cooler—even though you think of "being sweaty" as feeling hot.

GETTING PRUNEY?

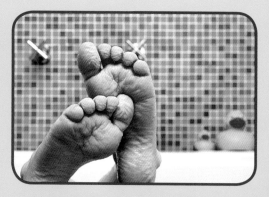

Next time you take a bath, check out your fingers and toes. If you see wrinkles, you're looking at a scientific puzzle! Why, exactly, do fingers and toes wrinkle after bathing?

One hypothesis suggests that the top layer of the epidermis on fingers and toes soaks up water, making it swell. But this layer is attached to inner layers that don't swell, so it wrinkles instead of puffing up.

A new theory suggests that wrinkling happens because blood vessels inside fingers and toes shrink after a long soaking. The wrinkly skin may help fingers grip objects in water and toes grip wet ground.

ADD IT UP

Your body makes about two cups (0.5 l) of sweat a day under normal conditions. If you exercise hard, or the weather is hot, your body produces more sweat. A runner might lose four cups (1 l) of sweat in just an hour.

Bet you didn't know

Sweat doesn't smell bad. A stinky "body odor" is caused when skin bacteria feed on sweat. Their waste products are what smell bad!

a microscopic view of a cross section of the skin's sweat glands

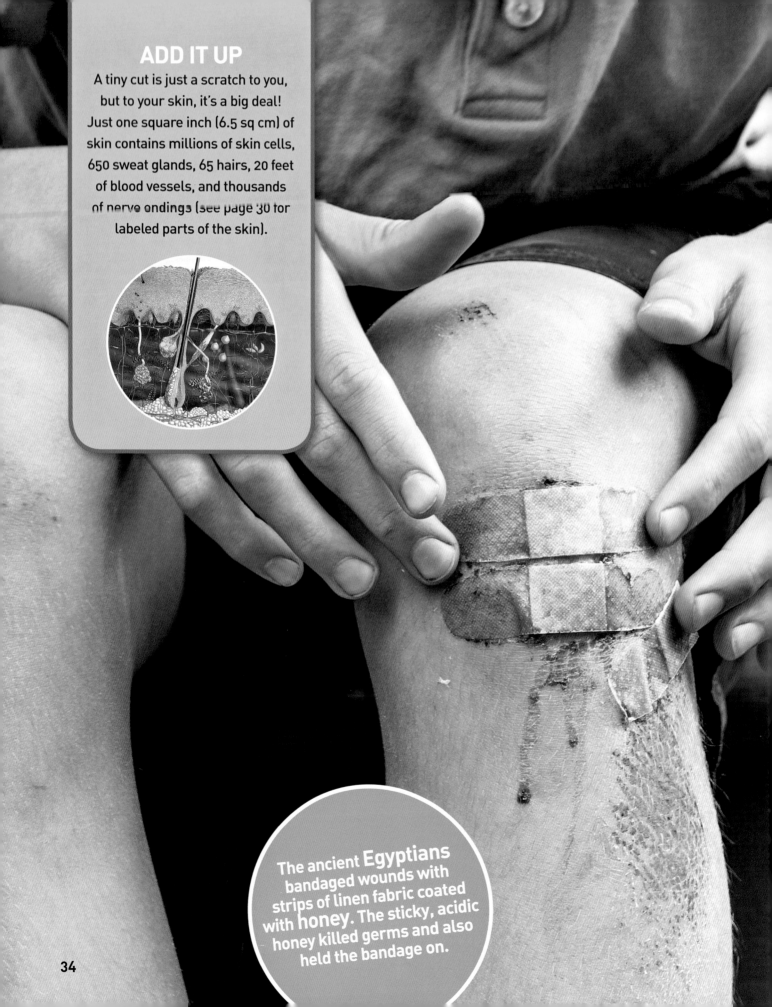

ADD IT UP

A tiny cut is just a scratch to you, but to your skin, it's a big deal! Just one square inch (6.5 sq cm) of skin contains millions of skin cells, 650 sweat glands, 65 hairs, 20 feet of blood vessels, and thousands of nerve endings (see page 30 for labeled parts of the skin).

The ancient **Egyptians** bandaged wounds with strips of linen fabric coated with **honey**. The sticky, acidic honey killed germs and also held the bandage on.

OUCH!
SCRATCHES AND CUTS

Skin is amazing armor even when it's damaged by cuts, bites, or other injuries—because it's armor that can repair itself.

Your skin reacts instantly when you scrape a knee or cut a finger. Substances in blood near the injured spot get busy making a "bandage" for the wound. Among these substances are special blood cells called platelets. Platelets stick together and work with proteins in the blood to activate a stringy material called fibrin. The fibrin then forms a net that traps more platelets. Over time, this action creates a clot—your built-in bandage.

The part of the clot you see dries out, hardens, and forms a scab. Leave that scab alone! Under it, your skin is busy making new skin and blood vessels. White blood cells dive in to destroy damaged or dead tissue as well as germs. When the patch-up job is done, the scab will fall off, revealing a brand-new bit of you.

SWITCHING STITCHES

People stitched large cuts long before the invention of modern-day sutures. Wounds were closed using thorns, hair, or plant fibers. In parts of Africa and South America, army ants with large jaws did the job! They were prodded into biting the wounded skin. Then their bodies were twisted off, leaving the jaws in place to hold the wound closed.

SKIN COLORS

Human skin ranges in color from pale pinkish white to very dark brown, with many shades in between. The color of skin is created by skin cells called melanocytes (muh-LAN-o-sites).

Melanocytes sit in the bottom layer of the epidermis. They make a color, or "pigment," called melanin. Melanin comes in two forms: brown-black and red-yellow. Different amounts of the two types of melanin produce the rainbow of human skin colors. The melanocytes of a fair-skinned person, for example, make less melanin than those of a dark-skinned person.

The grains of melanin made inside a melanocyte don't just sit there. The melanocytes pass the melanin along to skin cells in the upper layer. They are always making new melanin and shipping it into the upper layers, which is why your skin color doesn't rub off even though you shed millions of skin flakes each day!

Albinism is a condition in which the body produces no melanin. The hair, skin, and eyes of an albino human or animal are **colorless.**

FACING FRECKLES

Freckles are spots of skin where melanocytes are packed together instead of being evenly spread out. They're harmless, but that doesn't stop some people from trying to get rid of them. In the past, this led to some strange ideas.

More than 100 years ago in the southern United States, for example, some people believed that washing with rainwater that fell on the first day of June would wipe away freckles. Others, in Newfoundland, Canada, once believed that snow that fell in May had freckle-fading power.

ADD IT UP

An adult human being, no matter what color his or her skin is, has about 60,000 melanocytes in every square inch (6.5 sq cm) of skin. That adds up to more than 155 million melanocytes!

a color-enhanced microscopic view of a melanocyte, a melanin-producing skin cell

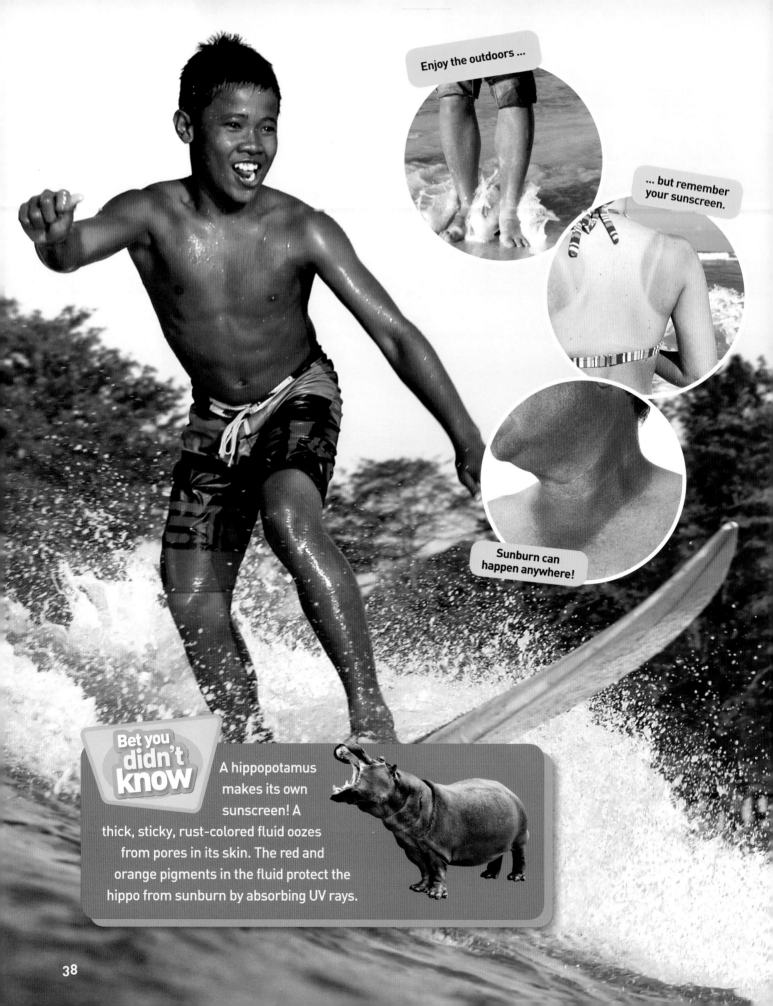

Enjoy the outdoors ...

... but remember your sunscreen.

Sunburn can happen anywhere!

Bet you didn't know

A hippopotamus makes its own sunscreen! A thick, sticky, rust-colored fluid oozes from pores in its skin. The red and orange pigments in the fluid protect the hippo from sunburn by absorbing UV rays.

SIZZLING IN THE SUN

The sun is both friend and foe when it comes to your skin. Your skin contains substances that turn into a form of vitamin D when exposed to sunshine. Then your liver and kidneys change the vitamin D so that your body can use it to help with functions such as bone growth and repair. But too much sunlight can harm your skin.

The damage comes from one of the many kinds of energy produced by the sun. Some of the sun's energy is light we can see. Some of it is heat we can feel. The skin-harming energy is ultraviolet (UV) radiation, which we can't see. UV rays can damage living cells and cause diseases such as skin cancer.

Luckily for life on Earth, our atmosphere filters out a lot of UV rays. The rays that do reach us, however, can burn skin. UV rays can be tricky, too—they can bounce off white sand and burn you while you sit under a beach umbrella. They can even burn you on a hazy, somewhat cloudy day because clouds block some, but not all, of the rays.

Your skin tries to protect you from UV rays by ramping up melanin production because melanin can absorb some of this radiation. But it takes many hours over many days for skin to "tan" or make extra melanin. In the meantime, the skin burns. It may even blister.

SAVE YOUR SKIN!

Tanning is your skin's way of saying, "Help! Put on sunscreen!" A sunburn is just what it sounds like—your skin, burned by sunlight. Studies show that sun damage suffered when you're young can lead to skin problems later in life. So protect your skin from the sun— and remember, all skin can burn, not just very fair skin.

- Always wear sunscreen that offers "broad spectrum protection." Look for SPF 30 to 50. (SPF stands for "Sun Protection Factor.")
- Put on fresh sunscreen at least every two hours and more often if you are going to be in the water.
- The blob of sunscreen you use each time should be at least as big as a golf ball.
- Sand, snow, and water reflect sunlight, making it easier for you to burn. (Yep, you read that right: You can burn in the snow!)
- Wear a hat or a cap to shade your face.

HEAR, HEAR FOR HAIR

You are covered with hair, just like other mammals. Your body is dotted with about five million hairs—approximately as many as a gorilla has! A gorilla's hair, however, is coarse and thick. Most of the hair on a human's body is soft and fine. (That's why a gorilla is furry, and you're not!)

All hair grows from bulb-shaped pockets in the skin's second layer—the dermis. These pockets are called follicles. Cells form in the bottom of the follicle. As new cells are created, they push the older cells up and out.

Like skin cells, hair cells fill up with keratin as they move upward. The hair that finally grows out of the follicle is made of dead cells. That's why it doesn't hurt when your hair is cut. The hairs you see are strings of dead cells without any nerve endings.

Your hair is there for more than just appearance. Scalp hair protects your head from the sun. It also helps keep you warm. Eyelashes and eyebrows help keep particles out of your eyes. Body hair helps you feel things, like a bug landing on your arm or a breeze blowing by.

SHEDDING SEASON

Hair on your scalp grows about half an inch a month. That's about six inches (15 cm) in a year. So how long would your hair grow if you never got it cut? That depends on what kind of hair follicles you have.

Your scalp contains 100,000 to 150,000 follicles. Most of them are busy growing hair, but some are resting. They're "sleeping on the job" because each follicle enters a resting phase every few years. When it "wakes up" again, it grows a new hair, which pushes out the old one. (You lose 25 to 100 hairs a day!)

Hair grows almost all over your body. Much of this hair is so short, soft, and fine, you can **hardly see it**. Among the only completely hair-free areas of skin are the soles of your feet, the palms of your hands, and your lips.

a microscopic view of a hair follicle

Bet you **didn't** **know**

Many animals raise the hairs on their body to look bigger when they're angry. They also fluff up their hair to stay warm. That's what your skin is trying to do when you get goose bumps!

Bet you didn't know

Electrical hair-curling machines invented in the early 1900s took hours to curl hair. The machines got so hot, stylists often had to fan customers to keep them cool! (Known as a "permanent" or "perm," this hairstyling process uses chemicals, heat, or both.)

COLORS, CURLS, AND COWL'ICKS

Just like skin, your hair gets its color from melanocytes. They add melanin to hair while it's forming in a follicle. The exact color of hair depends on the mixture of browns, blacks, reds, and yellows produced by these little melanin factories. Black is the most common hair color among humans worldwide, with brown taking second place. Blond hair is rare, and red hair is even rarer.

As people get older, melanin production in the follicles drops. This makes their hair turn gray. If the melanocytes stop making melanin altogether, a person's hair turns white.

The shape of hair is determined by follicles, too. Straight hair grows from round, straight follicles. Curly hair grows from flat, curved follicles, with the flattest follicles producing the most coiled locks. Wavy-hair follicles are somewhere in between.

Some patches of scalp hair seem to have a mind of their own and grow in a spiral! These patches are called whorls or cowlicks.

FREAKY STREAKS

A frightening experience or lots of worrying can cause changes in the body that make colored hair fall out and colorless hair remain. A condition called alopecia ariata, for example, makes hair suddenly fall out in patches. This condition can be made worse by anxiety and fear.

Scientists think the body's immune system, which protects you against diseases, may also go haywire under stress and attack the melanocytes. Likewise, stress may make lots of follicles go into their falling-out phase at the same time.

But can your hair turn white overnight after a terrible scare? No. This "hair scare" color change happens in stories and movies, but not in real life—at least, not in just 24 hours.

HARD AS NAILS

Your fingers and toes are tipped with nails. Fingernails protect the ends of your sensitive fingers. They also help you pick up tiny objects, peel fruit, and scratch itches on your skin.

Toenails aren't much use for peeling fruit, but they do protect your toes. You know how much it hurts when you bang your toe or drop something on it. Imagine how much worse the pain would be if your toenail didn't block some of the blow!

Both fingernails and toenails grow in much the same way that hair does. A nail is alive at its root, which is tucked under the skin at its base. New cells born here push older cells forward. The cells fill up with keratin as they grow. The part of the nail you see is made up of layers of dead, keratin-filled cells. Unlike hair, however, nails grow nonstop, without a resting phase.

If you stopped cutting your nails, they could grow to be more than six feet (2 m) long.

WRITE ON!

Fingernails grow about three times faster than toenails do. They grow faster in summer than in winter. And the nails on the hand you write with most likely grow faster than the nails on your other hand.

Are you scratching your head wondering why? Nobody really knows the answer for sure, but the leading hypothesis is that growth rate is affected by blood supply. The blood brings nutrients to body parts, and more blood flows to body parts when they are being used.

So if you are a "righty," you use your right hand the most. As a result, its nails grow faster. Your toes, safely tucked in your socks and shoes, don't move around as much as your fingers, so their nails grow more slowly. As for the seasons, less blood flows to fingers and toes when exposed to winter's cold, so nails grow more slowly in winter.

Bet you didn't know

A nail's growth begins deep in the skin. The part you can see lies on top of a sensitive area of skin called the nail bed. The underside of the nail is ridged. These ridges match up with ridges in the nail bed, a bit like a sliding window in a track.

a cross section of a fingernail under a microscope

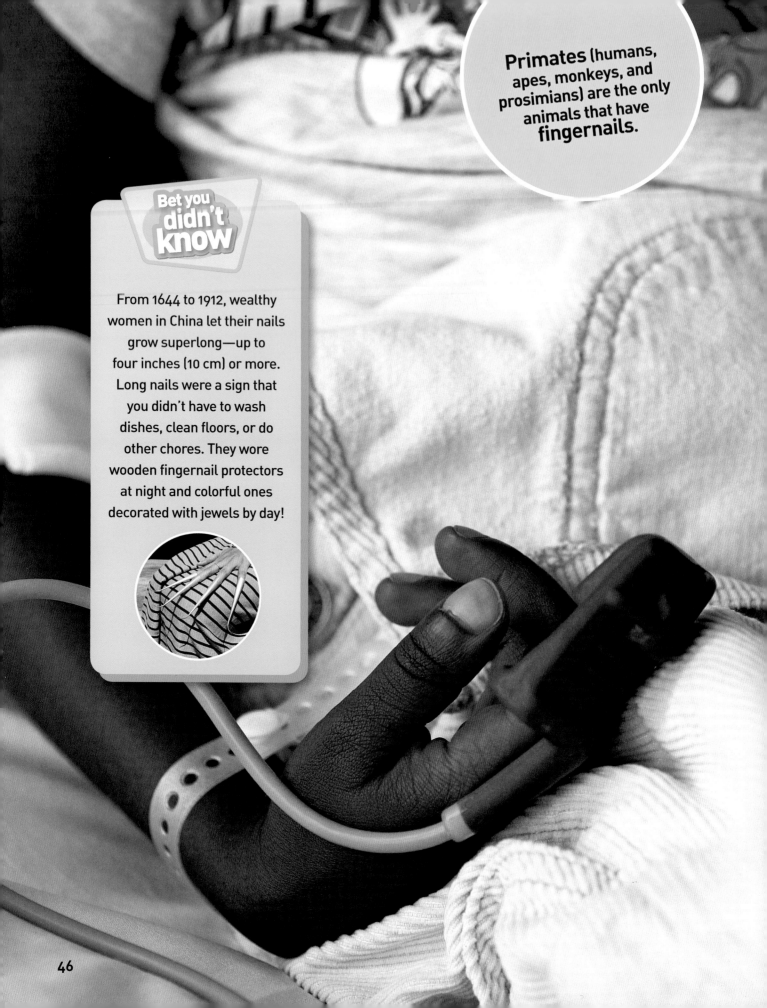

Primates (humans, apes, monkeys, and prosimians) are the only animals that have **fingernails**.

Bet you didn't know

From 1644 to 1912, wealthy women in China let their nails grow superlong—up to four inches (10 cm) or more. Long nails were a sign that you didn't have to wash dishes, clean floors, or do other chores. They wore wooden fingernail protectors at night and colorful ones decorated with jewels by day!

HEALTHY NAILS, HEALTHY YOU

Nails can provide a doctor with clues about a patient's health. Healthy nails are usually pale pink because blood in the nail beds shows through. They are stiff, not too soft or too brittle, and firmly attached to the nail bed.

Nails that are discolored, brittle, too thick, or separating from the nail bed are signs that something is wrong. For example, nails that get soft and form spoon-like scoops may be a sign that the body lacks iron. Thick, yellow nails may be a sign of a lung disease.

In hospitals, a patient's fingernails can help doctors check oxygen levels in his or her blood. A device called a pulse oximeter is clamped onto the patient's finger. It shines a beam of light through the fingernail to measure the oxygen content of the blood. Pulse oximeters are also used on other body parts, such as earlobes and toes.

Even without a pulse oximeter, low oxygen levels can be revealed by the nails. Nail beds look blue or purple if oxygen levels are low. Patients are told to remove their nail polish before getting an operation so that their nail beds can be seen clearly by medical professionals.

NAIL ANATOMY

Look at your thumbnail. Can you see a small, pale, rounded shape at its base? This mark is the "lunula," which means "little moon" in Latin. It's part of the nail's root, or "matrix," which produces nail cells. Each nail has a lunula, but it's often hard to see except on the thumb.

The lunula's whiteness comes from the crowds of new cells inside it. Its curve tends to match the natural shape of your fingernail's tip, if you allow it to grow without cutting it.

Do you see any white spots in the middle of a nail? If you do, you probably injured the bed of that nail a few weeks ago. A bang or a pinch to the nail bed harms the bit of nail growing at that time. This kind of spot is harmless and will go away as the nail grows out.

THE ZOO ON YOU!

Your skin looks smooth to your eyes. Viewed through a microscope, however, its surface is a landscape of ridges and canals, with hairs sticking up like vast tree trunks and pools of oil and sweat. This landscape is populated with living creatures—millions and millions of microscopic organisms.

This population includes single-celled organisms called bacteria. You are also home to different kinds of fungus and tiny organisms called viruses. They live in hair follicles, sweat glands, oil glands, and on your skin's surface, too.

Scientists call these organisms "skin microbiota." "Micro" means "small," and "biota" means "living things." Most people, however, call them germs.

Wait! Germs? Germs are bad, right? Not all germs! Most of the microbiota living on your skin are harmless. "Good" germs on your skin crowd out any "bad" germs trying to live there. Scientists have also discovered that certain skin bacteria help your skin fight off harmful germs. These bacteria stimulate the skin to make chemicals and prepare to fight an infection.

ARACHNID INVASION

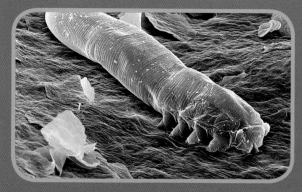

Most people's skin is crawling with tiny arachnids called skin mites. Arachnids are a group of eight-legged animals that includes spiders, scorpions, ticks, and mites. Skin mites live in hair follicles and the oil glands connected to them. They feed on skin cells and oil. They are most common on the face, especially in the eyelashes and eyebrows and on the forehead and nose.

Skin mites are so small, a lineup of 100 of them would be only an inch (2.5 cm) long. They can crawl, but not very far or fast. Even a speedy mite would take nearly a day to crawl from one side of your face to the other.

Skin mites are harmless to most people.

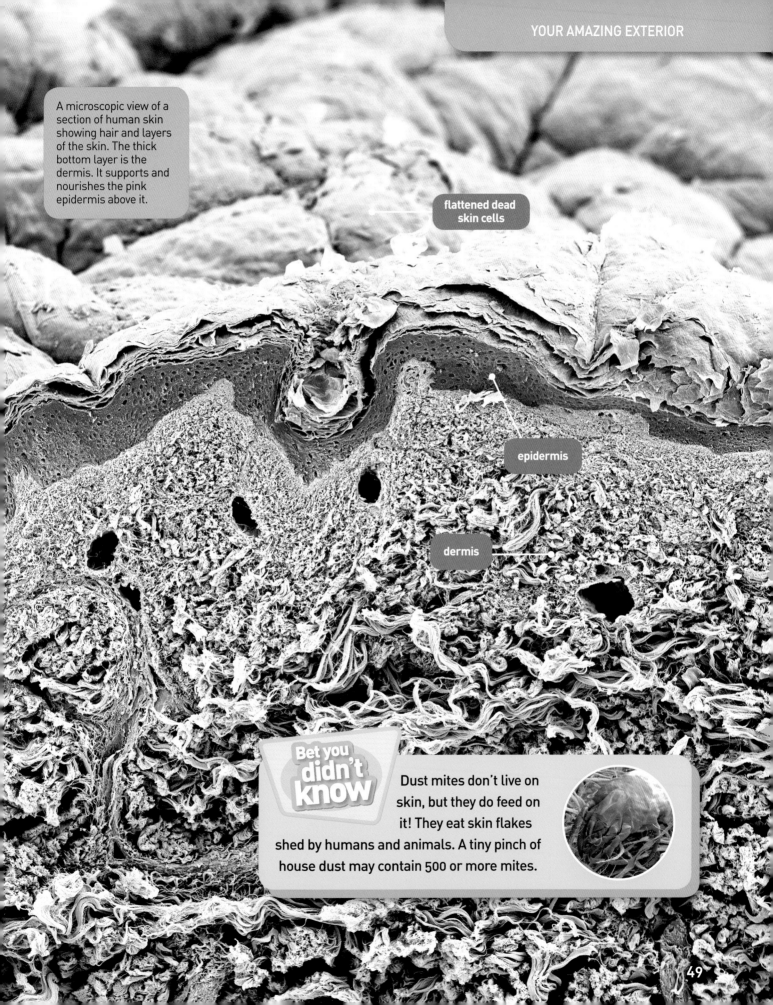

A microscopic view of a section of human skin showing hair and layers of the skin. The thick bottom layer is the dermis. It supports and nourishes the pink epidermis above it.

flattened dead skin cells

epidermis

dermis

Bet you didn't know

Dust mites don't live on skin, but they do feed on it! They eat skin flakes shed by humans and animals. A tiny pinch of house dust may contain 500 or more mites.

49

RUN, BEND, JUMP: US IN MOTION

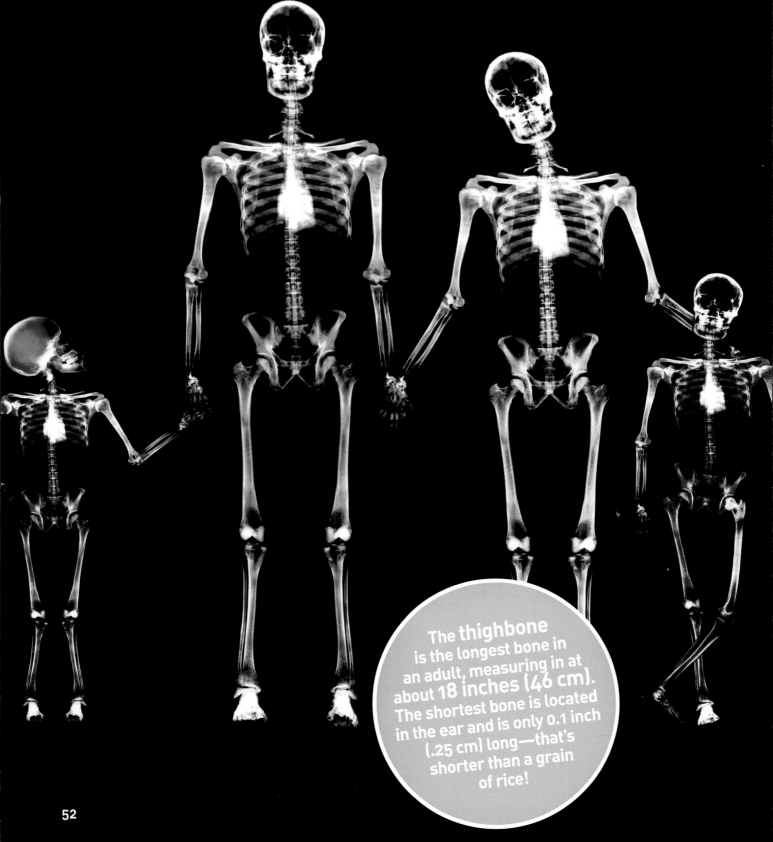

The **thighbone** is the longest bone in an adult, measuring in at about 18 inches (46 cm). The shortest bone is located in the ear and is only 0.1 inch (.25 cm) long—that's shorter than a grain of rice!

YOUR BONY BODY: THE SKELETON

Boo! There's a skeleton inside you!

This skeleton, however, is too busy to rattle around scaring people like the ones in horror movies. Your skeleton is a framework made of bones that supports your body and gives it a shape. Without your skeleton, you would be a jellyfish-like blob. Your skeleton protects your internal organs, too. The ribs, for example, form a sturdy cage around your lungs. Your skull protects your brain.

Your skeleton also makes it possible for you to run, crawl, jump, play ball, and more. Its bones move because muscles are attached to them. When a muscle pulls on a bone, the bone moves. Bunch your upper arm muscles, for example, and they raise your forearm like a lever. Contracting muscles in your leg likewise makes your foot move up.

But bones are more than stiff, strong rods for muscles to maneuver. Like other body parts, they are living, growing tissues that contain nerves and blood vessels. They can even repair themselves when they get damaged.

BABIES' BONES

A baby's skeleton is made up of about 300 bones. Some of these bones are hard whereas others are made of a rubbery material called cartilage. As a child grows, many cartilage bits turn into hard bone and fuse with the bony bits to form big bones. If you looked at an x-ray of a baby's hand, you would see big gaps between finger bones.

The gaps get smaller as the bones harden and fuse. This process wraps up by about age 25, leaving an adult with 206 bones. (A few rare people have 208 bones because they have an extra set of ribs!)

A BONE'S STRUCTURE

Press on the bone in your lower leg.

It feels rock-hard. But a bone is not stone. It is made of living tissue that teams up with minerals to make your strong, sturdy skeleton.

One important mineral in your bones is calcium phosphate. Your body gets this mineral from calcium-rich foods, such as milk, collard greens, and salmon. Inside your bones, the mineral sticks to the stringy, flexible fibers of a material called collagen. Collagen gives bones some flexibility, which prevents them from snapping easily, while the calcium gives them strength and hardness.

The job of making collagen belongs to special bone cells called osteoblasts. Osteoblasts remain embedded in the hard bone material after it forms. Then they turn into cells called osteocytes, the "bosses" of the bone factory! Osteocytes send chemical messages to new osteoblasts, telling them when to make new bone. They also tell "bone destroying" cells, called osteoclasts, when to break down bone material and recycle it. This stops your bones from growing too thick.

The hardest type of bone is called compact bone. It forms the stiff, strong outside. The inside is filled with a lacy material called spongy bone, which looks like a honeycomb. It's a web of sturdy bars with hollow spaces in between. The bars make the bone strong. The spaces help make the bone lighter, so your skeleton can move!

YOUR BLOOD FACTORY

A bone is coated with a very thin, skin-like covering called the periosteum. The periosteum contains many blood vessels and nerves. It keeps bone cells nourished so bones stay healthy. Bone cells also produce new bone cells to replace old ones, repair breaks, and make small humans grow bigger.

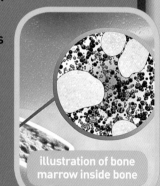

illustration of bone marrow inside bone

Some bones, such as the hip bones and ribs, also contain a jelly-like substance called red marrow. Red marrow is your own built-in blood factory. It makes about eight million new blood cells every second. These cells replace the millions of old red blood cells that your liver and spleen remove from your bloodstream.

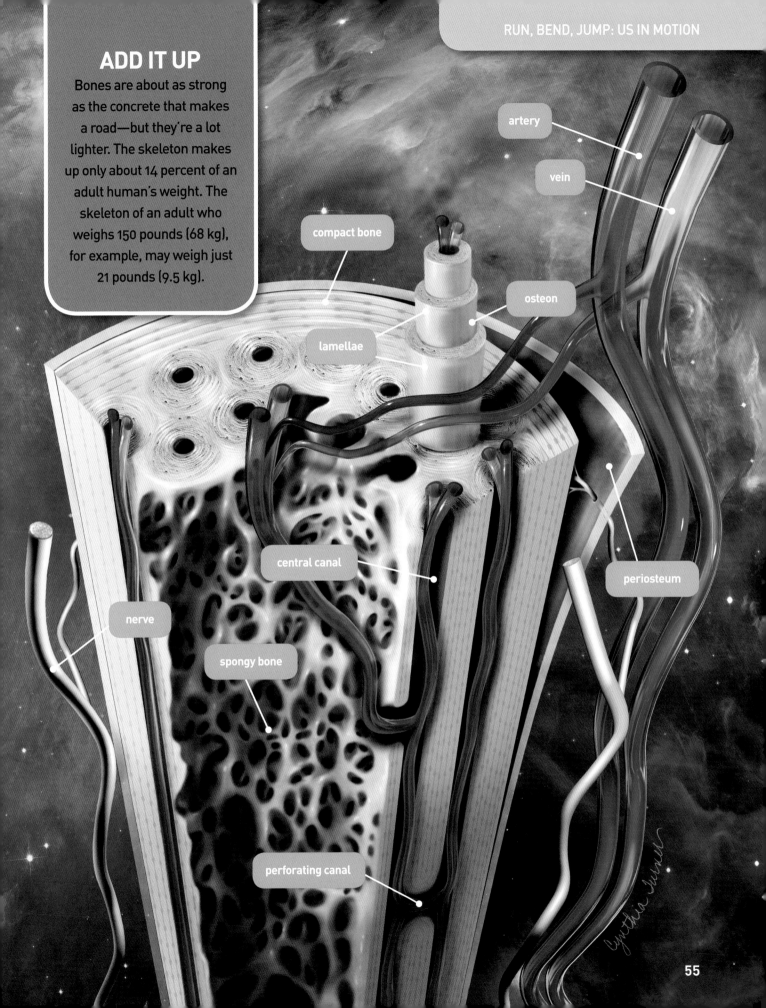

ADD IT UP

Bones are about as strong as the concrete that makes a road—but they're a lot lighter. The skeleton makes up only about 14 percent of an adult human's weight. The skeleton of an adult who weighs 150 pounds (68 kg), for example, may weigh just 21 pounds (9.5 kg).

artery

vein

compact bone

osteon

lamellae

central canal

periosteum

nerve

spongy bone

perforating canal

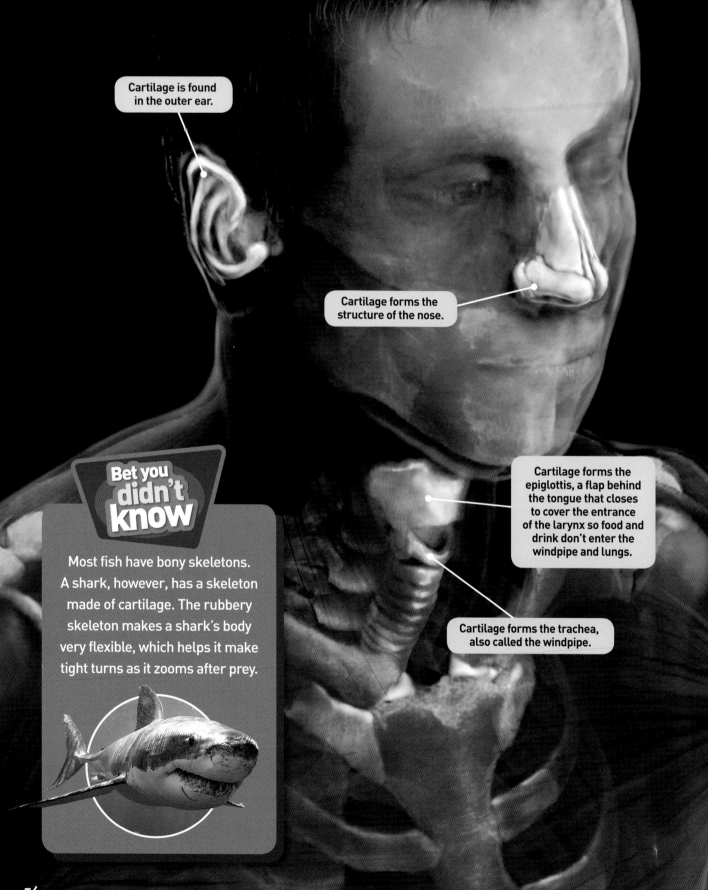

Cartilage is found in the outer ear.

Cartilage forms the structure of the nose.

Cartilage forms the epiglottis, a flap behind the tongue that closes to cover the entrance of the larynx so food and drink don't enter the windpipe and lungs.

Cartilage forms the trachea, also called the windpipe.

Bet you didn't know

Most fish have bony skeletons. A shark, however, has a skeleton made of cartilage. The rubbery skeleton makes a shark's body very flexible, which helps it make tight turns as it zooms after prey.

RUBBERY BONES: CARTILAGE

Pinch your nose. Can you wiggle it? What about your ears? These body parts are stiff enough to keep their shape, but flexible enough to be bent because they are made of a rubbery material called cartilage.

Cartilage is found not only in your nose and ears but also many other parts of your body. The bones that form your leg and arm joints, for example, are capped with cartilage at their ends. The cartilage helps the bones glide over each other as you move. The tubes that bring air deep into your lungs are held open by rings of cartilage. Your voice box is made of cartilage, too.

Thick pads of cartilage called spinal discs sit between the knobby bones in your backbone. They work as shock absorbers and also stop the bones from grinding against each other. A spinal disc is extra cushiony because it has a fluid-filled center, like a jelly doughnut.

HOT OFF THE PRESS

Cartilage is flexible and strong, but it can still be damaged by a fall or other injury. Sports also put a lot of stress on cartilage. Tennis and basketball players, for example, do a lot of twisting and turning when they run, which wears out cartilage in the knees. Cartilage also wears out over time simply due to age and everyday use. The result is pain and stiffness in joints.

Surgery can help many people with stiff, achy joints. The surgeon takes out damaged cartilage and makes holes in the bone. This causes cells in the bone to make new cartilage. But this healing takes a long time.

New technology that uses 3-D printers may solve this problem in the future. Scientists have experimented with printing thin, rubbery mats soaked with a mixture of cartilage cells. This material would be put inside the damaged joint. New cartilage could then grow on this framework so that the joint could work freely—and painlessly.

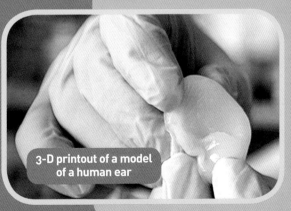

3-D printout of a model of a human ear

MAKING
—AND BREAKING—
BONES

The round, knobby ends of a kid's arm or leg bones are separated from the rest of the bone by an area of cartilage called a growth plate.

A growth plate makes the bone grow longer by forming new cartilage. Over time, this cartilage hardens and becomes new bone material. By the time you are an adult, the growth plate stops making cartilage and hardens, too.

If you break a bone, the repair work is done differently. The break heals a bit like a cut on your skin. First, a blood clot forms. Next, the break fills up with a tough substance called collagen. The collagen forms a net that links the broken ends. New spongy bone grows on this net, building a repair called a callus. After about two months, compact bone replaces the callus, and the bone is good to go.

If bones can heal on their own, why do doctors put them in casts? A cast helps keep a broken bone lined up properly so that it heals in the right shape. A badly broken bone might otherwise heal crookedly and become a source of future pain and disability. A bone in a cast also heals faster and is less likely to be reinjured during healing.

MASTER OF BONES

In the mid-1700s, after a ship sank in the ocean near Wales in the United Kingdom, one survivor, a young boy, was adopted by a local doctor, who named him Evan Thomas.

As Evan grew up, he helped the doctor in his work. He was especially good at setting broken bones. He was able to find breaks in patients' bones and fit them together neatly so they would heal better. He also figured out better ways to pull on bones so they would heal in the correct position.

Evan's work changed the way doctors set broken bones. Many of his children, grandchildren, and other descendants were "bone-setters," too. Some of them became doctors, including his great-grandson, Dr. Hugh Owen Thomas, who would become the "father" of modern bone surgery.

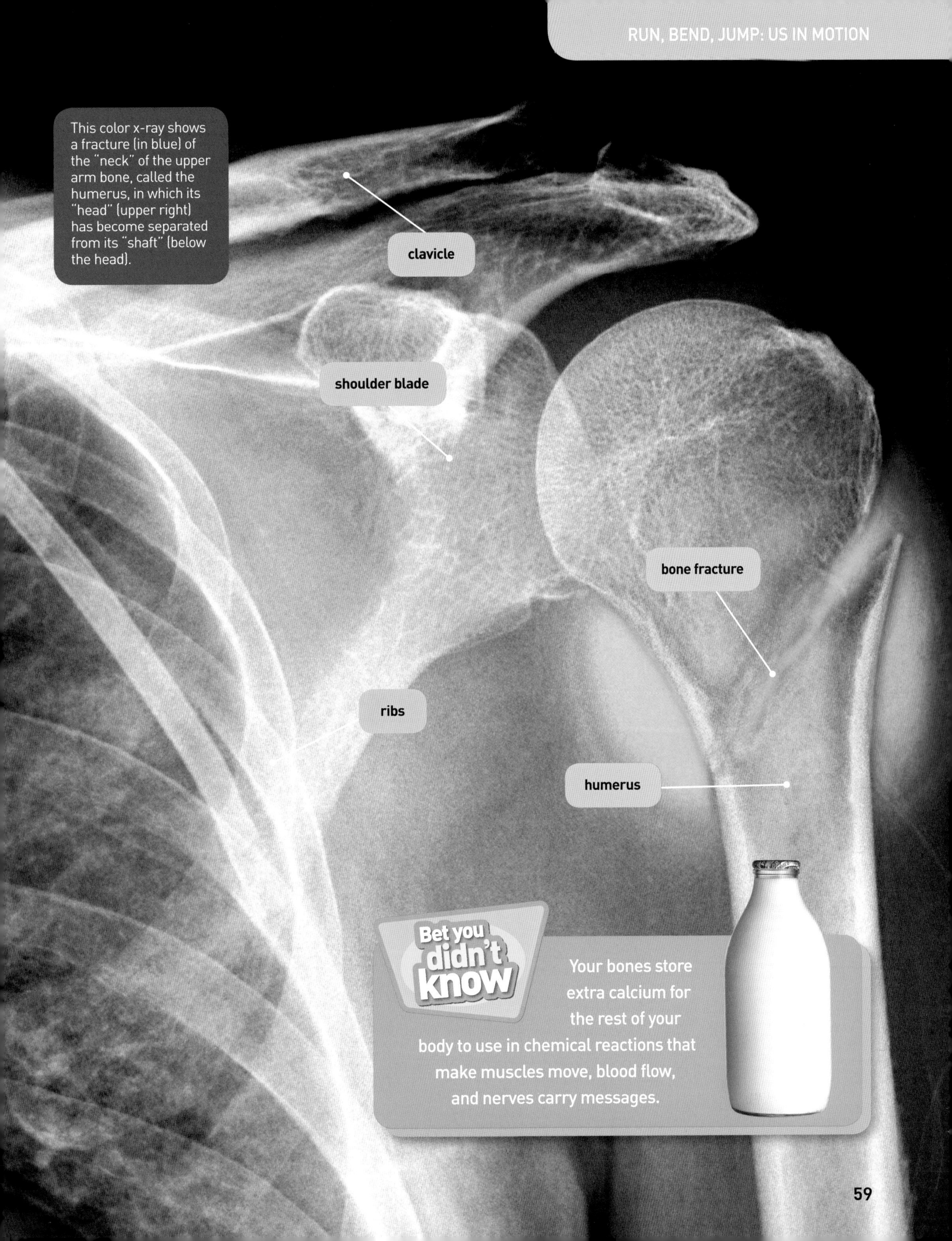

This color x-ray shows a fracture (in blue) of the "neck" of the upper arm bone, called the humerus, in which its "head" (upper right) has become separated from its "shaft" (below the head).

clavicle

shoulder blade

bone fracture

ribs

humerus

Bet you didn't know

Your bones store extra calcium for the rest of your body to use in chemical reactions that make muscles move, blood flow, and nerves carry messages.

59

Some people claim they can **predict the weather** based on how achy their joints are, but scientists aren't so sure. A sore knee doesn't always mean it's going to rain!

Bet you didn't know

Near the base of your spine are five bones called "sacral vertebrae." Early in life, they are jointed, like the rest of your spine. By the time you're 30, they've fused together to form one large bone, called the sacrum.

JOINED BY JOINTS

Can you walk without bending your knees or moving your hips?

Can you eat a bowl of cereal without bending your arms? You can try—but it won't be easy!

Luckily, your skeleton isn't just stiff and strong. It also bends easily at places where different bones meet. These places are called joints. Your body has more than 400 joints, and many of them are flexible enough to move up, down, sideways, or in a circle.

A freely moving joint is made up of two bone ends strapped together by tough cords called ligaments. The ligaments keep the bones in place, like sturdy ropes, but they're stretchy enough to allow movement.

The bones' ends are covered with smooth cartilage, which lets them glide easily. The joint also makes a special fluid that fills the area where the bones meet, making movement even smoother.

The joints in your backbone are less flexible, because they are attached to thick pads of cartilage. They bend enough to let you arch your back and twist while still protecting the nerves inside your backbone. Joints in your skull, however, don't move at all. They look like stitches holding your skull together.

RICE TO THE RESCUE

You're running across the park when suddenly your ankle folds sideways and you fall. Ouch! You've just sprained your ankle, and even though you can stand on it and move it, it really hurts.

When you sprain a joint, you've overstretched and torn its ligaments. These ligaments must heal before you can use the joint normally again. So how do you help them heal? With RICE!

RICE, in this case, doesn't mean fluffy grains. It stands for Rest, Ice, Compress, and Elevate.

1. **REST** the joint.
2. **ICE** it to help minimize swelling. You can use an ice pack or bag of frozen peas wrapped in a thin towel a few times a day for the first 48 hours after you sprain a joint. Never put ice directly on your skin.
3. **COMPRESS** the area once you're back on your feet with an elastic wrap made for sprains. Don't wrap it too tightly— ask an adult for help.
4. **ELEVATE** it. Put your foot up whenever you can to help reduce swelling.

HOORAY FOR HANDS!

The human hand is an amazing body part. It can throw a ball, pull on a rope, squeeze a lemon, and hold a hammer to bang nails into wood. It can also stroke a kitten's head, pick up a tiny bead, and paint a beautiful picture.

Your hands are both strong and sensitive, flexible and firm. They contain more than one-quarter of your body's bones: there are 27 in each one! The fingers and thumb together contain 14 of these bones. The rest are in the palm of the hand and the wrist.

Joints in your fingers let you bend them. A more flexible joint sits at the base of each finger and in your wrist. You can twirl your wrist and wag a finger thanks to these joints!

The joint at the base of your thumb gives it greater ability to move than your other fingers. The thumb can rotate and reach across your palm to touch the tip of each finger. A thumb like this is called an "opposable thumb" because it can turn to face, or "oppose," the fingers and touch them. Your other four digits can't swivel around to face each other.

THUMBS UP!

Humans aren't the only living things with opposable thumbs. Apes, lemurs, and many monkeys have them, too. Thumbs help these animals climb on branches, pick fruit, and (in the case of some apes) use tools such as sticks.

What makes human thumbs special is that they are much longer, in relation to the other fingers, than the thumbs of other animals. The human thumb also has larger muscles. With a long, flexible, strong thumb like this, you can use extra-fine control to pick up something. It also lets you firmly hold on to objects. Chimps and other animals have shorter thumbs and longer palms.

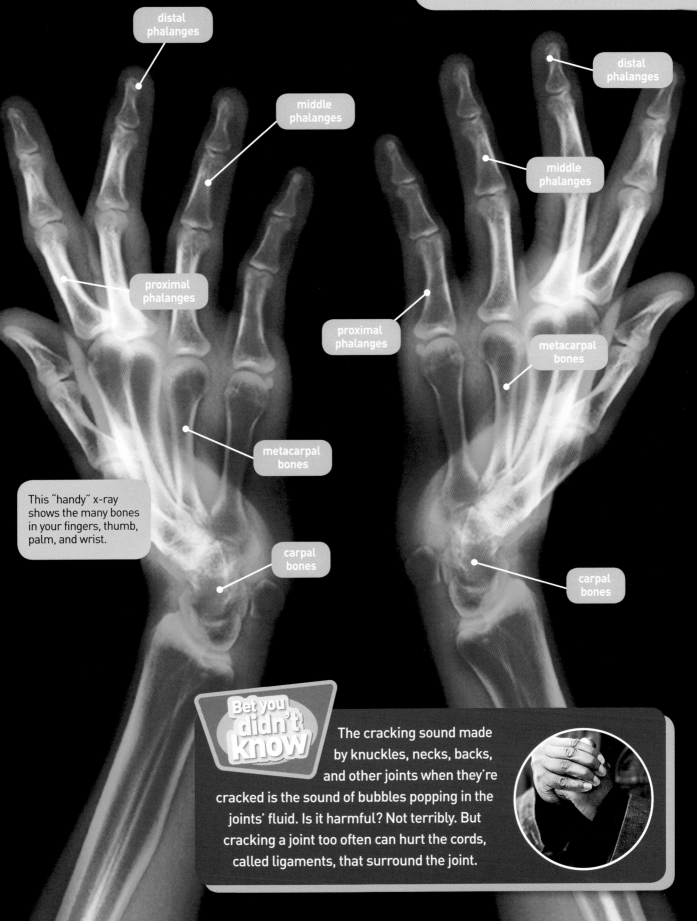

distal phalanges

middle phalanges

distal phalanges

middle phalanges

proximal phalanges

proximal phalanges

metacarpal bones

This "handy" x-ray shows the many bones in your fingers, thumb, palm, and wrist.

metacarpal bones

carpal bones

carpal bones

Bet you didn't know

The cracking sound made by knuckles, necks, backs, and other joints when they're cracked is the sound of bubbles popping in the joints' fluid. Is it harmful? Not terribly. But cracking a joint too often can hurt the cords, called ligaments, that surround the joint.

ADD IT UP

An average person walks about 100,000 miles (160,934 km) in his or her life. That's like walking around the world four times at the Equator!

Bears, raccoons, and mice are among the animals that walk on "flat feet" as humans do.

FANCY FOOTWORK:
BONES OF THE FEET

Like your hands, your feet contain a big portion of your body's skeleton. Each foot contains 26 bones. The toes, like your fingers, contain 14 of them. The rest of the bones form the sole and the ankle.

The bones in your feet are supported by strong muscles and ligaments. The ligaments wrap around part of the foot and the ankle, helping to hold everything in place. They work like the support bandages that athletes wrap around ankles and other joints.

Look at the sole of your foot, and you'll see a curve that runs from your heel to just behind your toes. This is your foot's arch. It has a tough, stretchy ligament that works as a shock absorber inside your foot.

Why does your foot need a shock absorber? Think about it: Whenever you step, stomp, jump, dance, and run, your weight travels down through your leg bones and into your foot's bones. The arch works like a big rubber band to absorb this pounding.

PICTURE-PERFECT FOOTPRINTS

What kind of feet do you have? Are they flat? Do they have high arches? It's very easy to find out! All you need is a little water, an outdoor area, a paper shopping bag or sheet of construction paper, and ... your foot.

First pour a little water on a flat, outdoor spot, such as a sidewalk. Step in the water with your bare foot. Then step onto the paper. Lift your foot and look at the print you've made. Compare it with the pictures on this page to see if you have a high, medium, or low arch.

A foot with a very low arch is known as a "flat foot." Some people with low arches suffer from tired, achy feet after lots of standing or walking. Very high arches, on the other hand (or foot!), put a lot of stress on the bones between the toes and ankle. Doing special foot exercises and putting arch supports inside shoes can help.

flat arch   medium arch   high arch

THE BRAIN BOX: YOUR SKULL

Have you ever worn a helmet? A helmet is a hat designed to protect your head. There are special helmets designed for sports, such as football, and jobs, such as construction. All these helmets protect your skull so it can do its job—protecting your brain!

Your skull is built to absorb the shock of a bang on the head. It's made up of 22 bones. Only one of these, your lower jaw, also called the mandible, can move. The rest are fused together to make a very strong built-in helmet.

Your skull is not only strong, but also light, thanks to air spaces in the bones around your nose and eyes. These spaces are called sinuses. These spaces may fill with fluid when you have a cold. That's why you feel "stuffed up."

Look at a skull, and you'll see lines that look like stitches. They are actually joints called sutures. At birth, a baby's skull isn't a solid, fused box. Its skull bones must be able to move and even overlap as the baby is squeezed and pushed out during birth. They are connected by flexible fibers. The bones fuse as the baby grows and form a solid skull by the time he or she is two years old.

HEAD-BANGING

People who design helmets for athletes and workers are always looking for ways to make the headgear even stronger. That's why they're studying an animal that spends its time whacking its head into tree trunks: the woodpecker.

A woodpecker pecks up to 12,000 times a day at high speed. Yet it never hurts itself because there is a pad of spongy cartilage between its beak and skull that works as a shock absorber.

This discovery inspired the invention of a superstrong, superlight bike helmet with a shell that looks like a cardboard honeycomb inside it. Like the woodpecker's cartilage, the cardboard shell contains pockets of air that absorb the shock of a bang. Helmets for other sports are in the works, too.

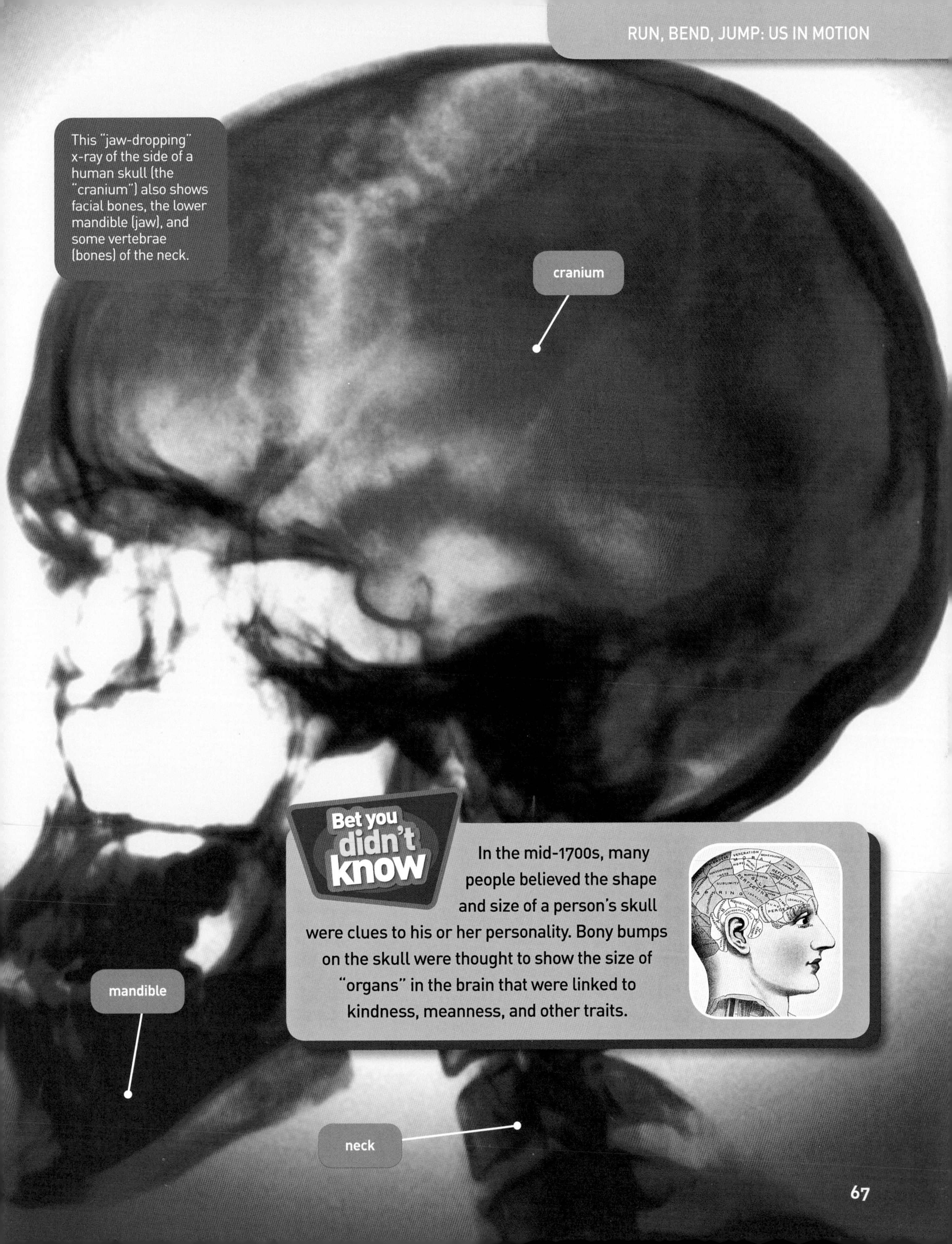

This "jaw-dropping" x-ray of the side of a human skull (the "cranium") also shows facial bones, the lower mandible (jaw), and some vertebrae (bones) of the neck.

cranium

mandible

Bet you didn't know

In the mid-1700s, many people believed the shape and size of a person's skull were clues to his or her personality. Bony bumps on the skull were thought to show the size of "organs" in the brain that were linked to kindness, meanness, and other traits.

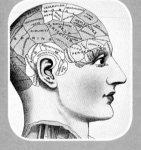

neck

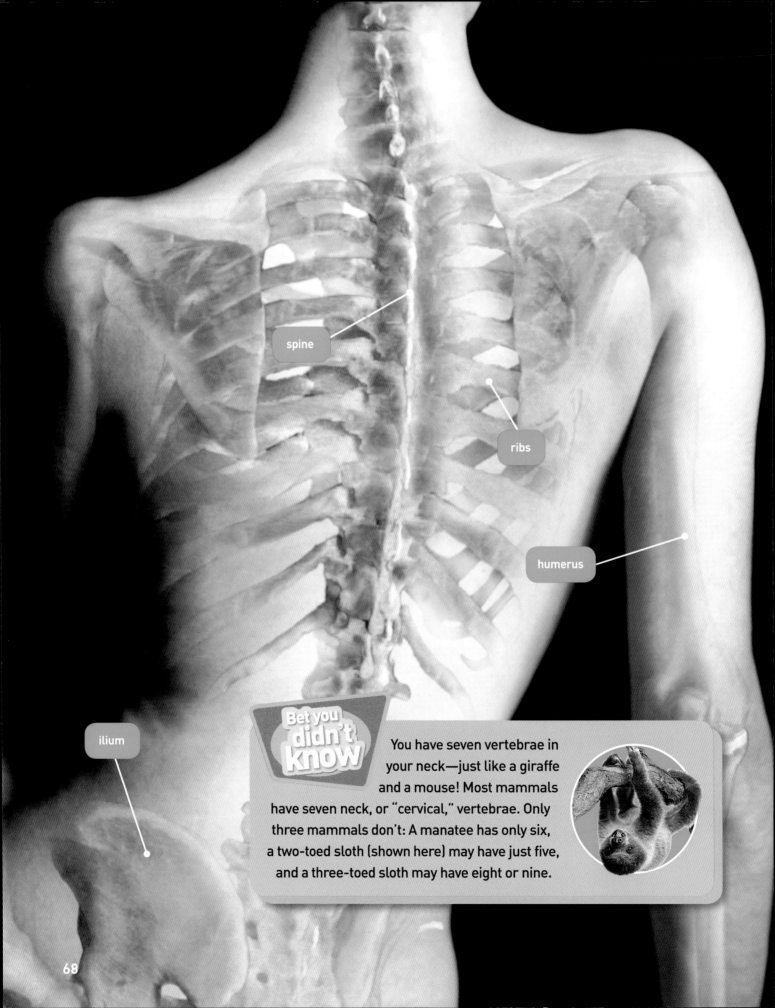

spine

ribs

humerus

ilium

Bet you didn't know

You have seven vertebrae in your neck—just like a giraffe and a mouse! Most mammals have seven neck, or "cervical," vertebrae. Only three mammals don't: A manatee has only six, a two-toed sloth (shown here) may have just five, and a three-toed sloth may have eight or nine.

YOUR SUPERFINE SPINE

Stacked in your back is a column of 26 bones called vertebrae. All together, they form your backbone, or spine. Like a column, your spine makes it possible for you to stand up straight. Unlike a column, your spine is flexible!

Joints made of cartilage fit between each vertebra. Each one can move just a little bit. When these movements are added up, however, they let your spine bend so you can reach down and touch your toes or twist from side to side. At the same time, your spine is also protecting the spinal cord, a bundle of nerves that runs from your brain to the base of your back.

Different sections of your spine also do other jobs. Your neck vertebrae hold up your head and let you move it up, down, and side to side. Your chest vertebrae are attached to your ribs. Big, strong vertebrae in your lower back help hold up your body.

Below that, there are five vertebrae that fuse into one bone, called the sacrum, as you grow. At the very base are two to four very small bones that fuse to form your coccyx, or "tailbone."

SERPENTINE SPINES

Stand with your back against a wall. Make sure your shoulders and your backside are touching the wall. Now slip a hand between your lower back and the wall. Slip your other hand between the back of your neck and the wall.

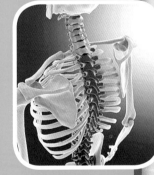

The spaces where your hands fit reveal that your spine has curves—even when you're standing up straight. The natural S-shaped curves of your spine make it work like a spring. Being a little bit "bouncy" helps your spine work as a shock absorber so that your skull and brain don't get jolted with every step you take.

MUSCLE POWER

With its strong bones and flexible joints, your skeleton is built to be on the go. But without muscles, it won't go anywhere! You need muscle power to make your body walk, run, skip, rub your nose, or even just sit up without toppling over.

The muscles that do these jobs are called skeletal muscles. You have about 650 of them, and you can control what they do. Sometimes, it takes a lot of skeletal muscles to make even a simple move. Your tongue alone contains eight muscles!

You also have muscles that work without your having to do a thing. Most of these muscles are called smooth muscles. Sheets of smooth muscle line your blood vessels, throat, stomach, intestines, lungs, and other organs. They are hard at work keeping your blood circulating and your food digesting while you're busy doing other things. And there's also that mighty muscle, your heart. It pumps thanks to cardiac muscles, which are found only in the heart (see page 119).

THE HIBERNATION MYSTERY

Very sick people often lie in bed for a long time as they recover. This lack of exercise weakens muscles—a process called "muscle atrophy." Preventing atrophy may be possible someday thanks to researchers who study hibernating animals.

Bears, for example, spend winter sleeping but do not suffer severe atrophy. When they wake up in spring, they're as strong as—well, bears! Scientists are studying the muscles and blood of bears, ground squirrels, and other hibernators to find out how they stay in  shape while sleeping. The answers may one day help people suffering from muscle atrophy when they're sick or in the hospital for a long time.

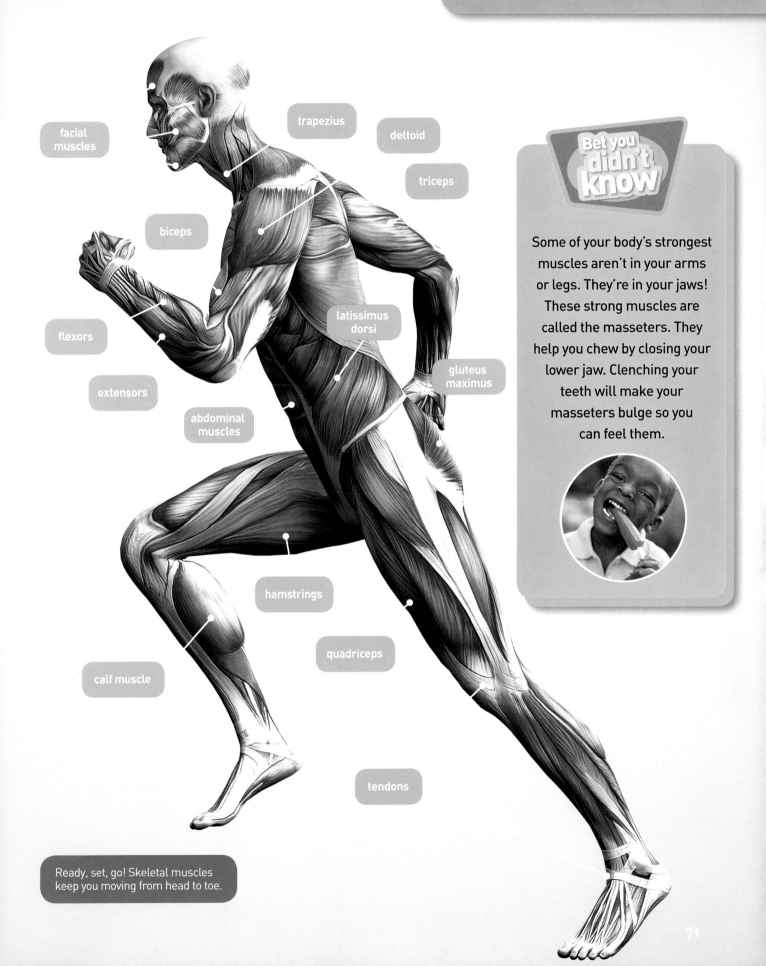

facial muscles

trapezius

deltoid

triceps

biceps

flexors

latissimus dorsi

extensors

gluteus maximus

abdominal muscles

hamstrings

quadriceps

calf muscle

tendons

Bet you didn't know

Some of your body's strongest muscles aren't in your arms or legs. They're in your jaws! These strong muscles are called the masseters. They help you chew by closing your lower jaw. Clenching your teeth will make your masseters bulge so you can feel them.

Ready, set, go! Skeletal muscles keep you moving from head to toe.

ADD IT UP

The fastest muscles in your body are the ones that make you blink. They can contract in less than one-hundredth of a second—as quick as a wink! In just one day, you may blink your eyes 11,500 times or more.

MAKING MUSCLES WORK

Bend your elbow and clench your upper arm. Do you see a bulge there? That bulge is your biceps muscle. It's the muscle that lifted your arm when you bent your elbow.

Like other skeletal muscles, your biceps is made up of many long, spaghetti-shaped cells bundled together. Each one is connected to a nerve and some blood vessels. When you want to raise your arm, your brain sends signals to the nerves in the muscle. The nerves, in turn, stimulate your muscle cells to get shorter and thicker. This is called contracting.

When the muscle contracts, it pulls on whatever is attached to it. Your biceps muscle pulls on bones to raise your arm. Muscles in your face pull on your skin to make you smile. If a muscle isn't pulling, it's relaxing. A muscle can't push.

Even though they're tiny in comparison, **caterpillars** have about **3,200 more muscles** than a human.

MUSCLE MAGIC

Try this trick to catch your muscles in the act of "remembering" a command!

1. STAND IN A DOORWAY. Lift your arms to the side so the backs of your hands are pressed against the door frame on each side.

2. NOW PRESS ON THE DOOR FRAME—HARD! Keep pressing for about half a minute.

3. QUICKLY STEP OUT OF THE DOORWAY. Relax your arms.

4. WATCH as they keep rising up without any command from you!

What's happening? When nerves tell a muscle to contract, calcium is released inside the muscle. Calcium kicks off the reaction that makes the muscle shorten. By pushing for so long against the door frame, you made lots of calcium build up in the muscles. So even though your brain isn't telling your muscles to move, the extra chemicals still spark some motion before being stowed away for future use.

TENDONS:
YOUR MUSCLES' ROPES

Bend your fingers to make your hands look like fierce claws. Do you see straight, hard cords rise up on the backs of your hands? These cords are tendons. A tendon is a tough, thick cord that links a muscle to a bone.

The muscle end of a tendon grows out of the muscle itself. The other end of the tendon is rooted in the bone. Its fibers reach through the bone's outer layer and sink into the bone's hard material.

Tendons look like ropes or flat sheets, depending on how wide their muscles are. They can also be quite long. Those tendons in the backs of your hands, for example, stretch from muscles in your forearm all the way into your fingers.

Some tendons are surrounded by a tunnel, or sheath, that protects them. The sheath makes oil that helps the tendon glide smoothly as it works. This keeps the tendon from getting irritated by rubbing against bones.

ACHILLES' HEEL!

Find the bones that stick out above your ankle. Just behind them, you can feel a tough, thick tendon. It's called the Achilles tendon. It links muscles in your lower leg to your heel.

Its name comes from an old Greek myth that stars a warrior named Achilles. When Achilles was born, his mother dunked him in a river called Styx. The waters of the Styx had magical powers. By dunking the baby boy, the mother had made him immortal. He would suffer no wounds and would never die!

Except ... she was holding him by his heel. That spot didn't get wet. Poor Achilles! His story ends with an arrow flying through the air and landing—you guessed it— right in his heel.

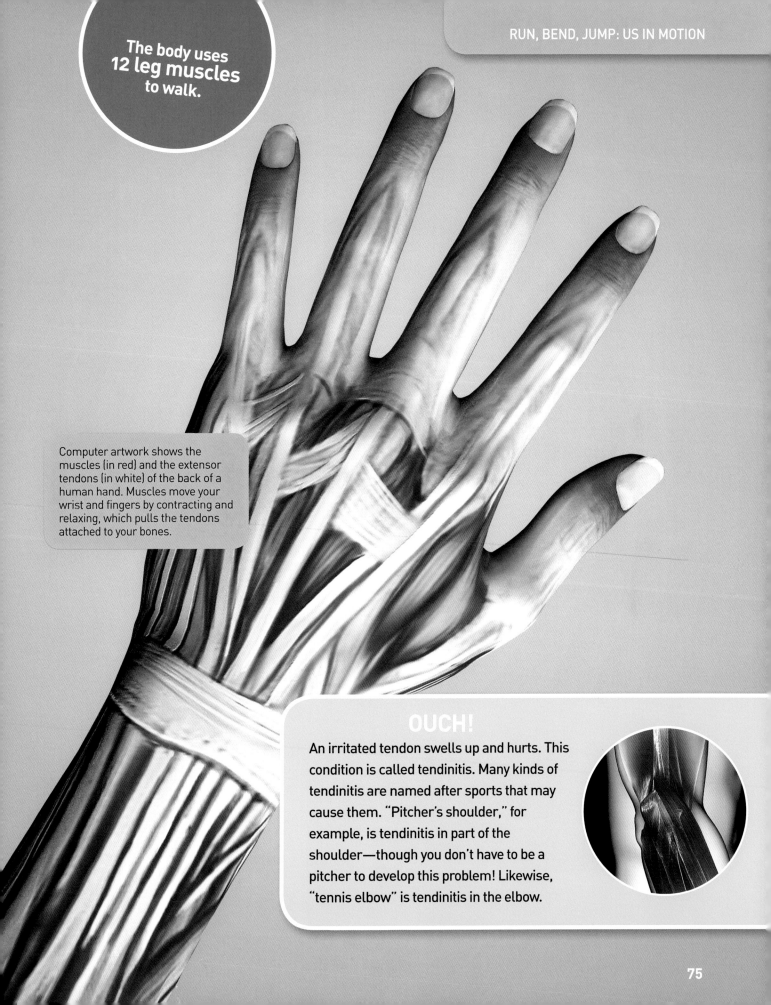

The body uses **12 leg muscles** to walk.

Computer artwork shows the muscles (in red) and the extensor tendons (in white) of the back of a human hand. Muscles move your wrist and fingers by contracting and relaxing, which pulls the tendons attached to your bones.

OUCH!

An irritated tendon swells up and hurts. This condition is called tendinitis. Many kinds of tendinitis are named after sports that may cause them. "Pitcher's shoulder," for example, is tendinitis in part of the shoulder—though you don't have to be a pitcher to develop this problem! Likewise, "tennis elbow" is tendinitis in the elbow.

ADD IT UP
About 30 to 40 percent of a woman's weight is made up of skeletal muscle. For men, skeletal muscle makes up from 40 to 50 percent of their weight.

ACHY MUSCLES

Have you ever ached all over after being very active? Maybe you've played an outdoor sport that you've never tried before, or worked very hard raking up leaves in your yard and the neighbor's, too.

Being extra active or working hard puts a great demand on your muscles. Scientists think it causes extremely tiny—we're talking microscopically tiny—tears in the fibers. This causes pain. But when the muscles heal, they're stronger than before.

This kind of pain is different from pain caused by an injury. Hurting a muscle causes a sharp, sudden pain. The injury may be a strain, which is also called a "pulled muscle." It means the muscle has been stretched farther than it should be, so the tears in it are bigger. Worst of all is a torn muscle. A muscle that's been badly torn needs to be taken care of by a doctor.

Our muscles got their name from the Latin word *musculus* for "little mouse." Romans thought a flexing muscle looked like a mouse moving under the skin.

WICKED STITCHES

You're running in a playground with some friends. Suddenly, you get a stabbing pain in your side. Ouch! The pain is so sharp, you have to stop running. What you've got is a stitch.

Experts aren't sure exactly what causes a stitch. It may be a cramp in the big muscle that lies between your chest and your belly. This muscle is called the diaphragm, and it's one of the muscles you use for breathing. Or it may be caused by an irritated nerve. Either way, when a stitch hits, the best thing to do is stop running for a bit, rub your side, and catch your breath.

FUELED BY FOOD: THE DIGESTIVE SYSTEM

CHAPTER

4

MAC & CHEESE, PLEASE!

Walking. Talking. Thinking. Blinking. Running, hopping, reading, shopping.
You need energy to do these activities and many more. Even sitting in a chair requires energy! This energy comes from food—your body's fuel.

Your body also needs building materials, which are supplied by food as well. And your body uses food to make you grow, heal your injuries, and build new cells and tissues to replace old ones that have worn out.

A banana muffin, however, can't fit inside a tiny cell. Your body needs to break down the muffin into simple ingredients that it can use. No, that doesn't mean flour, sugar, eggs, and the other ingredients you mixed to make the muffin! The ingredients your cells can use are chemicals called nutrients.

Your digestive system's job is to turn food into basic building blocks that can build more of YOU ... and keep you running, too.

LUNCHTIME

What's on your school lunch menu this week? Your answer could depend on where you are! If your school is in the United States, you might be expecting cheese pizza with a side of broccoli, or  maybe a chicken sandwich. If you're in South Korea, you might be enjoying *kimchi* (fermented vegetables) or potato pancakes, and in Denmark, roasted duck and potatoes. In Sweden? Smoked salmon. In Slovakia? Perhaps smoked mackerel. In Brazil, rice and beans. In Japan *goubou* (burdock root) salad, rice, fish, or *udon* (noodle) soup. No matter where in the world you are, a healthy lunch is the fuel that helps keep you going!

Most people spend about **five years** of their lives **eating.**

ADD IT UP

About 37 percent of Earth's land area is used for raising food. About two-thirds of this farmland is used as "range and pasture," where animals such as dairy cows, beef cows, sheep, and other animals feed. The rest of the farmland is cropland, which includes everything from fields of wheat to apple orchards.

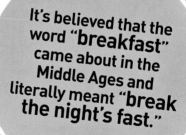

It's believed that the word "**breakfast**" came about in the Middle Ages and literally meant "**break the night's fast.**"

The land mammal with the most teeth is the giant armadillo of South America. It has from 80 to 100 teeth! The ocean mammal with the most teeth is the long-beaked common dolphin, which can have more than 200 teeth.

FIRST STOP: THE MOUTH

Chomp! **You bite into a crunchy apple.**
Crunch. Your teeth mash the apple into applesauce. *Gulp!* It slides down your throat, and you're ready for the next bite.

Your teeth are the hardest things in your body. They crush food so your body can digest it more easily. You have different kinds of teeth to get the job done: Sharp incisors and canine teeth in the front slice and shred food, while bumpy premolars and molars in the back grind it.

Though teeth are hard, they contain living tissue. Inside each tooth is a pulpy center that is filled with nerves and blood vessels.

Your muscular tongue not only tastes food, it also moves it around your mouth and senses the food's temperature and texture. (See pages 172–173 for more information about taste.) Amazingly, it manages to avoid getting bitten by your teeth (most of the time!). Your mouth also contains salivary glands, which produce saliva, or spit.

TOOTH ATTACK!

Your mouth is home to more than a billion bacteria! A typical mouth contains 75 to 100 or more different kinds. Some bacteria are harmless, but others cause tooth decay.

These bacteria feed on sugar in your mouth. Then, like all living things, they produce waste products. Their waste is an acid that eats away at the surface of your teeth. As their numbers grow, a yellowy film called plaque forms on teeth—a yucky brew of bacteria, food, mucus, and acid.

Brushing at least twice a day and flossing once a day is the best way to keep these bacteria under control and avoid getting cavities.

Slurp down a cold drink too quickly? Press your tongue to the roof of your mouth to make the "brain freeze" go away.

83

YOUR SPECTACULAR SPIT

Has your mouth ever watered when you smelled good food cooking? Your salivary glands are just getting ready for the meal they'll soon be helping you digest.

The slimy saliva sloshing around in your mouth is produced by three pairs of salivary glands. One pair sits under your tongue. Another pair is wedged back toward your throat. The third pair is in front of your ears.

Saliva trickles from these glands through small tubes into your mouth. Its job is to moisten food and make it easier to swallow. Saliva also contains chemicals called enzymes. Different enzymes speed up different chemical reactions in your body.

Your mouth also makes small amounts of saliva even when you're not eating. This helps keep your mouth moist. Saliva also contains materials that weaken acids made by cavity-causing bacteria.

One of the reasons your mouth produces spit is because food must be **dissolved** in water to have taste.

THE STRENGTH IN SPIT

There's an enzyme in saliva called salivary amylase that breaks down starchy food, such as bread, crackers, and rice. It starts digesting food right in your mouth! You can check it out with this simple spit test. All you need is two small glasses, a cracker, and your spit.

Save up some spit in your mouth. Spit it into a small glass. Then put water in another glass just like the first one, so that the water level matches the spit level.

Now put one cracker in the spit and another cracker in the water. They'll both get mushy, but you'll see the spit cracker starts breaking down. It's being digested!

Bet you didn't know

Your salivary glands produce from 2 to 6 cups (0.5 to 1.5 liters) of saliva a day. Six cups of saliva would come close to filling a big, 2-liter (67.6-ounce) soda bottle!

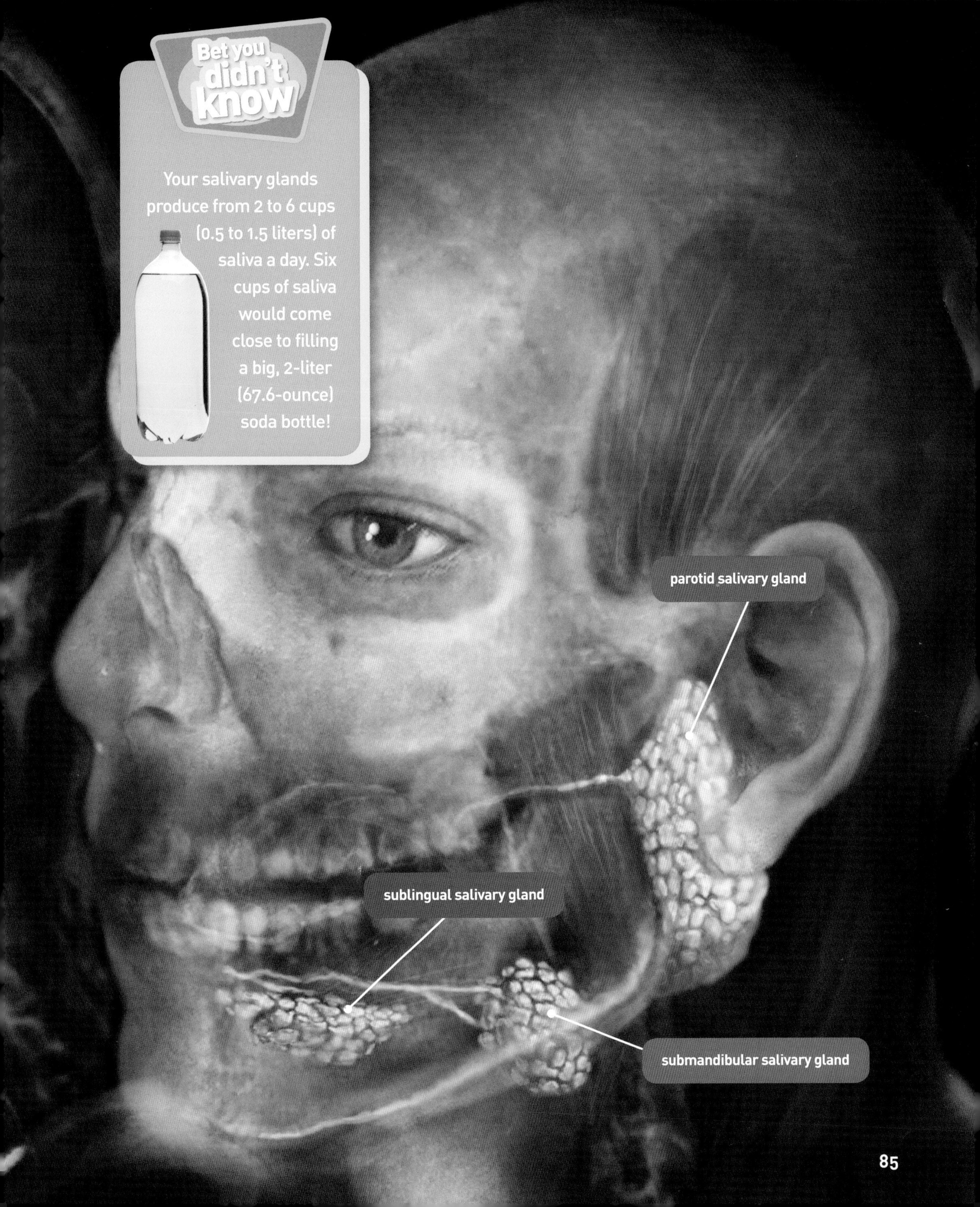

parotid salivary gland

sublingual salivary gland

submandibular salivary gland

It takes four to eight seconds for a lump of food to travel down your esophagus into your stomach.

Your **esophagus** scrunches up so that its inner walls touch when you're not swallowing.

DOWN THE HATCH: YOUR THROAT

You've chewed your food. Now it's time to swallow. This is where the tongue comes in. Your tongue moves the food to the top of your throat. Then, gulp! You swallow, and you're on to the next bite. Your throat, however, is busy taking care of that first gulp.

After you gulp, the rest of the swallowing process happens automatically. You don't have to think about it or do anything. As soon as the lump of food enters your throat, a flap of tissue called the epiglottis seals off the paths to your nose and lungs. Muscles move the food into the esophagus, a tube that leads to your stomach.

The esophagus is about ten inches (25 cm) long. Cells on its surface ooze slimy mucus to help food slip down it. Smooth muscles in its walls squeeze the food down to your stomach. This squeezing action is called peristalsis. Peristalsis moves food through your whole digestive system.

BE A HERO

Sometimes food goes down the wrong tube and ends up in the windpipe to the lungs. The food blocks the windpipe and causes choking. Choking can be deadly. Thousands of people die from choking each year.

In 1974, a doctor named Henry Heimlich invented a way to save choking victims. He taught people how to wrap their arms around a choking person from behind and press quickly and forcefully on a spot above the belly button. The method became known as the Heimlich maneuver. It has saved many people's lives. (See illustrations below.)

Even kids have saved lives using this maneuver. Find out about first-aid classes for kids in your area and see if you can learn it, too!

MEET YOUR STOMACH

The food you eat plops into your stomach, a muscular bag just under your ribs. When it's empty, this bag is crumpled into a blob no bigger than a baseball. But a stomach is stretchy, so when food arrives, it expands. It can stretch many times its empty size if stuffed with a big meal.

Smooth muscles in the stomach wall then get busy churning the food. Glands in the stomach walls pour digestive juices into the mix. Food spends up to four hours being sloshed and stewed in your stomach.

By now, the food looks nothing like what you ate. It's a soupy substance called chyme (rhymes with "time"). The stomach slowly squeezes chyme into the next part of your digestive system, where the nutrients will be absorbed.

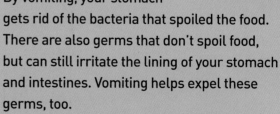

Some South American tribes thought **snakes** caused **stomachaches.** To help heal from them, medicine men made prayer sticks shaped like snakes.

UNPLEASANT UPCHUCK

Sometimes your stomach doesn't hold your meal very well. Instead, it sends it back up your esophagus and out your mouth again. This awful process is called throwing up, or vomiting.

It's really unpleasant to throw up, but it's one of your body's ways of protecting itself. Your stomach might reject a meal because it contains spoiled food. This illness is called food poisoning. By vomiting, your stomach gets rid of the bacteria that spoiled the food. There are also germs that don't spoil food, but can still irritate the lining of your stomach and intestines. Vomiting helps expel these germs, too.

You can also throw up if your stomach gets irritated, which can happen if you eat way too much. Sometimes motion can upset tummies, too, making you get seasick or carsick.

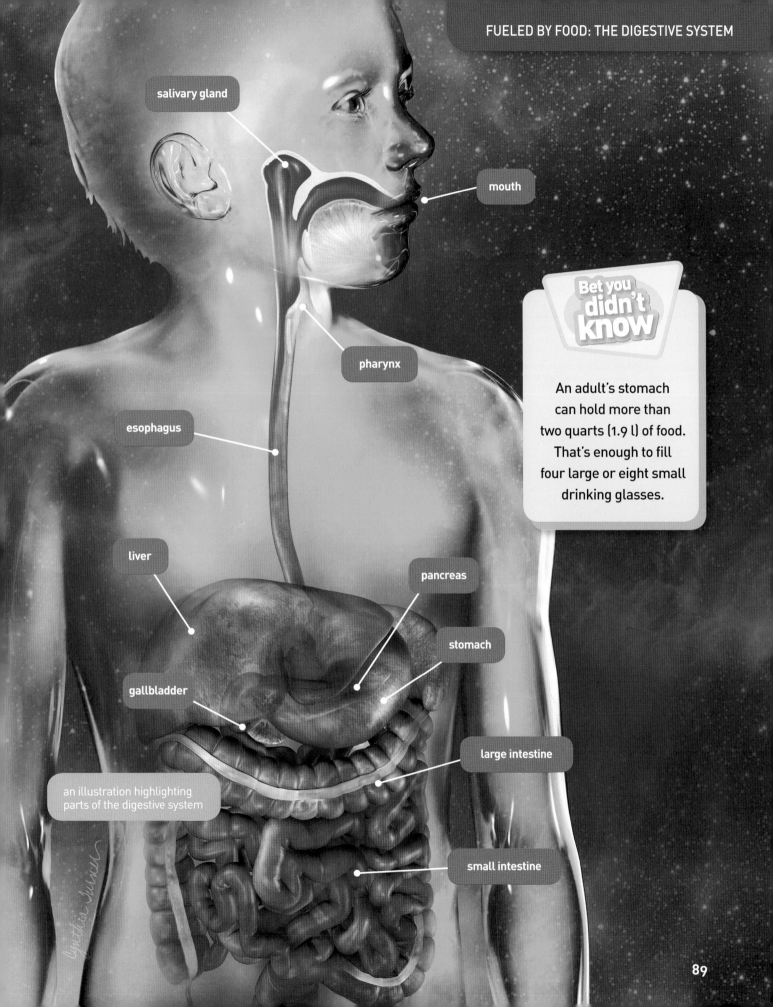

salivary gland

mouth

pharynx

esophagus

Bet you didn't know

An adult's stomach can hold more than two quarts (1.9 l) of food. That's enough to fill four large or eight small drinking glasses.

liver

pancreas

stomach

gallbladder

large intestine

an illustration highlighting parts of the digestive system

small intestine

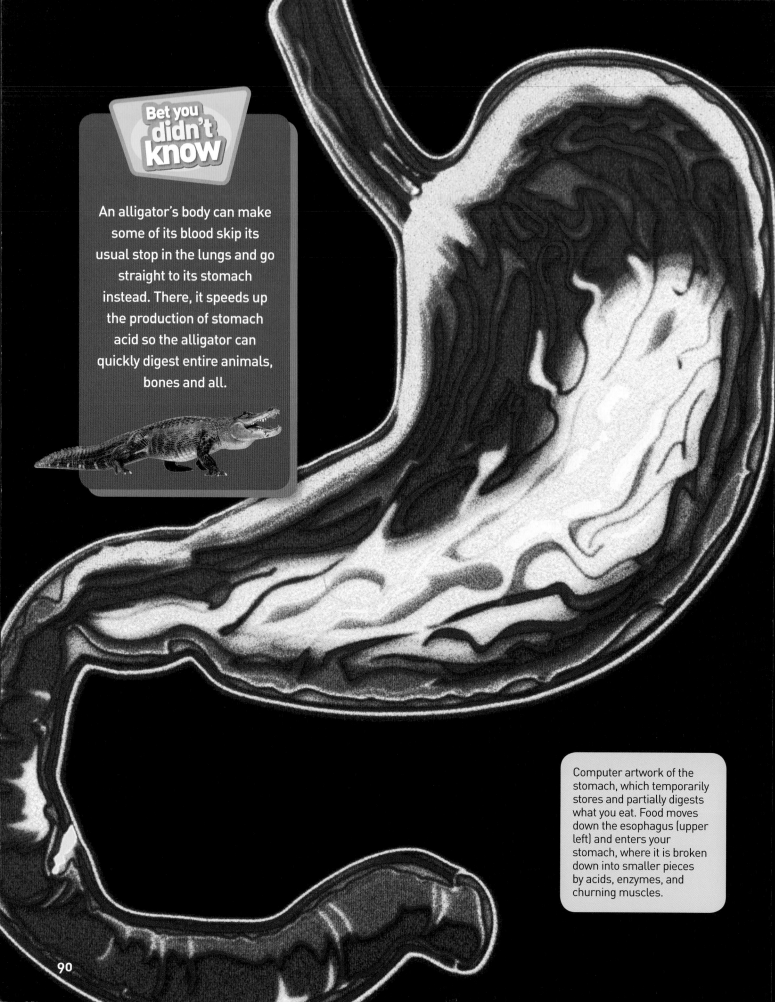

An alligator's body can make some of its blood skip its usual stop in the lungs and go straight to its stomach instead. There, it speeds up the production of stomach acid so the alligator can quickly digest entire animals, bones and all.

Computer artwork of the stomach, which temporarily stores and partially digests what you eat. Food moves down the esophagus (upper left) and enters your stomach, where it is broken down into smaller pieces by acids, enzymes, and churning muscles.

A BIG BATH OF ACID!

Your stomach has superpowers!

One of the juices that it makes is a powerful chemical called hydrochloric acid. This acid is so strong, it can dissolve an iron nail!

Inside your stomach, however, the acid works with other chemicals to digest protein in your food. It also helps your body absorb vitamin B12, which keeps your nerves and blood cells healthy. As if that's not enough, stomach acid even kills many germs that get into your tummy!

How does the stomach avoid digesting itself? Luckily for you, it doesn't just have acid glands. It also has glands that make protective mucus. The mucus they ooze protects your stomach from its own acid. The stomach also replaces its inner lining very quickly. Cells on the surface live only from three to five days and are constantly replaced by new cells, so any cells that are damaged by acid are rapidly replaced by fresh ones.

Snakes have long, expandable stomachs that help them digest their prey whole.

THE STOMACH PEEPHOLE

In 1822, Dr. William Beaumont cared for a patient who had been accidentally shot in the stomach. He tended to the injured man, saving his life. But even though the wound got better, it never closed fully. The man was left with a small hole on his left side. With the man's  permission, Beaumont used this opportunity to find out how digestion worked. He tied different kinds of food to bits of string. Then he lowered them into the man's stomach through the hole and pulled them out to check on them. The two worked together for ten years.

It sounds gross (and it was!), but Beaumont's research revealed how digestion worked. Before his discovery, it was believed that food was digested by rotting inside the stomach, like garbage dumped in a pit.

LOVE YOUR LIVER

Say hello to your body's biggest internal organ, the liver! By the time you're a grown-up, your liver will weigh about three pounds (1.4 kg).

This large, rubbery, reddish brown organ handles more than 500 different jobs. One of its most important tasks is processing the nutrients from food. Your blood picks up these nutrients from your small intestine and carries them to your liver. Then the liver decides what to do with them.

Some nutrients are broken down into smaller chemicals or made into new ones. Others, such as extra sugars, are stored for future use. Minerals such as iron and copper are stored, too. So are many vitamins.

Meanwhile, the busy liver is also breaking down harmful substances, such as alcohol, and turning them into less harmful chemicals. It's also destroying old blood cells, filtering out bacteria, and making a digestive juice called bile. Phew!

THE SUN'S CURE

After the liver destroys worn-out red blood cells, it's left with some garbage: a yellow substance called bilirubin. It gets rid of most of this bilirubin by adding it to the bile it makes.

When a baby is born, however, sometimes its liver isn't working at full speed yet. Bilirubin builds up in its blood. The baby's skin and eyes turn yellow. This condition is called jaundice.

In 1956, a nurse noticed that jaundiced babies became less yellow after they got some sunshine. Scientists then studied the use of light for jaundice. Light therapy, such as this fiber optic pad (above), is still used today to treat babies with jaundice.

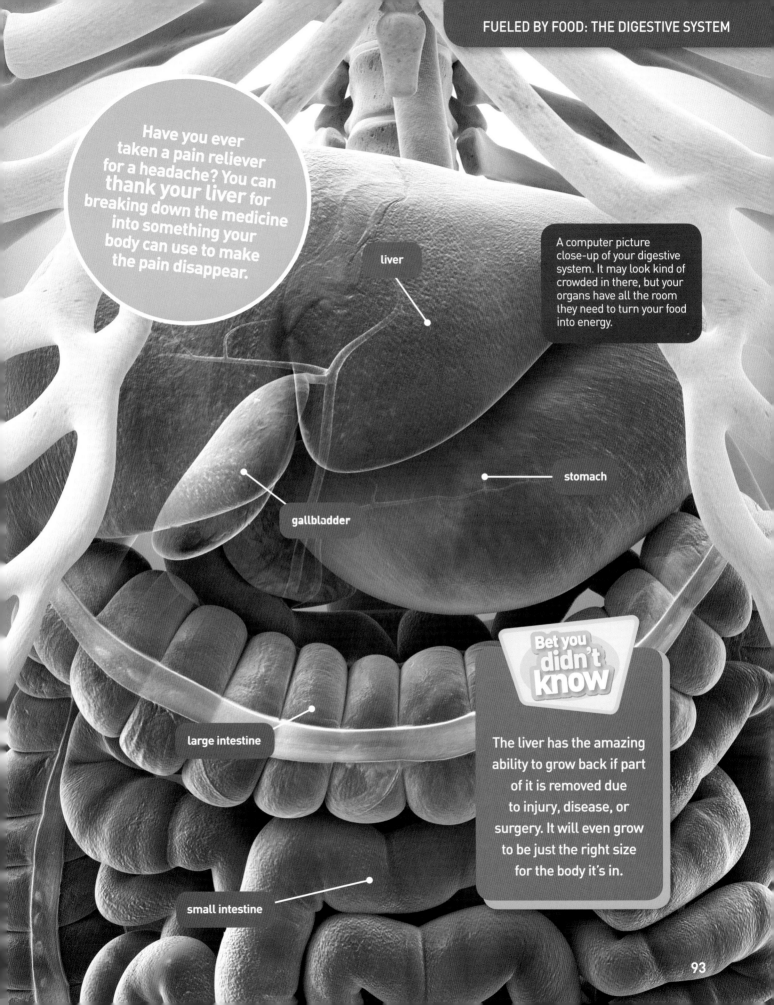

Have you ever taken a pain reliever for a headache? You can **thank your liver** for breaking down the medicine into something your body can use to make the pain disappear.

A computer picture close-up of your digestive system. It may look kind of crowded in there, but your organs have all the room they need to turn your food into energy.

liver

stomach

gallbladder

large intestine

small intestine

Bet you didn't know

The liver has the amazing ability to grow back if part of it is removed due to injury, disease, or surgery. It will even grow to be just the right size for the body it's in.

93

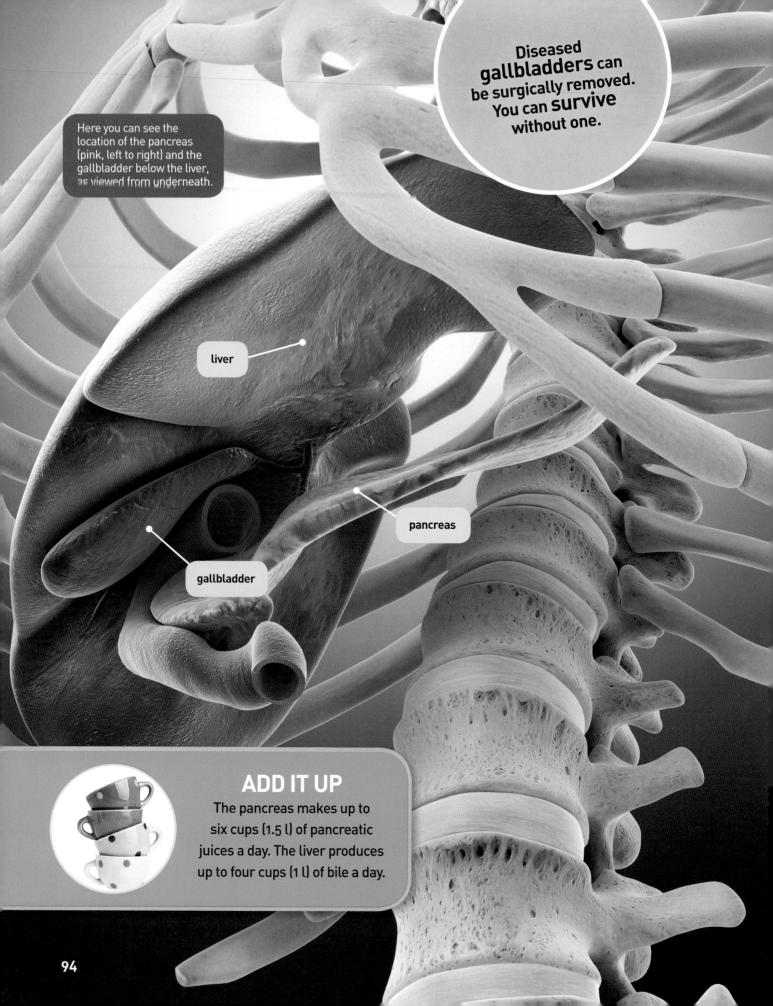

Here you can see the location of the pancreas (pink, left to right) and the gallbladder below the liver, as viewed from underneath.

Diseased **gallbladders** can be surgically removed. You can **survive** without one.

liver

pancreas

gallbladder

ADD IT UP

The pancreas makes up to six cups (1.5 l) of pancreatic juices a day. The liver produces up to four cups (1 l) of bile a day.

DIGESTIVE JUICERS: GALLBLADDER AND PANCREAS

You probably don't mention your gallbladder or your pancreas in everyday conversation. But they are vital parts of your digestive system.

The gallbladder is a green, baglike organ about the size of an egg that is tucked under your liver. Bile made by the liver flows through a tube into the gallbladder for storage. The gallbladder also removes some of the water in the bile, making it thicker and stronger.

Later, the gall bladder squeezes bile into the small intestine, which is the next stop on the digestion route. The bile helps digest fatty foods.

The gallbladder shares a tube leading into the small intestine with its next-door neighbor, the pancreas. The pancreas isn't a storage bag—it makes most of the enzymes your body uses to digest food. These enzymes break down the three main nutrients that come from the food you eat: fat, proteins, and carbohydrates. The pancreas also makes substances that control levels of sugar in your blood.

A SENSE OF HUMOR

About 2,000 years ago, in ancient Rome and Greece, people thought that your personality was related to the balance of fluids in the body. These fluids were called "humors." Two of the humors were bile—one yellow, one black. The other two were blood and phlegm (snot!).

If you had too much yellow bile, for example, you were very stuck-up and got mad easily. Too much black bile? You were crabby and sad. Too much phlegm meant you were sluggish. Too much blood, however, made you brave.

This belief in "four humors" hung on until the mid-1800s.

95

THE NOT-SO-SMALL
SMALL INTESTINE

Your stomach has finished churning up your food and turning it into a batch of gooey chyme. But the chyme still needs digesting. So your stomach squirts it into the next stop on its journey: your small intestine, which has one of the biggest jobs in your body. Its task is to soak up, or absorb, all the nutrients in your food.

The small intestine oozes digestive juices that go to work on the chyme. Bile and pancreatic juices drip into the small intestine, too. Meanwhile, muscles in the small intestine's walls squeeze the chyme, squishing it back and forth as it moves "down the pipe." This process is called segmentation.

If you could see inside the small intestine, it would look fuzzy. That's because its tunnel is lined with millions of little "fingers" called villi. The villi give the intestine more surfaces for absorbing nutrients. If you could iron the intestines and villi flat, they would cover a tennis court!

It takes about **three to five hours** for chyme to travel through all the twists and turns of the small intestine.

RUMBLING TUMMIES

Has your stomach ever growled? The rumbling, grumbling sounds you hear from your middle are called borborygmi. And don't blame your stomach: Most of the sounds actually come from your small intestine!

Air bubbles get mixed in with chyme as it travels through your body. They make burbling noises as your intestines squeeze them. You notice the burbling more when your digestive system is low on food. When there is food in your intestines, it muffles the noises, so you don't notice them as much.

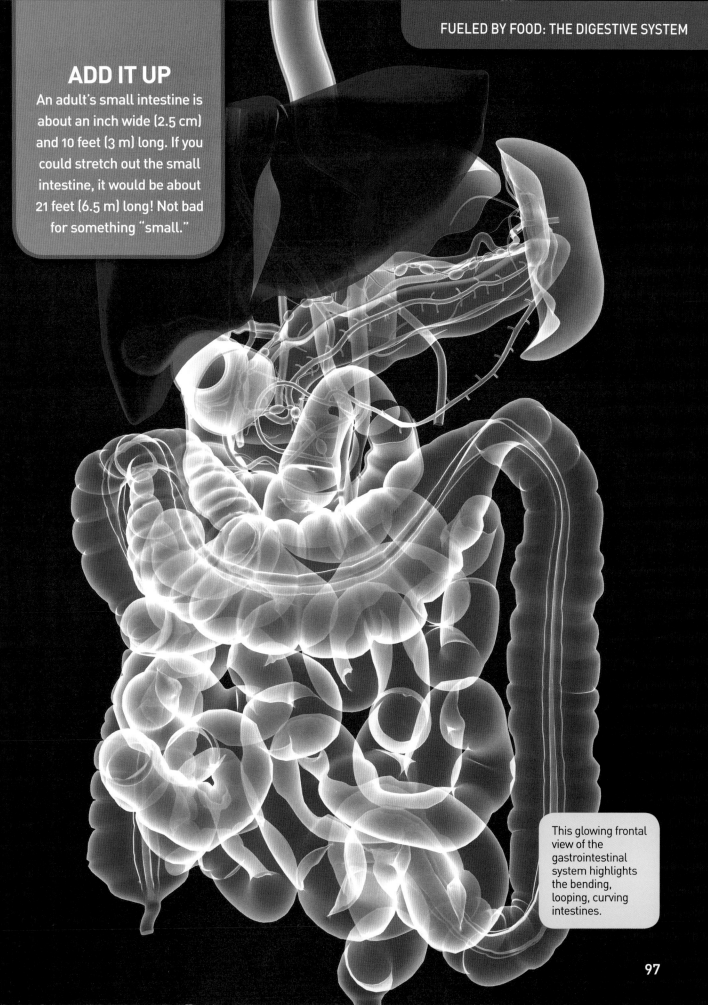

ADD IT UP

An adult's small intestine is about an inch wide (2.5 cm) and 10 feet (3 m) long. If you could stretch out the small intestine, it would be about 21 feet (6.5 m) long! Not bad for something "small."

This glowing frontal view of the gastrointestinal system highlights the bending, looping, curving intestines.

A sea cucumber is a sluglike ocean animal that's related to sea stars. Some kinds of sea cucumbers eject their intestines and other guts when fish attack them! The stringy organs are sticky and poisonous—and do a good job of repelling predators. The sea cucumber can survive without guts until they grow back in a few weeks.

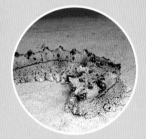

large intestine

small intestine

A person can become constipated if waste material moves through the large intestine too slowly.

The **large intestine** includes three sections: the cecum, the colon, and the rectum.

NEXT STOP:
THE LARGE INTESTINE

The coils and curls of your small intestine wind their way to your large intestine—which is shorter than the "small" intestine! An adult's large intestine is only about five feet (1.5 m) long. It's shorter than the small intestine because it isn't twisty.

The large intestine got its name because it's more than twice as wide as the small intestine. It's about 2.5 inches (6.5 cm) across. The large intestine differs from the small intestine in other ways, too. It doesn't make any digestive enzymes. It doesn't have any villi. Its surface looks smooth, not fuzzy.

The large intestine's main jobs are different, too. Its first task is to soak up any water left in chyme after it leaves the small intestine. It absorbs about two pints (1 l) of water a day, which prevents your body from becoming dried out, or dehydrated.

The other important chore handled by your large intestine is dealing with stuff your body can't digest. This stuff is turned into feces—otherwise known as poop.

THE MYSTERIOUS APPENDIX

The first part of your large intestine is a pouch called the cecum. It receives waste from the small intestine. Dangling from the cecum is a mysterious worm-shaped tube called the appendix.

The appendix is only three to four inches (8 to 10 cm) long. Most people only think about their appendix if it gets infected, swells up, and hurts. It must then be removed. People can live perfectly well without an appendix.

In the past, scientists thought the appendix was just a useless bit of tissue. New research, however, shows that the appendix may store "good" bacteria that help your digestive system work.

THE SCOOP ON POOP

Just what are feces, and why do we have to poop regularly? Feces are what's left after your digestive system has finished digesting your food. As food moves through your system, your organs work hard to extract nutrition from it.

Some parts of food, however, can't be digested. The human body simply doesn't make enzymes that can digest them, and it gets no energy or nutrition from them. This indigestible material is known as fiber, or roughage.

Fiber isn't just garbage, however. It's important for your health, because it keeps your intestines working properly. In your large intestine, for example, fiber keeps feces moving along, so you don't get "plugged up," or constipated.

Feces also contain water, dead white blood cells and intestinal cells, and bile, which gives them their color. Last but not least, about one-third of poop is made of—ick!—bacteria!

FAST FOOD

It takes about 24 or more hours for your food to travel through your body from end to end. The rate of digestion varies from person to person, though. Some people may turn soup to poop in just 16 hours while another person may take a day and a half. The rate varies by meal, too. A big Thanksgiving dinner may take as much as three days, while a snack of fruit may take just a few hours.

In general, a meal spends 2 to 3 hours in your stomach and another few hours in your small intestine. Then it takes its time trudging through your large intestine, spending 20 hours or even more inside this tube.

That's forever compared with the digestive rate of a hummingbird! A hummingbird that sucks up a meal of nectar may digest it and poop out the leftovers in less than an hour. A cow, however, may take from 70 to 100 hours to digest its food. That's because grass and hay are hard to digest. By keeping the food in its body for a long time, the cow is able to extract the most nutrients possible from it.

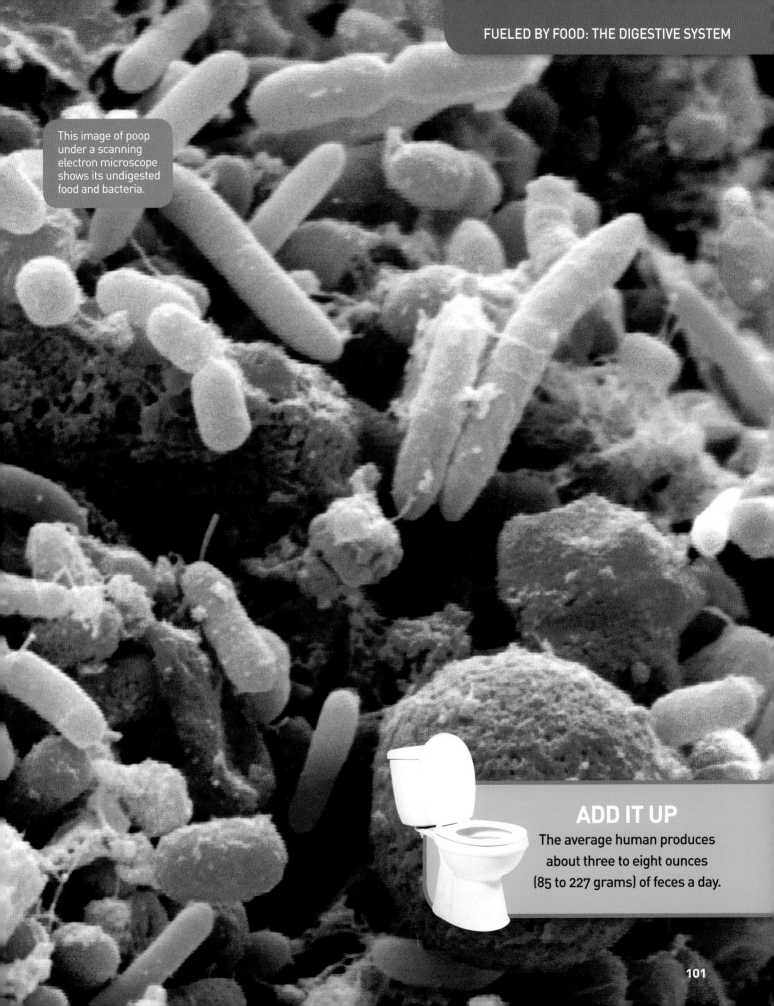

This image of poop under a scanning electron microscope shows its undigested food and bacteria.

ADD IT UP

The average human produces about three to eight ounces (85 to 227 grams) of feces a day.

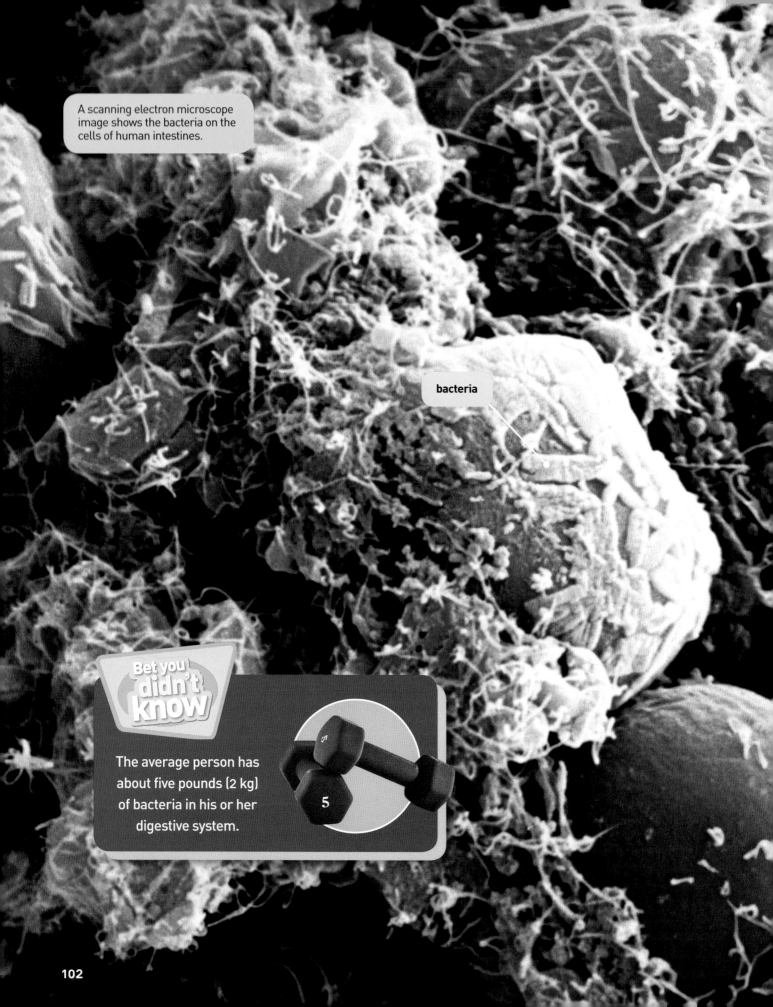

A scanning electron microscope image shows the bacteria on the cells of human intestines.

bacteria

Bet you didn't know

The average person has about five pounds (2 kg) of bacteria in his or her digestive system.

5

THE ZOO
INSIDE YOU!

If a third of the solid material in poop consists of dead bacteria—where are all the live ones? They're in your intestines—about 100 trillion of them!

Why would bacteria want to live in your intestines? From their point of view, it can't be beat: It's warm, it's wet, and there's a steady supply of food. Many bacteria also "pay back" the human they're in by doing useful jobs. Some intestinal bacteria, for example, make important nutrients, such as vitamin K. You get some vitamin K from food, but your bacteria make most of your supply.

Intestinal bacteria also digest some of the fiber that your organs can't. This bacterial breakdown wrings a few more nutrients from your food.

Your "gut flora" also crowd out germs that can make you sick. There is nowhere for the "bad" bugs to live if all the space is occupied by "good" bugs.

Escherichia coli bacteria live in your intestines along with other kinds of bacteria. Most strains of E. coli are harmless, and many help you by making vitamins. Bad strains, however, can make you very sick.

CUTTING THE CHEESE

All those bacteria busily digesting food in your intestines produce a side effect you could do without: stinky gas.

This gas has to go somewhere, so it exits your body from your backside. This process is called flatulating or "passing gas." The bad smell of the gas comes from sulfur, a substance released by the bacteria.

The average adult produces enough gas in a year to fill about 48 one-gallon (182 one-liter) jugs a year. People burp, too. But burping is usually the result of swallowing air when you eat.

MY STOMACH HURTS

Stomach bugs, bellyaches, barfing, puking, throwing up, "the runs" . . . people have lots of words to describe the misery of stomachaches, vomiting, and loose bowels, or diarrhea. These problems can be caused by everything from nervousness to serious diseases.

A dull pain in your belly and cramps in your middle, for example, may be due to nothing more than gas trapped in your intestines. It doesn't like being stretched and inflated like balloons, and it lets you know it! This pain often goes away when you poop.

A typical bout of "stomach flu," however, is usually caused by germs. This is the kind of "bug" that keeps you home from school for a day or two. You're miserable with cramps, vomiting, and diarrhea.

Why the diarrhea? Because just as your stomach gets rid of germs by vomiting, your intestines rush feces out of your body to get rid of germs. The feces are watery because your large intestine doesn't have time to absorb water the way it does when your guts are healthy.

SURVIVING A STOMACH BUG

A stomach bug makes you feel horrible. The last thing you feel like doing is eating or drinking anything.

But it's very important to make sure you drink plenty of fluids. Your body loses a lot of liquid when you vomit and have diarrhea, so you must replace it to avoid becoming dehydrated. Being dehydrated not only feels bad, it is also dangerous.

The best fluids are "clear" ones: water, ginger ale, broth, and watered-down juice. Drink small sips often instead of a whole glass. When your stomach feels a bit better, start eating again, but slowly and carefully. Good foods for starters are bananas, white rice, applesauce, toast, and plain crackers.

Make sure an adult knows where and how much you hurt.

Some animals, such as the turkey vulture, throw up on purpose to defend themselves. The vomit grosses out their enemies and keeps them away. *Eww!*

opening of the stomach

Norwalk virus

This computer image shows an infection of the gut caused by the Norwalk virus, a common sickness transmitted by contaminated food and water that causes diarrhea, vomiting, and stomach pains.

YOUR BLOOD, BREATH, AND BEATING HEART

CHAPTER 5

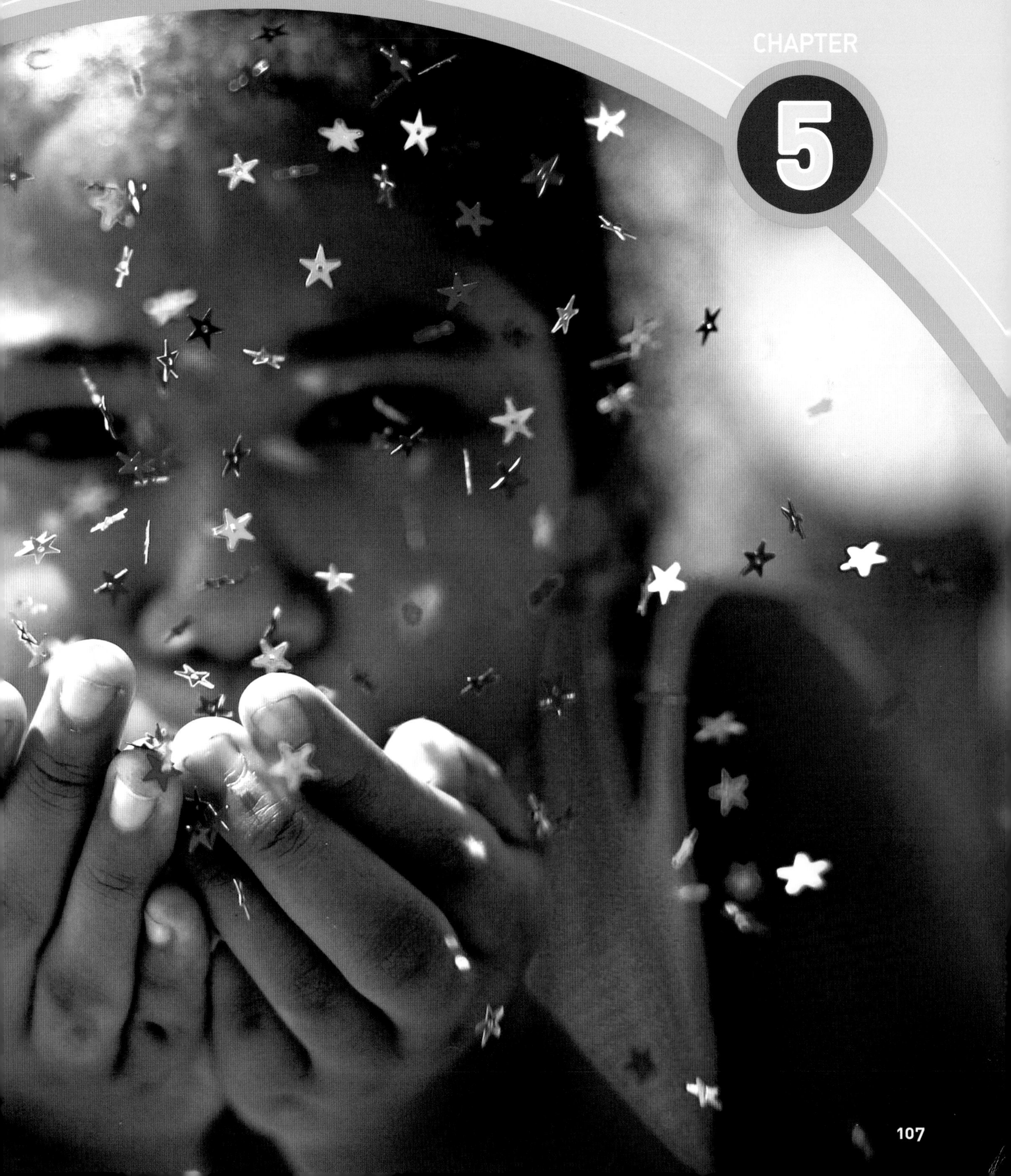

RIVER OF LIFE: YOUR BLOODSTREAM

Think about the most basic things you need to survive. Air is one, right? So is water. And food. You need these things because your body cells need them, too. Your cells can't work and keep you alive without oxygen, water, and nutrients.

Your body must somehow get oxygen, water, and nutrients from the outside of your body to the inside. Then it must deliver it to every single cell, no matter how small it is or how deep it is inside your body. This is the job of your circulatory system—the stream of blood that flows endlessly through your body.

The circulatory system is powered by your heart. It beats nonstop to keep your blood moving. Your circulatory system also teams up with your respiratory system, which is made up of your nose, throat, and lungs. Your lungs are responsible for bringing air into your body so your blood can grab the oxygen you need to stay alive.

The heart pumps blood through its largest artery at about **one mile an hour** (1.6 km/h). In tiny vessels, blood moves only 43 inches an hour (109 cm/h).

THE ABOs OF BLOOD

Every human's blood contains the same basic assortment of materials, but there are a few chemicals that differ from person to person. These chemicals are known as antigen A, antigen B, and the Rh factor.

A person whose blood contains antigen A is said to have type A blood. A person with antigen B has type B blood. Got both types? Your blood is type AB. If you don't have either, your blood type is O. You're also either Rh positive or Rh negative. About 85 percent of people are Rh positive.

All these blood types do the same job. Blood type becomes important mainly when a person needs a blood transfusion. That's when donated blood is added to a person's body. A transfusion might be necessary if a person has lost blood in an accident or is having an operation.

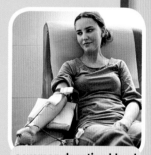
a woman donating blood

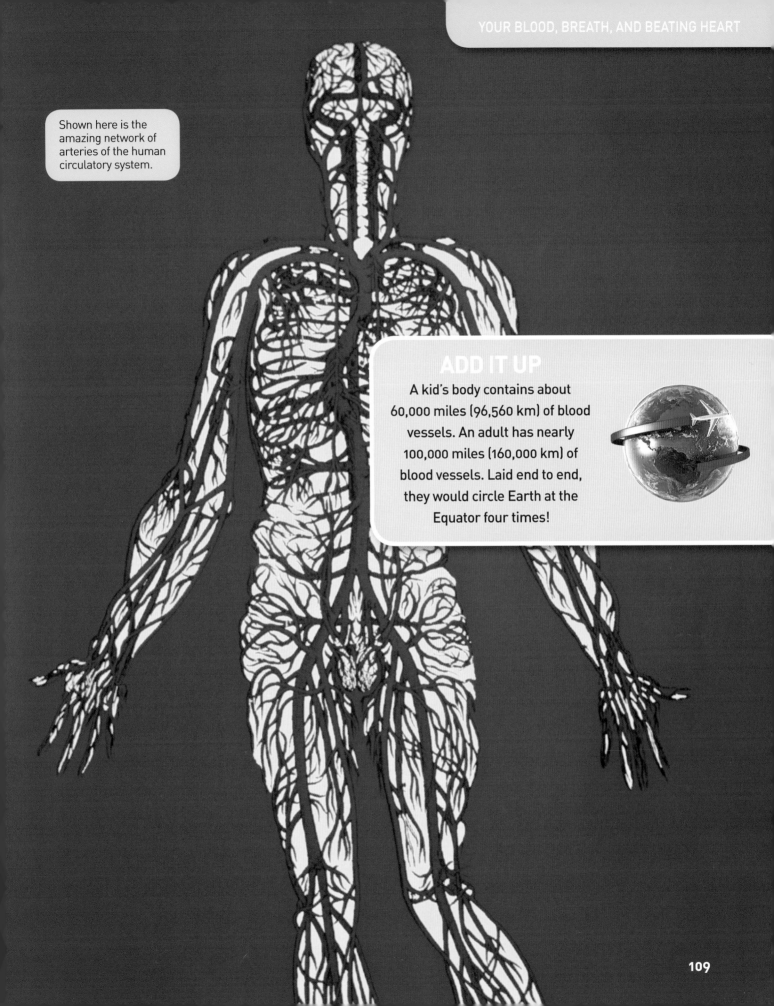

Shown here is the amazing network of arteries of the human circulatory system.

ADD IT UP

A kid's body contains about 60,000 miles (96,560 km) of blood vessels. An adult has nearly 100,000 miles (160,000 km) of blood vessels. Laid end to end, they would circle Earth at the Equator four times!

red blood cell

white blood cell

 **Bet you didn't know** Your blood flows about 12,000 miles (19,000 km) a day as it cycles through your body over and over again. That's like making a trip from east to west across the widest part of the Pacific Ocean.

WHAT IS BLOOD?

You probably don't think much about your blood until some of it oozes from a cut in your skin. But your blood is hard at work keeping you alive 24/7.

The amazing red liquid we call blood is actually made up of a few different substances.

A little over half of your blood consists of a yellow-white fluid called plasma. Plasma is a mixture of water, gases, minerals, nutrients such as vitamins, and chemicals produced by different organs in the body. Bobbing along like rubber ducks in the plasma are a variety of blood cells, which make up the rest of your blood.

All the blood in your body makes up about 8 percent of your body weight. For an adult, that's up to 6 quarts (5.7 l) of blood. That's enough to fill one and a half plastic one-gallon (3.8 l) milk jugs!

Your blood's main job is to pick up oxygen, water, and nutrients and deliver it to all your body's cells. Blood not only drops off these goodies, but also takes away "trash," whisking waste materials out of cells.

A MEDICAL BLUNDER

For thousands of years, people believed draining some blood on purpose was a good way to cure diseases. This process is called bloodletting. Blood was drained by cutting the skin or by putting bloodsucking worms called leeches on the body!

Bloodletting was done to treat everything from the flu to broken bones. The "treatment" often made patients weaker and sometimes even killed them. But at the time, doctors believed bleeding helped balance body fluids and restore health. It wasn't until the late 1800s that scientists showed how germs caused diseases, not blood.

RED BLOOD CELLS

Your blood is red thanks to its red blood cells. Red blood cells are red because they contain an iron-rich protein called hemoglobin. Iron combines easily with oxygen (that's how iron gets rusty and red).

Iron's fondness for oxygen makes hemoglobin the perfect substance for transporting oxygen. Red blood cells load up with oxygen in the lungs. Then, like little delivery trucks, they *whoosh* along in your bloodstream, dropping off oxygen supplies to the cells in your body along the way.

After the red blood cells have unloaded all their oxygen, they head back to the lungs to pick up some more.

You have more than enough red blood cells to get the job done. An adult human's body contains about 25 trillion red blood cells. There are about 5 million red blood cells in just one drop of blood! That's why people can donate blood for use in hospitals. They can spare a small amount, plus their bodies will quickly make new blood to replace it.

Blood is always **red**, but its shade varies by location in the body.

CIRCULAR MOTION

The ancient Greeks believed digested food was turned into blood inside the liver and that from there, blood flowed up or down to nourish the body. They thought the heart was a furnace that heated the body. Doctors, too, thought that was how the body worked for hundreds of years.

Then, in 1628, an English doctor, William Harvey, wrote a book about how blood moved in animals' bodies. It was based on his own scientific studies. Harvey showed how the heart pumped blood, pushing it around the body through veins and arteries. He described how blood went around and around inside the body. Harvey's discovery of circulation changed medicine forever.

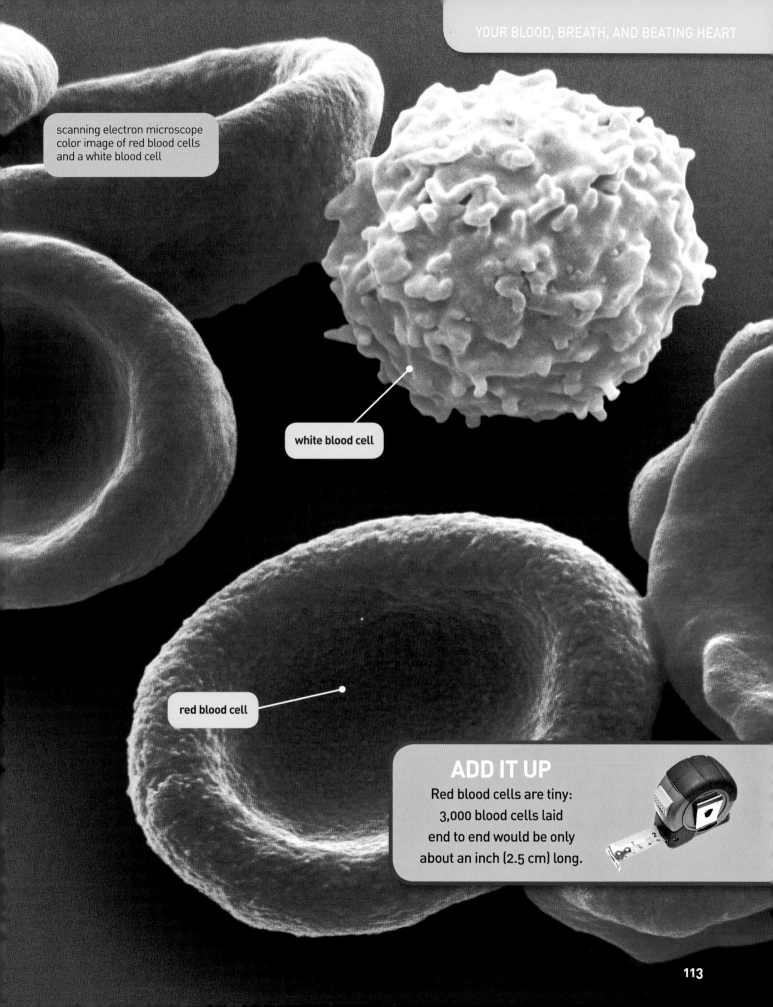

scanning electron microscope color image of red blood cells and a white blood cell

white blood cell

red blood cell

ADD IT UP

Red blood cells are tiny: 3,000 blood cells laid end to end would be only about an inch (2.5 cm) long.

Just one drop of blood contains about 10,000 white blood cells and 250,000 platelets.

platelet

white blood cell (leukocyte)

scanning electron microscope color image of a group of white blood cells and activated platelets in human blood

Most white blood cells are produced in a soft tissue called **marrow** inside bones.

RESCUE SQUAD:
OTHER BLOOD
CELLS

Red blood cells are the most plentiful kind of cell in your blood. But your blood also contains white blood cells—about 35 billion of them float in an adult's bloodstream. These cells don't transport oxygen. Instead, they help fight diseases and infections.

Some white blood cells gobble up bacteria. Others recognize viruses that have caused diseases you've had before, such as a certain kind of flu. They immediately produce chemicals that kill the virus and stop you from getting the disease again. This attack helps your body mount a fast, strong defense against the disease.

Last but not least are the platelets. Platelets are not whole cells—they're more like cell scraps. Their job is to help form clots. If you cut your skin, platelets rush to the scene. They attach to the sides of blood vessels and become spiky and sticky. They also release chemicals that attract more platelets, which add to the sticky pileup. The platelets also react with substances in the blood to form a sort of net that traps blood cells and forms a clot.

FANTASTIC FILTERS

Your body has a second circulatory system that you don't hear much about. It's called the lymphatic system. It's made up of vessels that carry a watery liquid called lymph.

Lymph vessels have two jobs. One is to soak up fluid from body tissues and return it to your bloodstream. The other is to fight disease. Like blood, lymph contains germ-fighting white blood cells. Lymph vessels also have bulges, called nodes, which filter germs from lymph. White blood cells in the nodes destroy the germs.

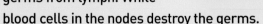

Your tonsils are part of your lymphatic system. They catch germs that try to sneak down your throat. Another lymph organ is the spleen, a potato-shaped organ near your stomach. The spleen filters germs and worn-out red blood cells from blood.

YOUR HARDWORKING HEART

Make a fist. Place it in the middle of your chest, just a little to the left. That's about how big your heart is, and where you'll find it in your body.

Your heart started beating before you were born. It will continue beating for your entire life—thumping 100,000 times a day. With each beat, it pumps blood around your body, keeping you alive.

This muscular organ is actually two pumps in one. The heart's left side pumps blood to your body. This blood is rich with oxygen. After its journey around your body, the blood returns to your heart. It enters the heart's right side, which pumps it to your lungs so it can pick up a fresh supply of oxygen.

Each side of the heart has two chambers. The top chamber is smaller and is called an atrium. The bottom chamber is bigger and is called a ventricle. Blood goes into the heart through the atria and is pumped out from the ventricles.

DECODING YOUR HEARTBEAT

Your heartbeat sounds like *lub-dup, lub-dup,* over and over again, when you hear it through a device called a stethoscope. These noises are made by flaps of tissue, called valves, inside your heart.

The valves' job is to stop blood from flowing "backward" in the heart. They make sure blood is always being pumped on its way to the body or lungs.

There is a valve on each side of the heart that separates the atria and the ventricles. After blood leaves an atrium and goes into a ventricle, the valve snaps shut. This stops the ventricle from pumping blood back into the atrium instead of into a blood vessel. That's the *lub* you hear.

After the ventricle pumps the blood out of the heart, a valve in the blood vessel snaps shut, too. This stops blood from leaking back into the heart. That's the *dup* you hear.

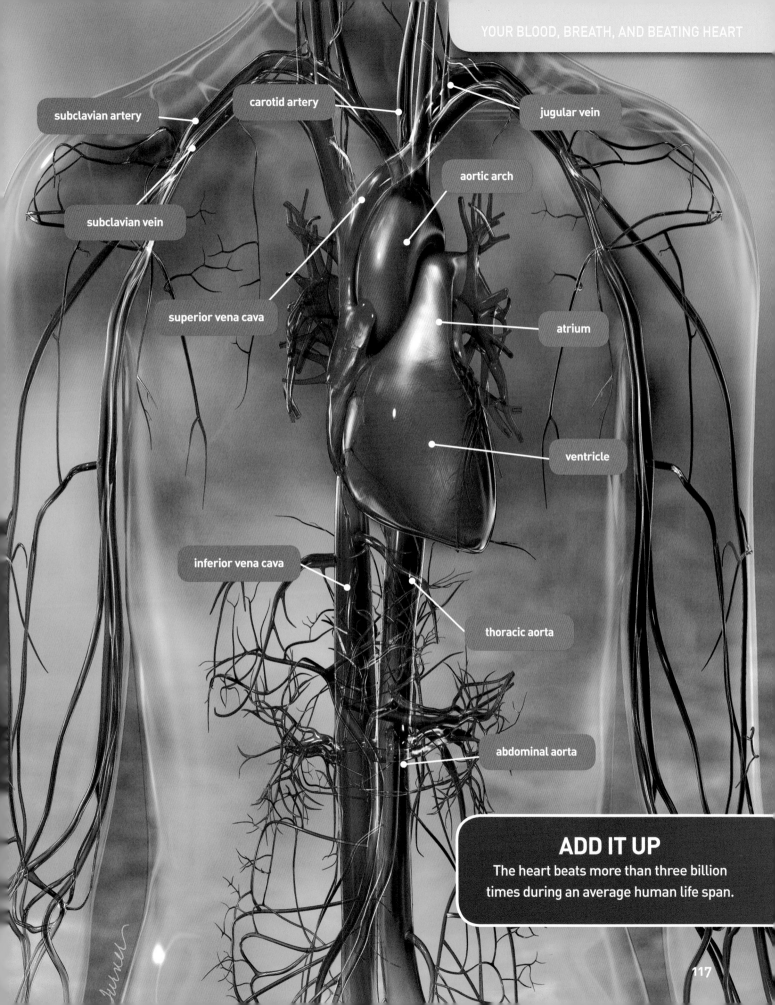

subclavian artery

carotid artery

jugular vein

aortic arch

subclavian vein

superior vena cava

atrium

ventricle

inferior vena cava

thoracic aorta

abdominal aorta

ADD IT UP
The heart beats more than three billion times during an average human life span.

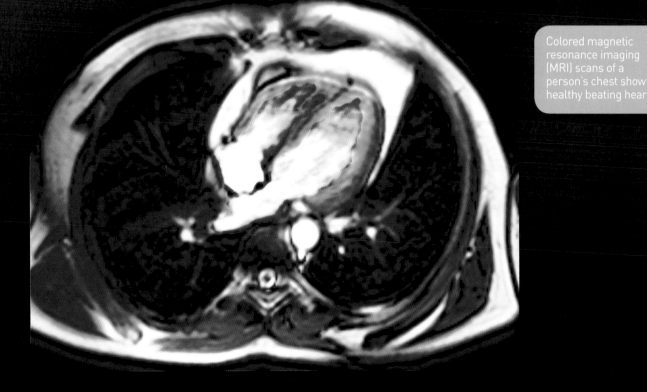

Colored magnetic resonance imaging (MRI) scans of a person's chest show a healthy beating heart.

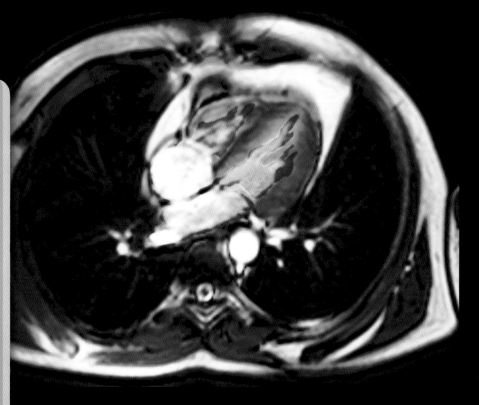

THE BEAT GOES ON

The heart is powered by cardiac muscles, which aren't found anywhere else in the body.

("Cardiac" means "of the heart.") These muscles look a bit like skeletal muscles, but work by themselves—you aren't able to "tell" them what to do.

Like other muscles, cardiac muscles work by contracting. They contract rhythmically and automatically thanks to your heart's own built-in electrical system. This system is based in a small piece of tissue that sits near the top of the right atrium. It sends out an electrical signal that makes muscle cells contract at the same time. It also tells another part of the heart to get ready to pump out the ventricles.

All that pumping is hard work, even for cardiac muscles that don't need a rest! Where does the heart get its energy? From the same source that other body parts do: the blood. When the heart pumps blood out to the body, some of it flows into a special blood vessel that leads back to the heart, to keep it supplied with oxygen and nutrients, too.

PRACTICE PULSE-TAKING

You can feel your heartbeat in your chest. You can also feel it in other parts of your body, such as your wrist or the side of your neck. The beating you feel in these places is called your pulse. A pulse is like an echo of your heart's beat. It's caused by your blood vessels throbbing as each heartbeat pushes blood through them.

You can "take your pulse" to measure your heart's rate of beating. You can gently press the inside of your wrist with two fingers, or rest your fingertips lightly on one side of your throat. Typical heart rates for a person at rest range from 60 to 100 beats per minute. What's yours?

THE BLOOD VESSEL HIGHWAY

Your body is laced with blood vessels, which are tubes made of muscle and other tissue. There are three main kinds of blood vessels:

- Arteries, which carry blood away from the heart
- Veins, which carry blood to the heart
- Capillaries, which connect arteries and veins

The heart's left ventricle pumps oxygen-rich blood into a big artery called the aorta. This big artery divides into smaller arteries, just like a highway map shows big streets branching off into smaller roads.

The smallest arteries feed into arterioles that then feed into even smaller capillaries. Capillaries are much finer than a human hair—so thin that red blood cells must squeeze through in single file! Oxygen, water, and nutrients ooze out of their thin walls and into body cells. In the same way, the cells' waste materials seep into the capillaries.

The tiny capillaries feed into tiny venules that then feed into veins, which lead to bigger and bigger veins and finally back to the heart. Then the heart pumps the blood to the lungs to get a fresh supply of oxygen, and the cycle begins again.

FILL IT UP!

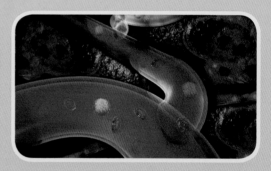

Arteries have stronger, more muscular walls than veins do. Arteries close to the heart are especially thick and sturdy because they receive blood rushing out of the pumping heart. An artery can also widen or narrow to adjust blood flow depending on which body part needs the most blood at the moment.

Veins are not as thick and strong. By the time blood is flowing through veins, it is moving slowly. Your movement and muscles help push it back to your heart.

Drop one hand to your side and let it hang. See how the veins fill up with blood? Now raise your hand to eye level and hold it sideways. You will see the veins shrink as blood leaves them.

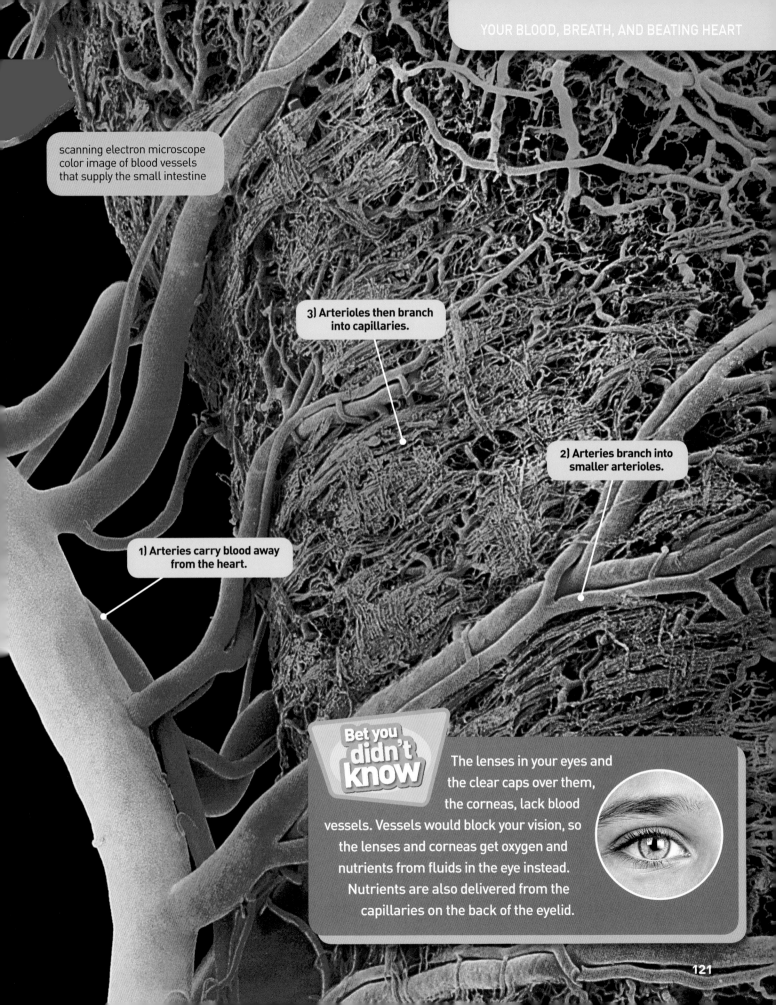

scanning electron microscope color image of blood vessels that supply the small intestine

3) Arterioles then branch into capillaries.

2) Arteries branch into smaller arterioles.

1) Arteries carry blood away from the heart.

Bet you didn't know

The lenses in your eyes and the clear caps over them, the corneas, lack blood vessels. Vessels would block your vision, so the lenses and corneas get oxygen and nutrients from fluids in the eye instead. Nutrients are also delivered from the capillaries on the back of the eyelid.

ADD IT UP

The air you breathe consists mostly of gases your body doesn't need. Only about 21 percent is oxygen. Some of this oxygen enters your blood. Exhaled air contains only about 17 percent oxygen.

TAKE A DEEP BREATH!

Every day, you breathe in and out about 23,000 times! With each breath, your lungs take in, or inhale, fresh air. This is the air that supplies your body with the oxygen it needs.

Breathing starts with the contraction of muscles in your ribs and the diaphragm, a big muscle below your lungs. (Breathe in and you can see and feel how your chest expands.) Air flows in first through your nose, then down through tubes into your lungs.

When you breathe out, or exhale, your rib muscles and your diaphragm relax. Your ribs move inward, your diaphragm curves upward, and your lungs shrink, squeezing out the air inside them.

Lungs, however, are not just empty balloons that inflate and deflate. They are spongy, stretchy organs filled with tiny airways and air sacs. This warm, moist area is where your body's air exchange takes place.

The word "lung" comes from a Germanic word meaning "light"; together your two lungs weigh only 2.5 pounds (1.1 kg).

LUNG HOUSEKEEPING

The air that enters your nose carries dust, pollen, and germs—things you don't want inside your lungs! Luckily, your nose is filled with hairs and sticky mucus that trap them. Your throat and the airways in your lungs produce mucus, too. You produce about 4 cups (1 l) of mucus a day. That's a lot of snot.

a colored image of the lung's lining taken by a microscope

Anything that makes it past the sticky mucus barrier into the lungs is attacked by wandering cells called "dust cells." The dust cells quickly surround and gobble up the invaders. Tiny hairs, called cilia, that line the airways then sweep the dust cells and their prey out of your lungs and into your throat, where you can cough them up.

123

INSIDE THE LUNGS

Your one nose with two nostrils is connected to more than 300 million tiny "air balloons" in your lungs!

When you breathe in, the air that flows through your nose goes down the back of your throat. It enters a stiff tube called the windpipe, or trachea. The trachea carries the air down to your lungs.

At the lungs, the trachea splits to form two tubes. These tubes are called bronchi. The right bronchus goes to the right lung, the left bronchus to the left lung. Inside each lung, the bronchi divide into smaller and smaller tubes called bronchioles.

At the tips of the smallest bronchioles are the tiny "air bubbles" called alveoli. Alveoli are covered with capillaries. The wall of an alveolus is just one cell thick. So is the wall of a capillary. Here, oxygen can enter the blood, and carbon dioxide—a waste gas—can leave the blood.

BREATHTAKING!

The air you exhale contains more than carbon dioxide, oxygen, and other gases. It also contains water! Your breath is moist because the inside of your lungs is moist. You exhale one to two cups (.25 to 0.5 l) of water every day.

You can easily see this water when the air is cold. The water in your breath, which is a gas called water vapor, turns into liquid water as it hits the cold air. Your breath forms clouds. If it's warm out, you won't see the water vapor that travels out with each breath.

The same thing happens if you puff breath onto a cool surface. Lean close to a mirror and exhale on it through your mouth. Can you see a patch of moisture on the mirror?

The left lung is about 10 percent smaller than the right because it has a notch where it curves around the heart.

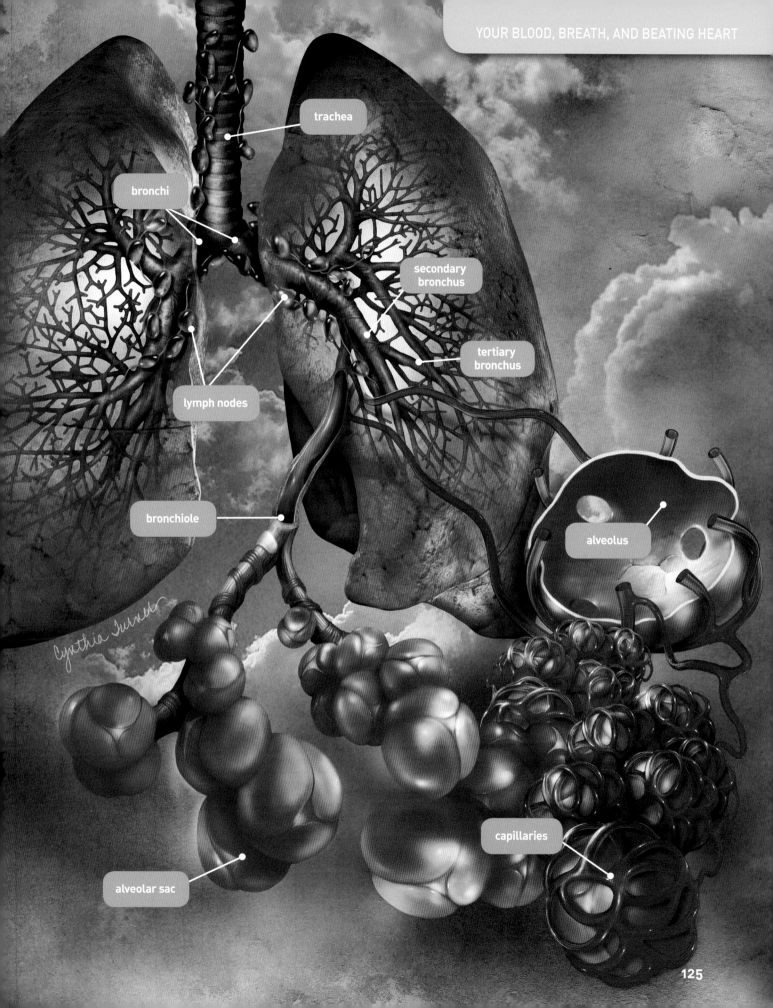

trachea

bronchi

secondary bronchus

tertiary bronchus

lymph nodes

bronchiole

alveolus

alveolar sac

capillaries

Cynthia Turner

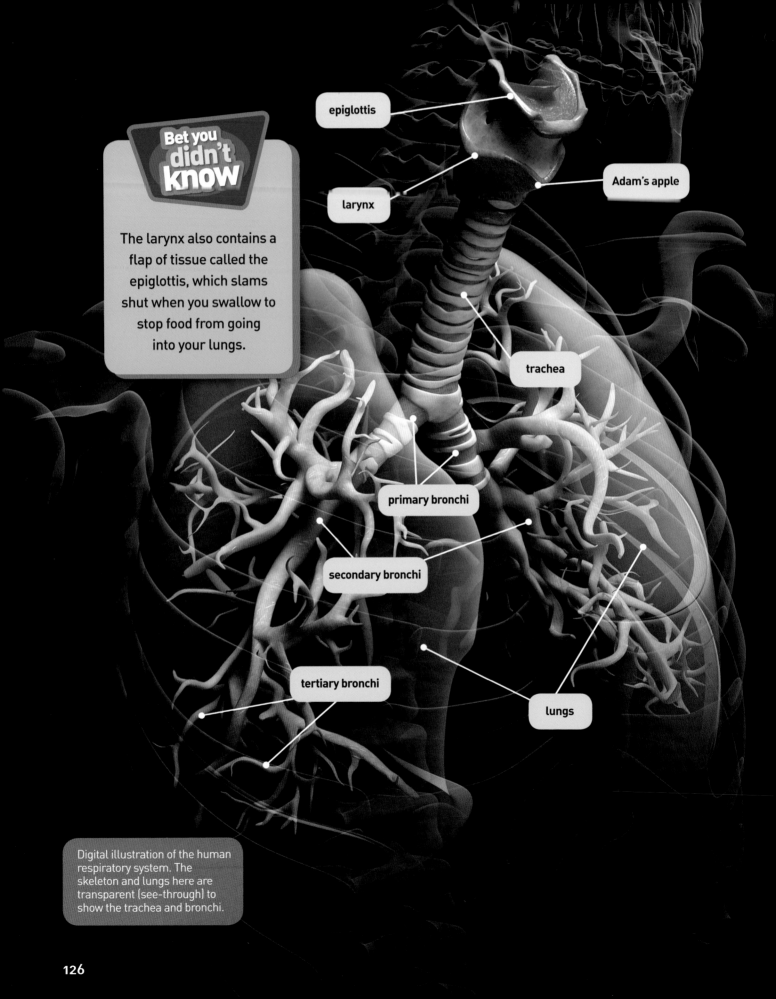

epiglottis

Adam's apple

larynx

The larynx also contains a flap of tissue called the epiglottis, which slams shut when you swallow to stop food from going into your lungs.

trachea

primary bronchi

secondary bronchi

tertiary bronchi

lungs

Digital illustration of the human respiratory system. The skeleton and lungs here are transparent (see-through) to show the trachea and bronchi.

SPEAK UP!

The air you breathe in and out powers your body, but that's not all. It also helps you speak.

The sounds you make to speak are produced inside your voice box, or larynx. The larynx sits in your throat, just above your trachea. You can easily find it. Put your fingers on your throat and hum! You can also feel it move up and down when you swallow.

The larynx contains two ligaments, called vocal cords. When you're silent, your vocal cords are relaxed, leaving an opening for air to flow out easily. When you speak, the cords are pulled tight. Now the air you breathe squeezes through a narrow slot. The vocal cords vibrate, making sounds.

By moving muscles, you can change the sounds. By moving your mouth, tongue, cheeks, and lips, you can shape the sounds into words.

You use a mere **2 percent** of the air you exhale to **speak.** A singing bird, however, uses almost all the air flowing through its voice box.

SOUNDING SQUEAKY?

The faster vocal cords vibrate, the higher the pitch of the sound they make.

Kids usually have high-pitched voices. Their vocal cords may vibrate more than 300 times per second. Many women have high-pitched voices, too. Their vocal cords usually vibrate at about 200 times per second. A woman who sings professionally, however, may be able to hit extra-high notes. Her vocal cords can vibrate up to 2,000 times per second!

When boys and girls go through puberty, their voice boxes grow larger, but for boys the change is more significant. A boy's vocal cords lengthen and thicken to make his voice deeper. As he adjusts to this growth, his voice usually "cracks" when he speaks. Men have larger vocal cords, which vibrate more slowly. They usually vibrate about 115 times per second. A really low voice may be produced by vocal cords vibrating just 60 times per second.

127

AH-CHOO!
COLDS, COUGHS, AND SNIFFLES

Sometimes your breath comes out gently, like when you blow a soap bubble. Other times it comes out quickly, like when you puff the seeds off a dandelion. And sometimes it whooshes out at 100 miles an hour (161 km/h)!

That's how fast air rushes from your mouth and nose when you sneeze or let loose a powerful cough. A sneeze is your body's way of getting rid of dust or other irritants that get in your nose. Your ribs contract, forcing air out of your lungs and through your nose.

Likewise, a cough gets rid of bits that get into your lungs. Your ribs and diaphragm contract while your vocal cords stay shut. This is like putting a cork in a volcano! Pressure builds up behind the closed cords, so when they open, the air rushes out very quickly.

RECOVERING FROM COLDS

Your nose is running. Your head is plugged up. Your throat hurts. You cough and sneeze and feel very tired. Yuck! You have a cold.

Your body works hard to fight off germs. Sticky mucus in your nose traps many of them. Cells in your lungs destroy germs that sneak past your nose and throat. Still, sometimes cold viruses get past these defenses and make you sick.

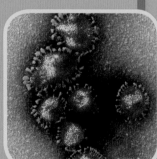

There is no "shot" to prevent one, because there are more than 200 different cold viruses!

The best way to recover is simply to get plenty of rest and drink lots of fluids. Nice, hot soup will soothe your throat and help unblock your nose. Some medicines can help you feel better as you recover by temporarily drying up sniffles or cooling a fever.

You may sneeze to clear out your nose, but sometimes **dogs sneeze** simply because they're **excited** and want to **play!**

Bet you didn't know

You hiccup when your diaphragm twitches, or spasms. The spasms make you breathe in sharply, which makes your vocal cords snap shut.

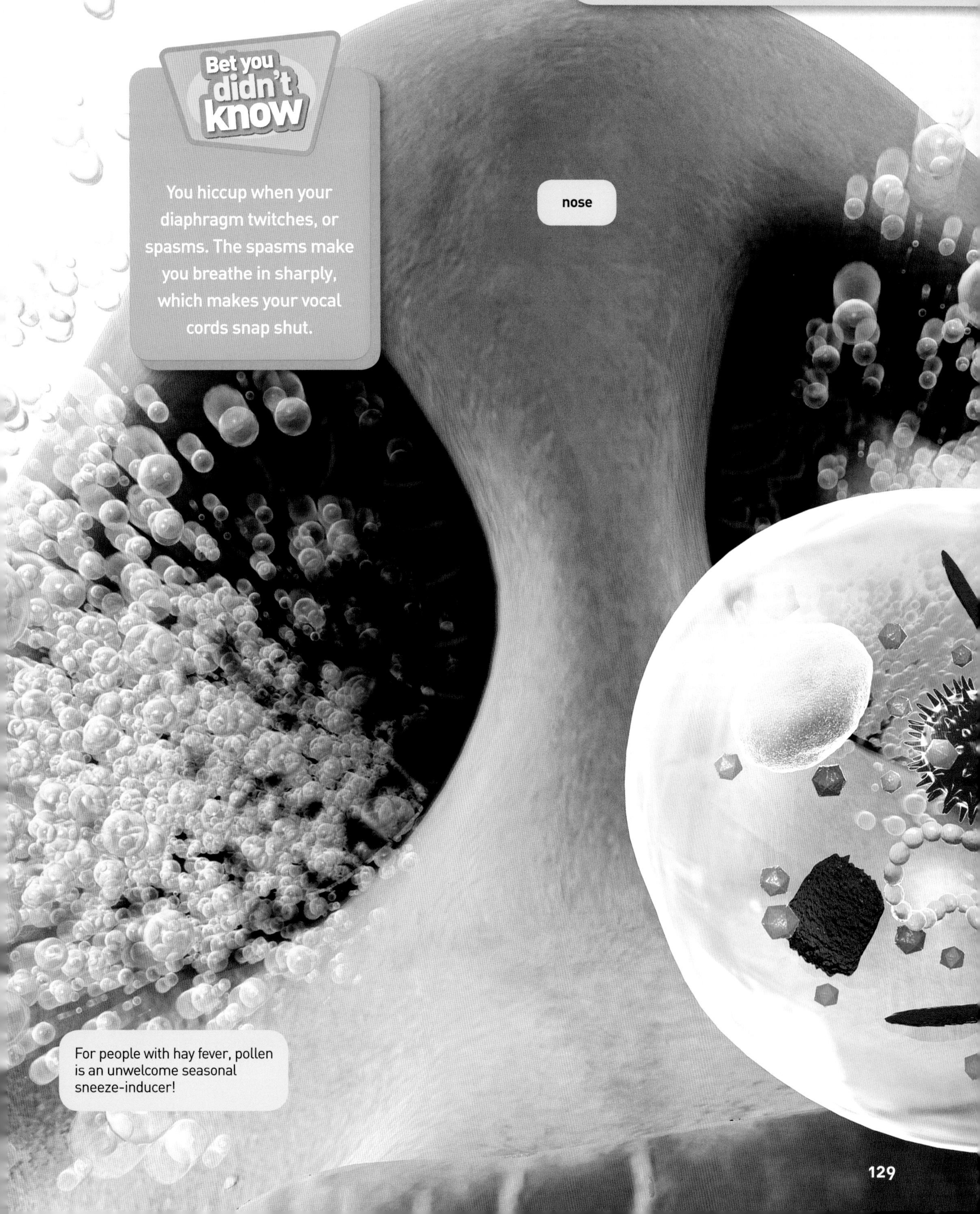

nose

For people with hay fever, pollen is an unwelcome seasonal sneeze-inducer!

129

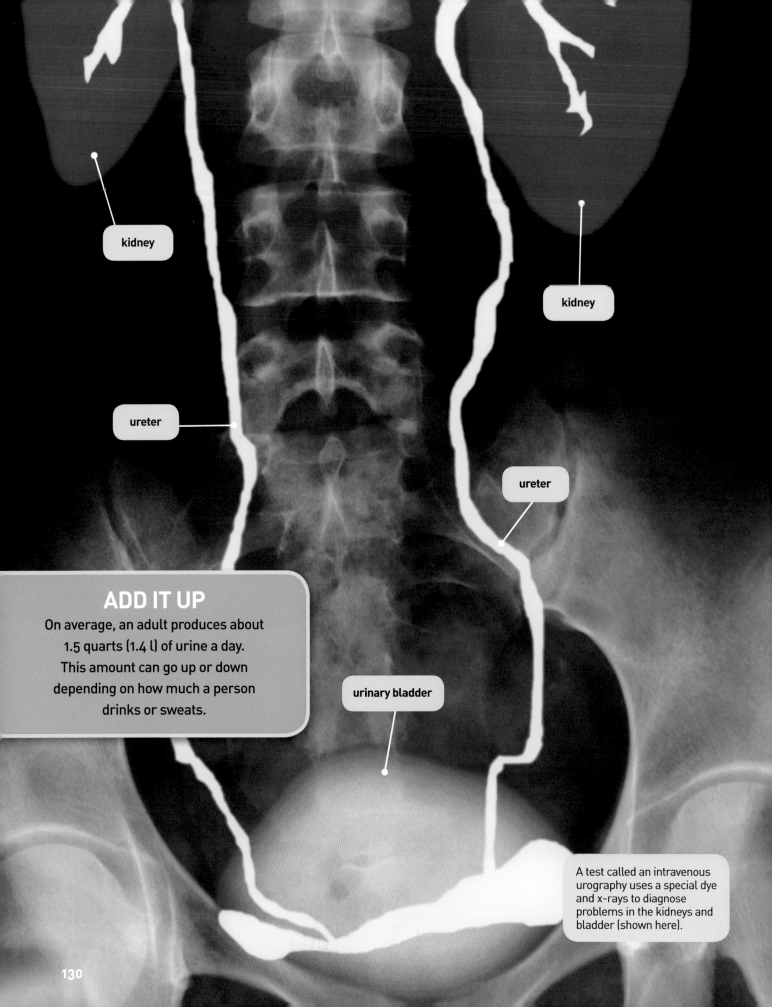

kidney

kidney

ureter

ureter

ADD IT UP
On average, an adult produces about 1.5 quarts (1.4 l) of urine a day. This amount can go up or down depending on how much a person drinks or sweats.

urinary bladder

A test called an intravenous urography uses a special dye and x-rays to diagnose problems in the kidneys and bladder (shown here).

GOTTA GO:
THE URINARY SYSTEM

You may wonder why the urinary system is here in the chapter about your blood and breath. Wonder no more—it's in the right place! The urinary system's main job is to filter and clean your blood.

The filters are your two kidneys, which sit on either side of your spine in the middle of your back. Each kidney is about the size of your fist. Each one contains about a million tiny filters, called nephrons. A nephron is made up of a capsule, which holds a clump of capillaries, and a tiny tube.

Inside the capsule, the body's waste products are filtered out of your plasma. Inside the tube, most of the water, salt, and nutrients in the plasma are reabsorbed into your bloodstream. What does not get reabsorbed flows through tubes into a holding chamber called the bladder. This liquid is called urine and is made up of water, salt, and waste products.

Your kidneys are also in charge of making sure your blood contains just the right amount of water to keep your body working properly. Sometimes they get rid of excess water, which makes urine look pale yellow. Sometimes they hold on to water, which makes urine look darker.

UR-INE TROUBLE!

Urine is often examined to find out about a patient's health. A sample is tested with a small stick with bands of different colors. The colors change when they react with substances in the urine. A color change may signal, for example, that there's too much sugar in the urine—a sign of a disease called diabetes. Other diseases that can be discovered in urine tests include kidney infections and muscle diseases.

Dogs may be able to identify disease, too. Scientists have trained dogs to detect sickness in a urine sample by smell. This research has inspired the invention of machines that do the same job. One has sensors that "sniff" gases given off by urine when it is heated. It shows the chemicals it detects on a computer screen.

YOUR AMAZING BRAIN

WHAT A BRAINIAC!

What makes you... you? If you had to pick just one part of your body that holds the essence of who you are, it probably wouldn't be your heart or lungs or belly button. It would be your amazing brain. This wrinkly organ inside your skull is your body's master controller and what makes you uniquely you.

The brain is always busy. It controls things your body does that you don't actively think about, such as breathing, digesting food, and pumping blood. It processes the sights and sounds that connect you to the world. It tells your arms and legs when and where to go. It stores your memories and makes choices. It fills you with happiness, sadness, and fear.

Because it's so important, the brain is sheltered inside a hard skull and wrapped in membranes. Blood vessels run through and around it. Your brain is also hungry! It uses one-fifth of the blood in your body to fuel itself. Put another way, the brain makes up only 2 percent of the body's weight but gobbles up 20 percent of its energy.

In the fourth century B.C., the philosopher Aristotle believed that the brain was a kind of "radiator" that cooled the heart.

MAPPING THE BRAIN

In the 1950s, a neurologist (brain doctor) named Wilder Penfield was trying to treat patients with severe epilepsy. He sent mild electrical currents to different areas of the brains of his (awake!) patients so he could figure out which part of their brain was causing their seizures. While doing this, Dr. Penfield saw that stimulating different parts of the brain had different effects on his patients and, because they were conscious, he also could ask them questions and they could answer! From his remarkable research he was able to create the first detailed "maps" of the primary motor and sensory areas of the human brain.

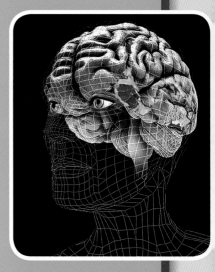

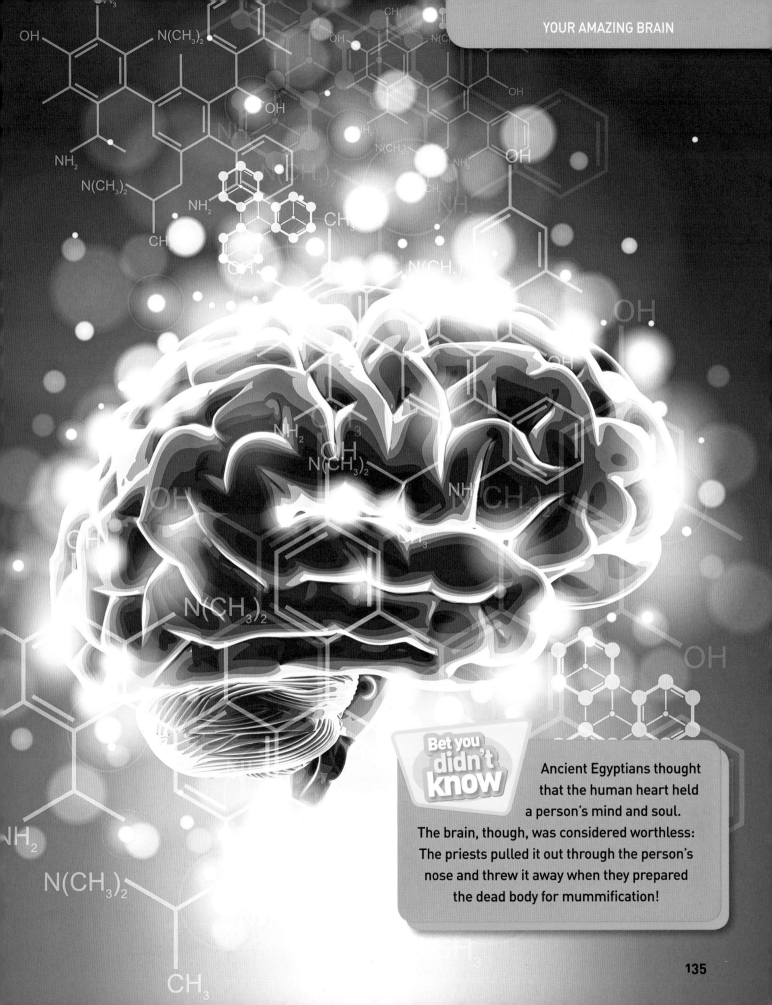

Bet you didn't know

Ancient Egyptians thought that the human heart held a person's mind and soul. The brain, though, was considered worthless: The priests pulled it out through the person's nose and threw it away when they prepared the dead body for mummification!

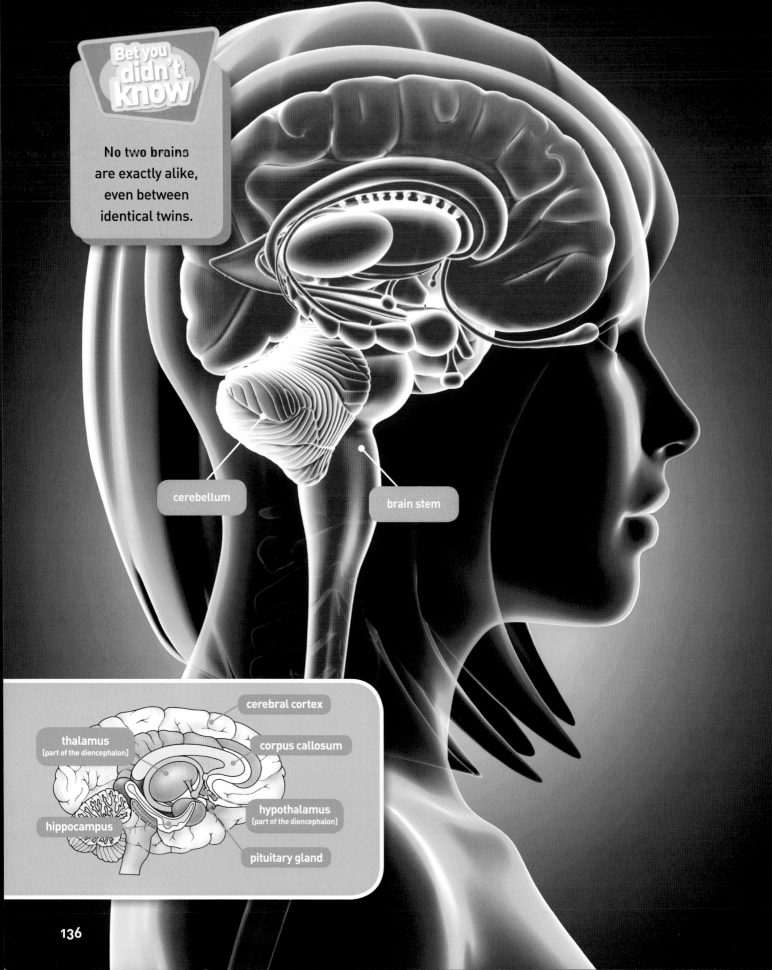

cerebellum

brain stem

cerebral cortex

thalamus
[part of the diencephalon]

corpus callosum

hypothalamus
[part of the diencephalon]

hippocampus

pituitary gland

YOUR MAGNIFICENT MIND

The brain doesn't look like much, but this amazing organ is among the most interesting and elaborate things known to humankind.
Weighing in at about three pounds (1.4 kg), the brain comprises different regions that control different parts of your body and different kinds of thinking. Regions of the brain include the brain stem, diencephalon, cerebellum, and cerebrum.

BRAIN STEM Way in back, where your skull meets your spinal cord, is the brain stem. It looks like, well, a stem and is in charge of basic body functions including reflexes, heartbeat, and breathing. Some people think of the spinal cord as an extension of the brain stem.

DIENCEPHALON Containing the thalamus and hypothalamus and located right above the brain stem is the diencephalon. The hypothalamus controls many of the body's automatic and essential responses, including hunger, thirst, and body temperature. It produces hormones, chemical messages that affect behavior. Your hormones regulate your body clock—telling you to get tired at night and to wake up in the morning. Hormones are also in control of your "flight or fight" response (how you react if you are faced with danger). The thalamus receives and sends sensory information from the sense organs to the cerebral cortex.

CEREBELLUM Behind and above the brain stem, toward the back of your head, is the cerebellum. This little knob is in charge of your movement and balance.

TRY IT!

Want to experience your cerebellum in action? Try this!

RAPID FINGER MOVEMENT TEST:

- Sit down.
- Rapidly touch the tip of each finger, in order, to the thumb of the same hand.
- Keep going. How fast can you do it?
- Try the other hand.

What happened? Did you find that you could quickly touch each fingertip to your thumb in a steady motion? This is an example of your cerebellum at work!

PUT ON YOUR THINKING CAP:
THE CEREBRUM

The biggest part of your brain—more than 80 percent of its mass—is the cerebrum, or your executive brain. Billions of neurons (nerve cells) make up its thin surface layer, the cerebral cortex, also called "gray matter." Neurons communicate with other neurons through dendrites and axons (see page 142), which form the inner part of the cerebrum, or "white matter." You make decisions and store your memories in this part of your brain. Sensory neurons send information from your eyes, ears, skin, mouth, and nose—your sense organs—to your brain, and your cerebrum makes sense of your senses. Your emotions—happy, angry, sad—are all controlled by your cerebrum.

Divided down the middle into two halves called hemispheres, the cerebrum is further divided into four areas called lobes that control different brain and body functions. Here's what each lobe does:

The parietal lobe controls how your body reacts to sensations. It tells your brain, "Mmm, that cat fur feels soft and cozy." Or, "Ouch, that cat has sharp claws!"

The frontal lobe controls thoughts, reasoning, emotions, planning, and problem-solving.

The occipital lobe processes the information coming in from your eyes.

The temporal lobe handles the sounds coming in from your ears as well as some parts of your memory.

AMAZING DISCOVERY

In 1848, a railroad foreman named Phineas Gage had a very unfortunate accident: An explosion drove a tamping iron right through his skull. (Gage is holding the iron in the photo.) Amazingly, 25-year-old Gage survived and even managed to chat with the doctor who treated him, John Harlow. Gage lost his left eye, but that's not all that was different.

Those who knew him observed that, before the accident, Gage had been a likeable, reasonable man; afterward, he was rude and unpleasant. Why the change?

Upon examining Gage's skull after his death, Dr. Harlow believed that the accident had damaged the part of Gage's brain that controls personality. This notion eventually helped scientists discover that behavior can be tied to areas of the brain.

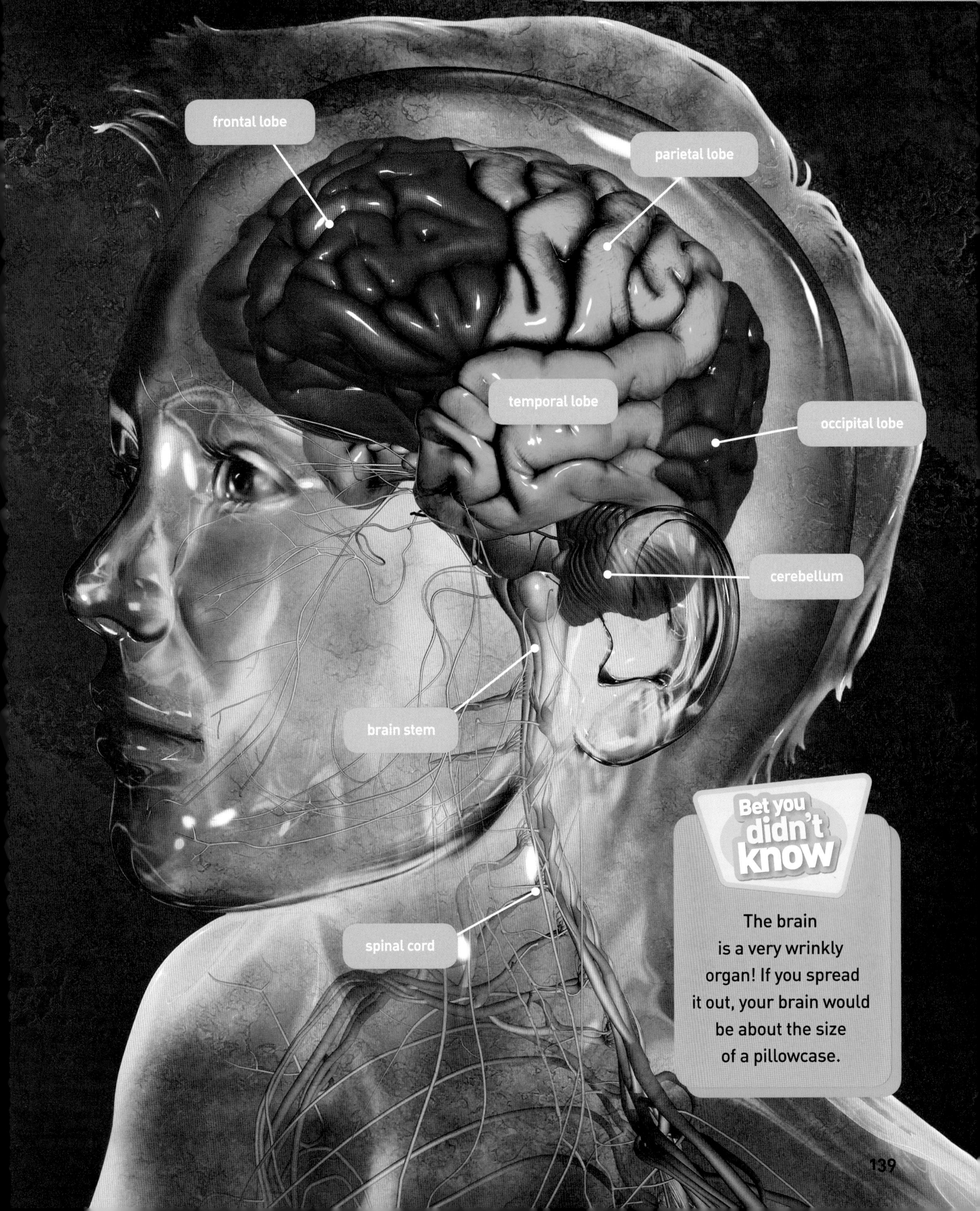

frontal lobe

parietal lobe

temporal lobe

occipital lobe

cerebellum

brain stem

spinal cord

Bet you didn't know

The brain is a very wrinkly organ! If you spread it out, your brain would be about the size of a pillowcase.

Human brain specimens are collected, stored, and distributed by the Harvard Brain Tissue Resource Center, the world's largest brain repository. The "Brain Bank" makes tissue available to scientists for use in their research on the functions and disorders of the human brain.

an x-ray showing a top view of the human brain

The human brain is made up of 78 percent water.

TWO SIDES
OF THE BRAIN

If you could see your brain from above, you would notice that it is divided right down the middle, into two hemispheres. The two parts of your brain can speak to each other through a thick band of millions of nerve fibers called the corpus callosum. The right side of your brain controls muscles on the left side of your body, and the left side of your brain controls muscles on the right side of your body.

In general, the right brain is more involved with spatial awareness—things like reading a map, having a sense of direction, and recognizing shapes. The right brain is also engaged when people recognize a face, perform visual activities like painting, or play a musical instrument.

What's left for the left hemisphere to do? Plenty! The left brain is more involved with math and logical reasoning. It is also engaged when a person is speaking and with language learning and listening. The left brain is often thought of as the more verbal part of the brain.

Though each of the hemispheres has its own functions, research done by neuroscientists (brain doctors) in 2013 seems to dispel the long-held idea of "left brain" versus "right brain" personalities. Studying brain scans of more than a thousand patients, they found no evidence that people use their right-brain network or their left-brain network more often. Though we may prefer to use one brain region more than another for certain tasks, it's just not true that one side of our brain dominates the other. They really do work together.

BRAIN SCANS

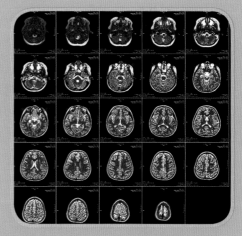

Technology helps neuroscientists better understand how the brain works. Some of their tools include:

EEG (electroencephalogram): records electrical signals from the brain

CAT/CT (computerized axial tomography): x-rays the head from different angles to create cross sections of the brain

MRI (magnetic resonance imaging): magnetic field maps the shape of the brain (see brain MRI slide above)

fMRI (functional magnetic resonance imaging): detects changes in blood flow and oxygen, showing which parts of the brain are engaged in different activities

YOU HAVE A LOT OF NERVE!

Different parts of your brain control different activities, but how does your brain tell all the parts of your body what to do? And, in return, how do your eyes, ears, and nose tell your brain what they see, hear, and smell? The answer is your nerves!

Nerves—thin, threadlike structures—carry messages between your brain and the rest of your body, in both directions. Nerves run down your spine and branch out all the way to your fingers and toes. This system of nerves controls your body, tells your muscles to move, and lets you experience the wonderful world around you. Nerves are part of your nervous system, which also includes your brain and spinal cord.

Your nerves are made of cells called neurons. Neurons send and receive messages between your brain and the other parts of your body by sending out alternating electrical and chemical signals.

Messages flash from neuron to neuron along your nerves and inside your brain. Signals from your eyes might tell the brain, "There's my school bus." The brain then sends signals that zoom from cell to cell making sense of the message. Then the brain sends signals back down to the nerves connected to your leg muscles to say, "Run to the bus stop!"

TOUR A NEURON

Neurons have four parts:

CELL BODY Contains the nucleus, which controls the activity of the cell and contains its DNA, or deoxyribonucleic acid

AXON Fiber that transmits impulses from cell body to another nerve cell

DENDRITE Branchlike fiber extending from cell body that receives signals from other neurons

MYELIN A fatty covering around the axons that insulate the axon, giving the white matter its characteristic color

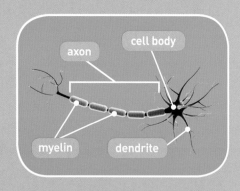

axon

cell body

myelin

dendrite

axon

synapse

an illustration showing how neurotransmitters behave in a synapse between neurons

dendrite

cell body

ADD IT UP

The human brain has about 100 billion neurons—that's 100,000,000,000! For the most part, humans are born with all the neurons they will ever have.

The connections between neurons in the brain create a network that resembles a spiderweb.

143

A reflex is a nerve message that doesn't go through your brain. When you touch a hot stove, for example, a sensory neuron picks up the message ("Hot!") and passes it to a motor neuron in your spinal cord. The motor neuron then sends a message to your hand, telling it to move ("Quick!").

an impulse being passed from one neuron to another

The nerve signal that tells your muscles to move is superfast! It zooms at **250 miles an hour** (402 km/h), as fast as the fastest race car.

BODY ELECTRIC

Your body is just humming with electricity. Nerve cells from head to toe speak to each other through electrical signals. The electrical signals zap down each nerve cell and, when they get to the end, jump across a tiny gap called a synapse (see photo, right). How does the signal jump across the gap?

The nerve produces special chemicals that can flow across the gap to the next cell. There a new electrical charge travels down the next nerve. Messages jump from neuron to neuron in a chain of electrical-chemical-electrical-chemical signals until they reach their destination.

Because nerves don't actually touch, they can change the path of their signals easily. They can make new connections and break old ones. This is how your brain learns and stores new information.

BUNDLE OF NERVES

A 1.2-inch (3-cm) section of your brain stem (called the medulla oblongata) controls some of your body's most important functions, such as breathing and heart rate. Amazingly, it also contains your body's motor and sensory nerves and is where nerves from the left and right sides of your body cross each other on their journey toward your cerebrum. **SENSORY NERVES** pull in information from nerve endings in your eyes, ears, skin, hands, and other parts of your body and then send this information to your brain. **MOTOR NERVES** send messages from your brain to your muscles, telling them to contract, to run, or to walk.

145

THE HAPPY CHEMICALS IN YOUR HEAD

While your neurons send messages through electrical impulses, your endocrine system sends messages through chemicals called hormones that tell your cells what to do. Some of these cells, called glands, are located in your brain. (See the "Body Atlas" for more on the endocrine system.)

Remember the hypothalamus (page 137)? Well, it not only produces hormones that affect behavior, it also tells the pituitary gland what hormones to release into the bloodstream.

The pituitary gland, located under your brain, is only the size of a pea but is often called the "master gland" because it is in charge of so many functions. It's not only in charge of the growth of your bones and tissues, it also sends out chemicals that can reduce pain and make you feel happy.

The pineal gland is located in the middle of the brain. It sends out chemicals that help you sleep at night and stay awake during the day. The pineal gland has held a lot of mystery for philosophers and ancient people. The ancient Greeks believed it was our connection to the "realms of thought" and philosophers have called it the "seat of the soul." In some religions, the pineal gland is thought to be the "third eye" or "all-seeing eye."

ANCIENT BRAIN SURGERY

Recent studies of ancient brain surgery in Bronze Age Turkey (that was 5,000 years ago!) show that early neurosurgeons could be skilled and precise.

Skulls discovered by an archaeologist had clean, rectangular cut marks, signs that the brains were likely operated on. The instruments used to make the cuts were thought to be shards of glass. Further studies of the skulls showed that the majority of patients operated on were likely to have survived.

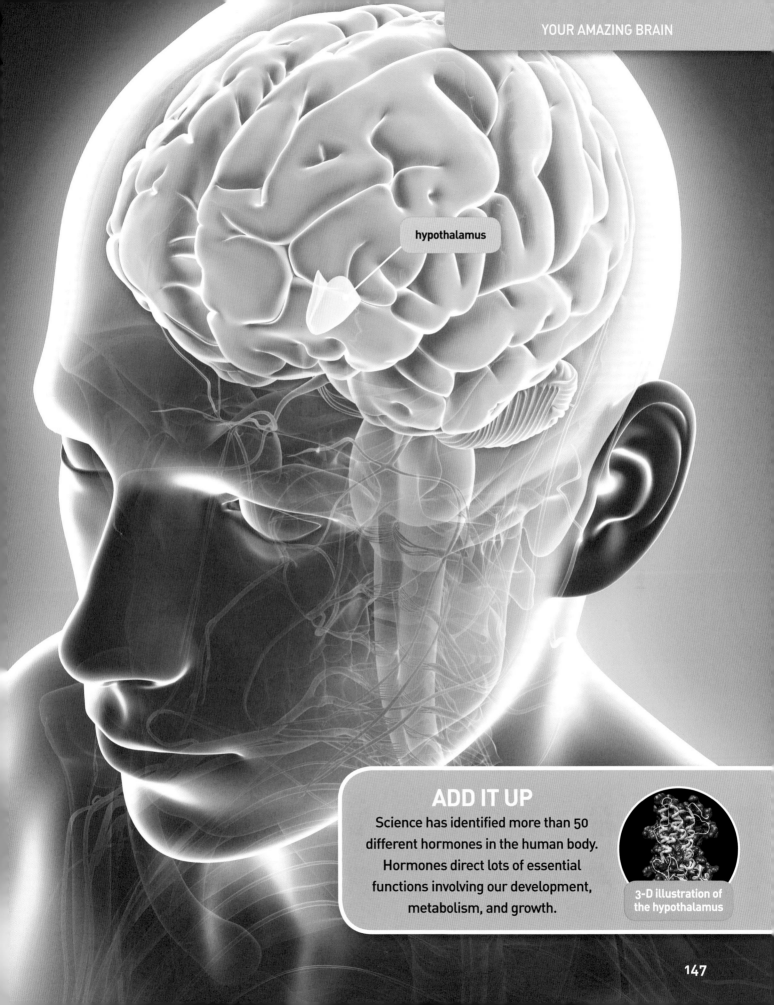

hypothalamus

ADD IT UP

Science has identified more than 50 different hormones in the human body. Hormones direct lots of essential functions involving our development, metabolism, and growth.

3-D illustration of the hypothalamus

A **phobia** is an **intense, irrational fear** of something. There are many kinds of phobias, from fear of snakes (ophidiophobia) to the fear of colors (chromophobia).

ADD IT UP

An average adult human brain uses about 12 watts of power—80 percent less than that 60-watt lightbulb in your desk lamp!

EMOTION IN MOTION

Your brain controls everything you think, everything you do, *and* everything you feel. Think about the different ways people express their emotions. A teenager slams his door. A runner leaps in the air when she beats her best time. Your grandparents celebrate their wedding anniversary. Emotions—anger, happiness, love—can be strong and are not always easy to control.

But your brain does control your emotions, mostly out of an area in your temporal lobe called the amygdala. The amygdala decides what kind of emotion you'll have when something happens. If you see a mountain lion while hiking, your amygdala decides if you will react with fear and back away. Other parts of your brain also play a role in your emotional reactions. Have you ever noticed how your heart pumps faster and your blood pressure rises when you get excited? That's because your amygdala has sent an SOS to your hypothalamus, which controls your autonomic nervous system (things like your breathing and heartbeat). The hypothalamus sends signals to the rest of your body that ensure you will react quickly when you spot that mountain lion. Your brain also controls your memories, which play a role in whether you'll still be afraid of the mountain lion if you see it later at a safe distance in a wildlife preserve.

FEAR FACTOR

Did you ever notice that when something really scary happens, you tend to remember it clearly? That's because two parts of your brain control your fear emotions—the amygdala and the hippocampus (see page 245), a curly little structure that moves your memories into long-term storage and remembers everything about the situation for next time!

REMEMBER TO REMEMBER!

If you couldn't remember what you did yesterday, or your likes and dislikes, would you be the unique person you are? Dealing with your memories is one of the most important functions of your brain. Most memories don't last long. Unimportant stuff, such as where you're sitting right now or a song you hear in passing, would likely be stored only briefly as short-term memories. They're forgotten in a day or so, but where do they go? Do these unimportant memories just disappear? No. These memories are stashed in the top layer of the cerebrum.

More important memories—or those that we keep thinking of over and over—will go into long-term memory storage, guided by the hippocampus. Many of these memories are stored in the front of your cerebrum.

A memory isn't stored all together like a book on a shelf. When your brain retrieves a memory, it pulls pieces of it from different places. It might grab the image of a warm body, the color brown, the name "Max," the sound of barking, and the feeling of happiness from different parts of the brain. All these combine to form "my dog Max."

SEE FOR YOURSELF

Do you know the rule of seven? It says that most people can't hold more than seven items in their short-term memory. That's why phone numbers (not counting the area code) are no longer than seven numerals.

Try it out. Start at the top of this list of numbers, read each one, then cover it with your hand and say it out loud. Where do you start to have trouble remembering it? Is it when you get to the number with eight numerals? Or can you beat the rule of seven?

3125
66578
332454
2109935
0498172
86663209
802541913
3892058218

"Tip-of-the-tongue" is the experience of feeling like you know the word you're looking for but you just can't recall it.

ADD IT UP

Have you ever heard that humans use only 10 percent of our brains? That is 100 percent incorrect! We may not always be demanding our brain's "higher" functions (say, multiplication), but even the most basic daily chores—such as brushing your teeth or walking the dog—activate areas across your entire brain.

ADD IT UP

Adult humans spend about 33 percent of their lives asleep. But that's nothing compared with some other animals! That python at the zoo? It spends about 75 percent of its life sleeping. And your devoted dog? About 44 percent.

GOOD MORNING! GOOD NIGHT!

Every night you close your eyes and lose all awareness of what's around you. Every morning you open your eyes and see the world again. What happens during those hours in between? As you slumber, you move through "sleep cycles": four stages of deeper and deeper sleep in which the electrical activity in your brain decreases, followed by stages in which your brain's electrical activity begins to increase, eventually reaching REM (rapid eye movement) sleep, in which much of your dreaming occurs. This sleep cycle lasts about 90 minutes and is repeated multiple times per night. (For more on sleep stages and REM, see page 154.)

OK, but why does the body even need to sleep? Amazingly, we don't completely understand why we sleep, but we do know that lack of sleep can negatively affect our coordination, our immune system, and our ability to make decisions. Sleep gives our active bodies time to rest and our busy minds time to make sense of what we learned that day. And sleep is a time when the brain sorts through its memories, putting some into long-term storage. People who are deprived of sleep have a hard time learning and remembering new information. They're also really cranky—wouldn't you be?

"HALF" ASLEEP

Like us, dolphins are mammals that have to breathe air to live. So what happens when they sleep? How do they know to go up to the surface of the water every few minutes to breathe? It's easy. First, they rest on the surface of the water in an action called "logging." It's called that because they look like logs floating on the water. Then, only one side of their brain falls asleep. The other side is just awake enough to remember to come up for air every few minutes, and to keep a look out for danger. Most other ocean mammals also engage in this half-brain sleeping.

DREAMING
THE NIGHT AWAY

Have you ever heard someone say, "I don't dream"? While it's true that not everyone remembers their dreams, everyone, in fact, dreams. Your body needs to sleep and your body needs to dream.

When you dream, the logical patterns your brain follows when you are awake are not in service. That's why your dreams may seem so weird.

The brain goes through several cycles of sleep each night. A sleep cycle has two main parts—REM sleep and non-REM sleep. Dreams occur during REM. Non-REM sleep is made up of four stages:

STAGE 1: The body is falling asleep. You may actually feel like you're falling. This lasts from 5 to 10 minutes.

STAGE 2: This is light sleep. The body relaxes. This lasts from 10 to 25 minutes.

STAGES 3 AND 4: These are periods of deep sleep. The brain moves at a different pace than when you are awake. This stage lasts from 20 to 40 minutes.

REM sleep occurs about 90 minutes into your sleep cycle. Brain patterns are similar to when you are awake. This is the time during the sleep cycle when dreams take place. The cycle repeats during the night, with your REM dream sleep becoming longer and longer. By the end of the night, your REM sleep may last for a full hour.

AMAZING DISCOVERY

A group of scientists is creating a device that can predict what people are dreaming based on their brain patterns. Scientists watch the images and patterns of a person's brain while they sleep. Then they wake up the person mid–sleep cycle and ask what they are dreaming about. The machine collects the information and tries to make connections.

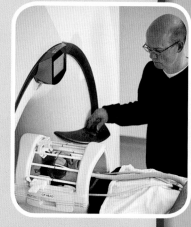

For instance, the machine may record that whenever the person's brain has a certain set of patterns, the person reports dreaming about a red barn. So the device notes that a particular brain pattern may mean "red barn." Using this information, the device is able to predict what people are dreaming about 60 percent of the time. As more information from more people is collected, the device will be able to make better and better predictions.

Bet you didn't know

People who stay up late are more likely to have nightmares than people who go to bed early.

A dreaming brain is just as **active** as a brain that is awake.

155

Bet you didn't know
To your brain, watching someone else do something is almost the same as doing it yourself. For example, the same brain cells are active when you watch someone else dance as when you dance yourself.

HANDLE WITH CARE

Your brain is protected by a skull, membranes, and cerebrospinal fluid that acts as a cushion for its tissue. Sometimes, however, when you bang your head really hard—if you are in a car accident, or get tackled too hard playing football, for example—the force of the impact can cause your brain to bounce off the inside of your skull. When that happens, you can end up with a concussion, which is like a brain bruise.

If you get a concussion, you might have a headache, or start to feel dizzy or sick to your stomach. You may feel drowsy or "out of it." A concussion may knock you out for a few seconds or a few minutes. With a concussion or any serious head injury, you need to see a doctor right away to make sure you're all right.

Your best bet for avoiding brain bumps? Use your head! Always buckle your seat belt in the car. Wear a helmet whenever you ride your bike, skateboard, or play contact sports. Be safe when you have fun. (See page 66 for more on bike helmets.)

NOURISH YOUR NOGGIN

Your brain is a vital organ and it's important to keep it healthy. These superfoods can help keep your brain in top shape.

1. **BERRIES** Blueberries, strawberries, and raspberries work hard to keep inflammation down. In studies, older people who ate berries had better memory and brain function.

2. **FATTY FISH** Fish like salmon and trout have a kind of fatty acid that keeps your nerve cells healthy and lets messages travel quickly between your body and your brain.

3. **NUTS** Nuts are a good source of vitamin E, which attacks chemicals that damage brain cells. Some nuts are also good sources of magnesium, which may help improve your memory.

4. **DARK CHOCOLATE** Dark chocolate helps you pay attention and boosts blood flow to the brain, helping you think faster and perform better.

MAKING SENSE OF THE SENSES

YOUR BODY MAKES SENSE

The spectacular beauty of a sunset. The ringing of a cell phone. The acrid scent of a fire. The yummy sweetness of ice cream. The roughness of a twisted rope. The senses—seeing, hearing, smelling, tasting, and touching—are your body's ways of explaining the world to your brain. Your senses help you make sense of the world, and they help keep you safe in it.

Most of your sense organs are located in your head. Your eyes give you vision. Your ears let you hear. Your nose provides smell, and your tongue adds taste.

Your other sense, touch, is spread throughout your body: in your skin, in your bones, and in most of your internal organs, too. Because it doesn't need a special organ, touch is called a "general sense." You have several kinds of general senses, a couple of which you'll learn about in this chapter.

UNUSUAL SENSES

Did you know that some people can taste a song? Or feel a color? No, they don't have superpowers, but they do have synesthesia, a rare brain condition in which a perception by one of your senses nudges a sensation by another sense at the same time. So, for example, when someone with synesthesia hears "Yankee Doodle Dandy," they may also taste vanilla. Or when they see the word "friend," they may  see it in the color blue. Or when they smell coffee, they may hear a train whistle. Or when they feel pain, they may smell lemons. Pretty much any combination of senses can happen, though usually not more than two at once. Synesthesia is automatic and not something people learn; it is part of who they are.

Bet you didn't know Crickets have "ears" on their legs—actually, thin bits of membrane that pick up sounds. Snakes can smell by flicking their long, forked tongues into the air.

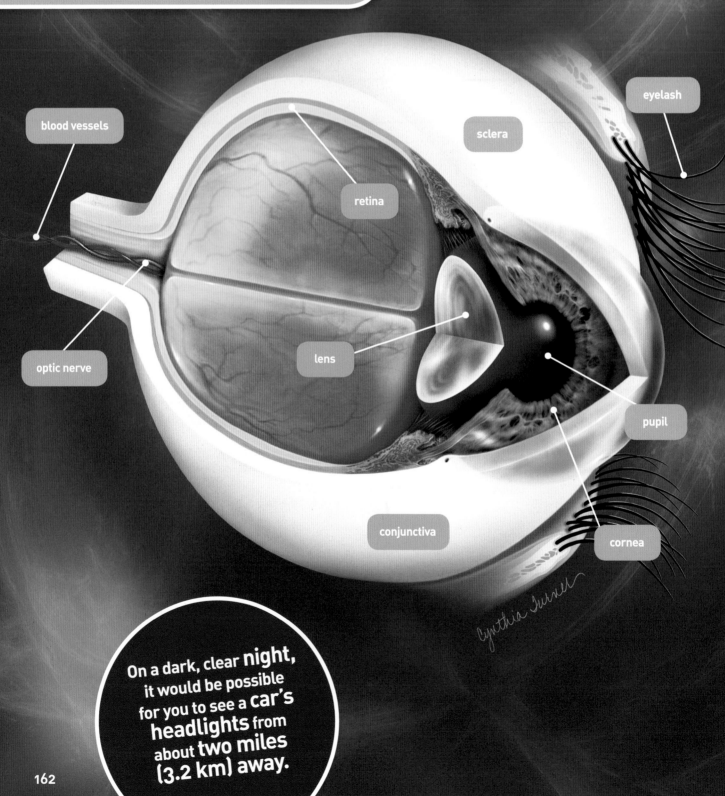

blood vessels

retina

sclera

eyelash

optic nerve

lens

pupil

conjunctiva

cornea

On a dark, clear **night**, it would be possible for you to see a **car's headlights** from about **two miles (3.2 km) away.**

LOOK OUT!

Your eyes are two of the most amazing organs in your body. These small, squishy, fluid-filled balls have almost three-quarters of your body's sensory receptors. They're like two supersmart cameras, but more complex.

So how do you see the world around you? It begins when you open the protective cover of your eyelid and let in the light. Light enters your eye through the window of your cornea and passes through the aqueous humor, a watery fluid that nourishes the eye tissue. It enters the black circle in the iris (the colored part of your eye), called the pupil. Because people need to be able to see in both bright and low light, muscles in the iris automatically make the pupil smaller when the light is strong and wider when the light is dim. Light then travels to the lens, whose muscles adjust it to be able to see objects both near and far. Then the light goes through the vitreous humor (a clear jellylike substance) to the retina. The retina, a layer of about 126 million light-sensitive cells, lines the back of your eyeball. When these cells absorb the light, they transform it into electrical signals that are sent along the optic nerve to the brain. The brain then makes sense of what we are seeing.

A TOPSY-TURVY WORLD

Turn this over in your mind: You're looking at the world topsy-turvy, and you don't even know it. Like other lenses, your lens focuses light, creates an image, and turns it upside down. Yep, when your lens focuses light inside your eye, it flips the image so it lands on your retina upside down. But, your brain knows to flip the image automatically to match your reality. But what if your reality suddenly changed? A well-known experiment in the mid-20th century in which a person wore special light-inverting goggles showed that his brain actually adjusted to the new, inverted world by eventually seeing the reversed view as normal! It is thought that newborns see the world upside down for a short while, until their brains learn how to turn things right-side up.

camera lens

163

SEEING IS NOT BELIEVING

When you look around, it might feel like you are looking at the world "as it is." In reality, you are looking at a picture of the world that is constructed by your brain. Without you even realizing it, your brain is constantly sifting and organizing your vision. Almost half of your cerebral cortex is engaged in visual processing.

When you look at something—let's say, someone tosses you an apple—signals speed from your eyes to your brain. These signals spread out in the visual area in the brain. Some signals make sense of color. Others recognize edges and shapes. Some signals pick up movement. Your brain receives all these signals and combines them to say "Red apple coming at you!"

So your brain is continually interpreting the information your eyes are collecting, but sometimes there's a mismatch between what your eyes see and what your brain perceives. Pattern, color, and light can be manipulated to create an optical illusion, an image that "fools" your brain into seeing something that is not actually there or somehow different from the way it actually is. Because your brain has learned to automatically process what it sees, when it encounters something different, it attempts to match what it is seeing with what it expected to see.

HEAVY SHIFTING

Your eyes get an intense workout, moving three times a second, every day. Three pairs of muscles allow your eyes to rotate up and down, side to side, and all around (see side view of muscles, right). When you're looking at something 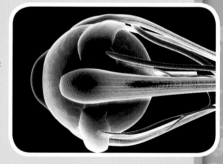 that's still, they make small and quick movements, and when you're viewing something in motion, they make larger and more fluid movements. All this activity can sometimes make your eyes tired, or strained. When this happens, you may get a headache or burning or itching eyes, or you may have trouble reading or concentrating. Try taking a break to give your eyes a chance to rest. If you keep having symptoms, though, you may need to see an ophthalmologist, a doctor who specializes in eye care.

Bet you **didn't know**

Heterochromia is a condition in which people have different color eyes. It's rare in humans, but common in dogs!

Your **eyes** can pick out about **ten million** different colors. Think you've **seen them all?**

AWESOME OPTICAL ILLUSIONS!

Ready to work your brain and show your visual alertness? Ponder these puzzling pictures to see what you see!

Which Circle Is Bigger?

Both of these circle clusters have an orange circle surrounded by purple ones. But which orange circle is bigger? The answer may surprise you: neither! The two orange circles are the same size. The one on the right may appear bigger because it's surrounded by purple circles that are smaller than it is. The one on the left seems smaller because it's surrounded by purple circles that are larger than it is.

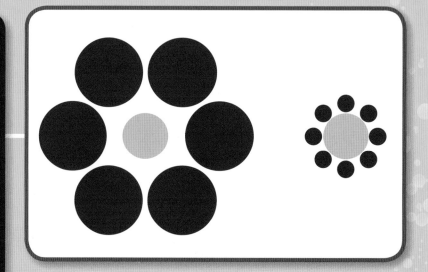

Guess the Direction

Which direction is this cube pointing? Down and to the left? Up and to the right? Or do you see it facing both directions alternately? Yup: It's both. Your visual system "guesses" that the cube is facing one direction, then it "guesses" that it is facing another. You can't see both at once because it can't settle on which of the two is the better "guess."

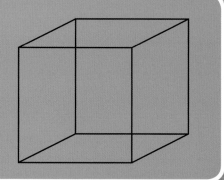

Spinning Circles

Do you see all the spinning circles? Don't look too long, or you might get dizzy! This illusion plays with your peripheral vision (vision from the sides of your eyes, not the middle). Sometimes when you look out the sides of your eyes, you see movement where really there are only patterns.

Rabbit or Duck?

It's a duck! Or is it a rabbit? Can you see it both ways? A recent study using this illusion suggests that the more easily people can switch back and forth between the two images, the more creative they are.

Most people who are **color-blind** can't tell the difference between **green** and **red**.

167

DO YOU HEAR WHAT I HEAR?

Bzzzzzzzz. Why does that itty-bitty mosquito sound so loud? Blame your excellent ears. They're designed to scoop up even tiny noises and turn them into signals for the brain.

Your ears have three parts—outer, middle, and inner—that play a game of "pass the sound." It starts when sound—which is vibrations, or waves, in the air—enters the outer ear. There, the waves bounce off the tightly stretched skin of the eardrum.

Now your middle ear gets into the action. The vibrating eardrum makes three teensy bones in your middle ear wobble.

The wobbling bones shake the liquid inside a curling tube called the cochlea, located in your inner ear. Tiny hairs lining the cochlea wave back and forth. This tickles nerve cells at their base. Then the nerve cells send a message to the brain to say, "Hey, I'm hearing something."

Meanwhile, your ears are busy doing a second job. In the inner ear, special liquid-filled canals help you keep your balance. The liquid sloshes back and forth when your head moves. Little hairs and nerve cells in the canals feel the sloshing liquid. They make sure that the liquids in both ears are lined up and equal to each other. Keeping the liquid even tells the inner ears that your body is keeping its balance. As you move, the nerves in your ears tell your brain that you're on the go.

THE WAX FACTS

Ever wonder why in the world you have yellow and brown gunk in your ears? Cerumen—what we call earwax—may be kind of icky, but it has an important function. It lubricates your ears so they don't get itchy and dried out. Its stickiness helps keep dirt, water, and bacteria from reaching your eardrum.

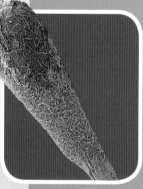

colored scanning electron micrograph (SEM) of a cotton swab with earwax (in red)

Some people can **hear** their **eyeballs** moving.

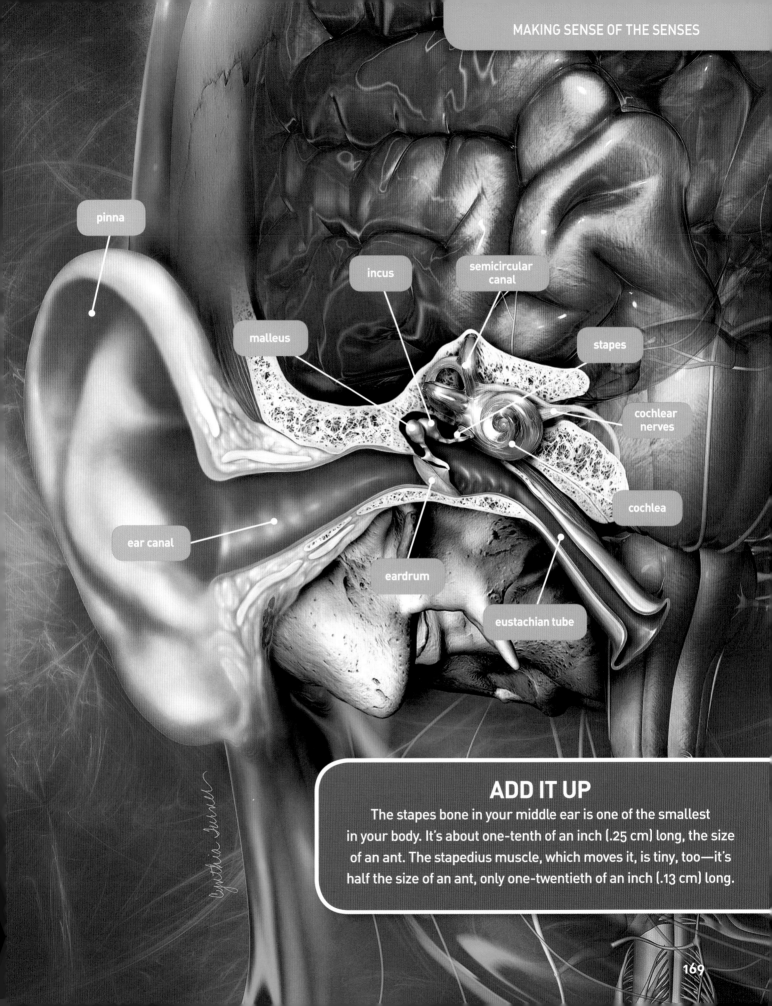

pinna

incus

semicircular canal

malleus

stapes

cochlear nerves

ear canal

cochlea

eardrum

eustachian tube

ADD IT UP

The stapes bone in your middle ear is one of the smallest in your body. It's about one-tenth of an inch (.25 cm) long, the size of an ant. The stapedius muscle, which moves it, is tiny, too—it's half the size of an ant, only one-twentieth of an inch (.13 cm) long.

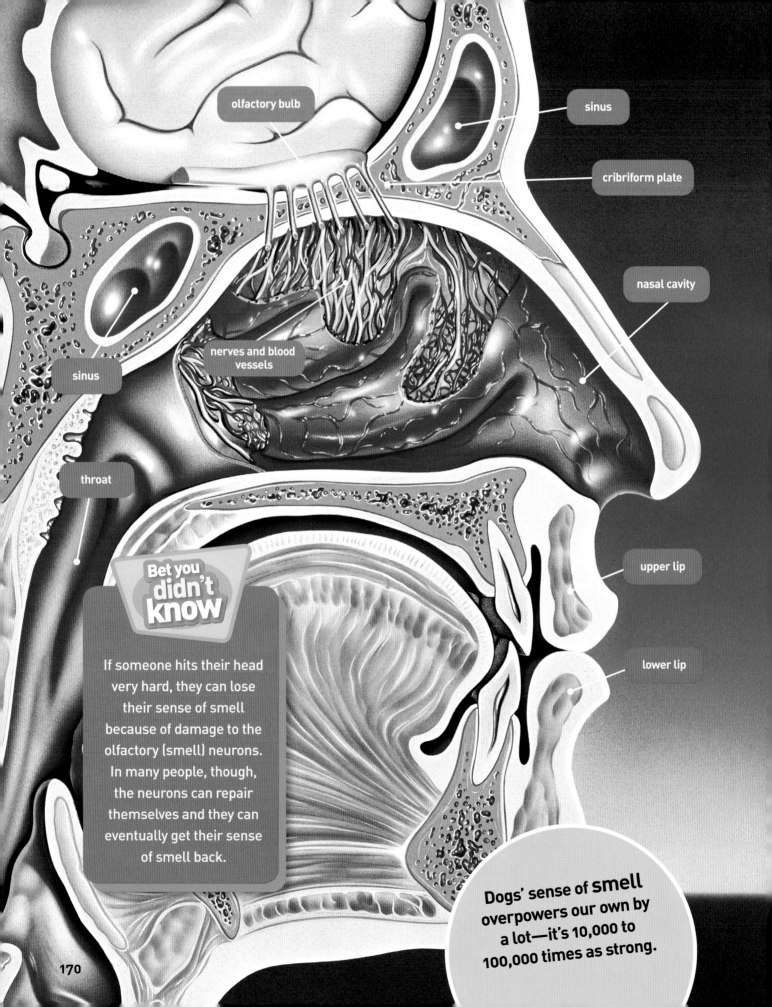

olfactory bulb

sinus

cribriform plate

nasal cavity

nerves and blood vessels

sinus

throat

upper lip

lower lip

Bet you didn't know

If someone hits their head very hard, they can lose their sense of smell because of damage to the olfactory (smell) neurons. In many people, though, the neurons can repair themselves and they can eventually get their sense of smell back.

Dogs' sense of smell overpowers our own by a lot—it's 10,000 to 100,000 times as strong.

THE NOSE KNOWS

Your nose knows how to let you know about the world around you.

It pulls in the air you breathe. It blocks out dust and germs. It helps shape sound when you talk. And it senses 10,000 different smells, from the sweet aroma of chocolate chip cookies to the yucky stink of garbage.

Smelling happens when you inhale (breathe in). Air goes in through your nostrils, up your nose, and then through your nasal cavity (an open space behind your nose), before heading on down to your lungs. While passing through the nasal cavity, the air goes by a postage-stamp-size piece of tissue packed with about 40 million tiny smell receptors. The smell receptors search the air for smelly chemicals, and, if they find any, they send the information to your brain. Your brain then sorts out the information and tells you what you smell.

Smell helps us out in lots of ways. It helps us figure out what's for dinner, but it also warns us of danger. Smell neurons (nerve cells) tell you, "Don't eat that rotten food!" or, "Something's burning! Find out what!"

TEST THIS SMELL

Do you have a great sense of smell? Well, you could smell for a living. Some companies employ odor testers to sniff their perfumes, shampoos, and makeup products and rate their scents. But being a smell taster can occasionally get stinky: Some companies hire deodorant testers to smell people's armpits to judge how well their deodorants are working. *Ewww.* If this is too up close and personal for you, take heart. Crazy about cooking? Our sense of taste is about 80 percent smell, so chefs need to have a particularly polished nose guiding them in the creation of new and delicious dishes.

THE BUMPY ROAD TO TASTE

Your tongue may not be the prettiest part of your body. But without it, a sweet, chocolaty brownie would taste like chewy sawdust. Lemonade would seem like water-ade. Life would be a lot less tasty.

Why can you taste food with your tongue but not with, say, your fingers? Your tongue is covered with thousands of sensory organs called taste buds. Individual taste buds are so small that you can't see them, but if you stick your tongue out and look in a mirror, you can see the little pink bumps where groups of taste buds are gathered. These bumps are called papillae.

When you pop food into your mouth, it starts to dissolve in your saliva (your spit). The taste buds on your tongue sense the chemicals swishing around in that liquid and send a signal to your brain. The brain then decides how to react: "Eat it up!" or, "Yuck! Spit it out!"

Taste buds pick up one or more of five basic taste qualities: sweet, sour, bitter, salty, or umami. This last one is a tangy, meaty flavor. ("Umami" is the Japanese word for "delicious"!)

But how do you taste so many flavors if your tongue can taste only five things? The reason is that taste is only one component of a food's flavor. The flavor is the combination of the different tastes, plus scent, texture, and temperature. Your sneaky brain combines all these parts together without you even knowing it.

TASTE TEST!

Find out if you need your sense of smell to really taste something. Gather a few friends and some foods such as different-flavored baby food, different-flavored jelly beans, and slices of fruits or veggies.

First, taste the foods as you normally would. Notice how you can easily pick out the flavors.

Next, blindfold one person at a time and have that person hold her nose. Ask her to taste the foods again. Without being able to smell, can she tell one flavor from another?

If you and your friends couldn't taste as well, it's because your sense of smell is an important part of tasting food. Without your nose working, you can't tell what the food is from just the texture alone.

The body can detect taste in .0015 seconds—that's faster than the blink of an eye.

backward-facing, scale-like projections called filiform papillae, which sense pressure

fungiform papillae, which contain the taste buds

ADD IT UP

We have about 10,000 taste buds, each with about 50 sensory cells. Though friction and heat regularly damage them, our taste buds actually renew themselves about every ten days.

colored scanning electron micrograph (SEM) of the surface of the human tongue

173

Bet you didn't know

You can't tickle yourself. At least, you can't do it and make yourself laugh. Why? Your brain is already one step ahead, awaiting the feeling your wiggly fingers might trigger.

FEELING
YOUR WAY

Your body has developed special organs to see, hear, smell, and taste things in the world. But what about touch? Your body doesn't use one special sense organ; it uses lots of different body parts. You can touch with your fingers, your elbows, your nose, even your rear end!

Touch is one of your "general senses"—a sense you have all over your body. General senses are very important because they keep track of what's happening all around your body, even when you aren't paying attention. When you feel your cell phone buzz in your pocket, or an itchy mosquito bite on your arm, or a cold winter wind on your cheeks, it's because your general senses are doing their job.

One of the most important general senses is pain. Pain feels really, really bad, but believe it or not, that's exactly the point! Pain is one of the ways your body keeps you out of danger. Without it, you would never learn to avoid sharp knives, broken glass, or hot stoves!

Awareness of position is another kind of general sense (called proprioception, meaning "to be aware of yourself"). Signals from your muscles and joints join signals from your eyes and your inner ear to tell your brain where your body parts are. This awareness is what lets you touch your finger to your nose, even with your eyes closed!

TESTING YOUR TOUCH

Want to try out your proprioception? Here's a twisty test you can do with a friend. Stretch out both arms, with your palms facing forward. Cross one arm over the other. Turn your palms toward each other and lace your fingers together. Bend your elbows and pull your clasped hands back toward your body under your chin.

Now have your friend point to one of your fingers without touching it. Can you move the finger?

Some people move the finger on the wrong hand, because their brain gets confused. It sees a hand on the left and a hand on the right, but it doesn't realize the two hands have switched places. Give it enough time, and your brain will learn from its mistakes!

AMAZING ANIMAL SENSES

Now you know about the ways your body and your brain make sense of the world around you.

But how about other living things? Animals, with different bodies and different brains, sense the world differently. Some have fewer, weaker senses—blind mole rats, for example, are born blind and never see a thing their whole life—and some have much stronger senses. Some animals have extra senses. It's hard for us to imagine how these senses "feel," because we aren't set up to feel them. But to us, it might seem like having superpowers. Check out these four amazing animal senses!

Infrared

Did you know that some snakes can "see" heat? All living things give off waves of energy called infrared light. Infrared is invisible to most animals, including humans. But some snakes, like the pit viper, have special organs in their faces, called pits, that can sense these waves and their locations—even in the dark. Pits come in handy when the snakes go hunting for prey, especially at night!

green pit viper

Echolocation

Bats, dolphins, and whales have supersensitive hearing, and they've developed a really cool way to hear where things are. It's called echolocation.

Echolocation works just like it sounds. Some animals use echoes—sounds bouncing off the things they hit—to locate the objects around them. This natural navigation helps bats, whales, and dolphins find food, make sense of where they are, and be aware of what (and who!) is around them.

southern right whale

shortfin mako shark

Electrical Field

Remember how your brain uses electricity to "talk" to your muscles? (See pages 144–145 in Chapter 6.) It turns out that sharks use electricity, too. If prey is nearby, they will feel the animal zapping and buzzing with electricity. Sharks can sense electricity in minuscule amounts, and they can sense it only when they are within three feet (0.9 m) of the source.

pigeon

Magnetic Field

Have you ever used a compass? If you have, you know that the compass's spinning needle works by pointing to the Earth's magnetic north.

Pigeons have something like this compass inside their heads. They have no spinning needle, but they do have tiny particles that respond to the magnetic forces in the Earth, just like a compass. Their magnetic sense helps them figure out which direction they're flying. Scientists think that many animals that migrate long distances rely, at least in part, on magnetism to find their way.

With their bills, **platypuses** can feel the **electric fields** put out by other animals.

THE LIFE CYCLE

GENES: WHAT MAKES YOU, YOU

You are truly one of a kind—there's no one else exactly like you, even if you have a twin. You may look like the members of your family (or act like them, or have the same interests), but there are "instructions" inside you that make you uniquely you. These instructions—called genes—are inside the trillions of cells in your body and have been there since before you were born.

Your genes are located on your chromosomes—threadlike structures that contain your DNA (deoxyribonucleic acid). Your DNA contains your genetic "code"—the blueprint for who you are, including what traits you have (such as eye or hair color). Your parents pass along their traits to you through their genes: You inherit one set of 23 chromosomes from your mother and one set of 23 chromosomes from your father. Nearly every cell in your body has 46 chromosomes, or 23 complete pairs. (See sidebar photo of pairs of chromosomes.)

After you were born, many of these traits were noticeable: Maybe you had brown hair like your dad's. Maybe as you got older and became a kid, people commented that your nose looked just like your mom's. As you continue to get older and become a teenager, you may notice even more ways you are like your parents. Your genes will be with you your entire life. And if you have children of your own someday, you will pass your genes along to your kids, too.

THAT'S EVOLUTIONARY!

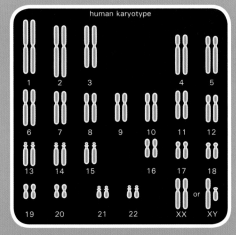

human karyotype

Your genes don't just contain specific information about traits like your eye and hair color. They carry the most basic instructions that make you a person to begin with. What makes you a boy instead of a bear? Or a girl instead of a gazelle? Your genes!

But the difference between us and some other animals is smaller than you might think. By studying both human and animal DNA, researchers are able to see how much alike we are to our animal relatives—how closely related (or not) we are to them. This makes DNA also important to the study of human evolution.

Bet you didn't know

Of our 23 pairs of chromosomes, 22 of them are the same in both boys and girls. But the 23rd pair is different. In that pair, girls have two copies of the X chromosome, and boys have one X and one Y chromosome.

DNA molecules

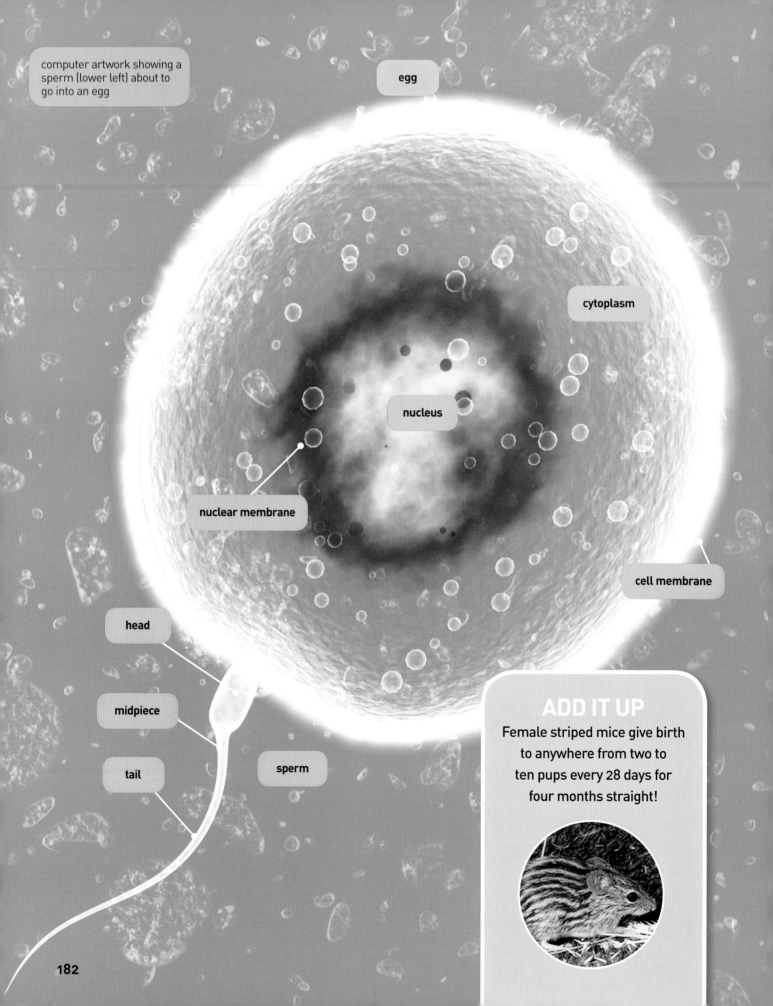

computer artwork showing a sperm (lower left) about to go into an egg

egg

cytoplasm

nucleus

nuclear membrane

cell membrane

head

midpiece

tail

sperm

ADD IT UP

Female striped mice give birth to anywhere from two to ten pups every 28 days for four months straight!

REPRODUCTION

Male and female bodies are mostly alike on the inside:

Most of our bodies' systems—such as our digestive systems, our circulatory systems, and our respiratory systems—work the same way. But one of our body systems is different: the reproductive system. The reason for this is that it takes a male's reproductive system and a female's reproductive system working together to make a new life (a baby), in a process called conception.

A male's reproductive system produces cells called sperm, and a female's system produces eggs, which live in her two ovaries. Each month, one of the female's ovaries releases an egg (sometimes more than one—see sidebar on twins), which travels down her fallopian tube. If along the way it meets a male's sperm cells, the egg can be fertilized by one of the sperm, meaning the sperm and the egg join together. This fertilized egg will continue down the fallopian tube, settle into the lining of an organ called a uterus, and grow into a baby.

Though all sperm cells contain your father's chromosomes, and all eggs contain your mother's chromosomes, each sperm and each egg carry a different combination of your parents' genetic information. If they didn't, every child in a family would look exactly alike! So when a sperm carrying a father's chromosomes joins with an egg carrying a mother's chromosomes, they create a unique new cell (you!). In 36 hours this one cell divides into two cells, each an exact copy of the other. And those cells divide again, and again, and again. And your life inside your mother's body has begun!

TWINS!

Sometimes a mother's ovary will release more than one egg at a time. If this happens, there is a possibility that the two (or more!) eggs released could all be fertilized. When two eggs are fertilized and become babies, they are called fraternal twins. Because fraternal twins come from two different eggs that joined with two different sperm, 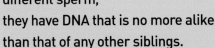 they have DNA that is no more alike than that of any other siblings.

Sometimes an egg that has been fertilized will split in half, creating identical twins. Because identical twins come from the same egg and the same sperm, they have nearly identical DNA. Identical twins are always of the same gender: either both boys or both girls. Even so, there are plenty of ways they are different—including their fingerprints!

BEFORE YOU WERE BORN

It's hard to imagine, but all people—including you!—started life as a single cell. That cell created more cells, all copies of each other and containing the same DNA in the nucleus. By dividing over and over again through a process called mitosis, they eventually created a ball of cells called an embryo. For about 40 weeks (9 months), you grew in your mother's body in a process called pregnancy, during which you got bigger and bigger, until you were developed enough to be born.

During the 8 weeks you were an embryo, you began to grow important body parts like your brain, your beating heart, and your other organs. By week 16, you had already developed your facial features, including your lips, your eyelids, and your ears. You could make faces and maybe even suck your thumb!

By 20 weeks, you were the size of a grapefruit and getting stronger: Your mother might have even been able to feel you kicking! You also had started doing other kinds of things you do now, like blinking, swallowing, sleeping, and waking up. Ten weeks later, at 30 weeks, you could already hear sounds and might have noticed light if the light outside was bright enough. And you were starting to look more and more like a baby.

Although babies can be born at different "weeks" and still be healthy, starting at 39 weeks a baby is considered "full term," meaning fully developed and ready to be born.

NO BONES ABOUT IT!

Would you believe that when you were born you had three different skulls? Well, not exactly. It was more like your cranium (skull) was in three main pieces that had not grown together yet. This is nature's way of helping a baby to be born, so that its head can more easily fit through its mother's body.

Your skull is not the only bone that changes. Babies have around 300 bones and cartilage when they are born, but adults have 206 bones! What happens to the rest of them? As you get older, small bones "fuse" together to become bigger bones, like your cranium does to become one skull. Part of the reason it is so important that babies—and kids!—get the nutrients they need, like calcium, is to help these bones fuse into a strong skeleton.

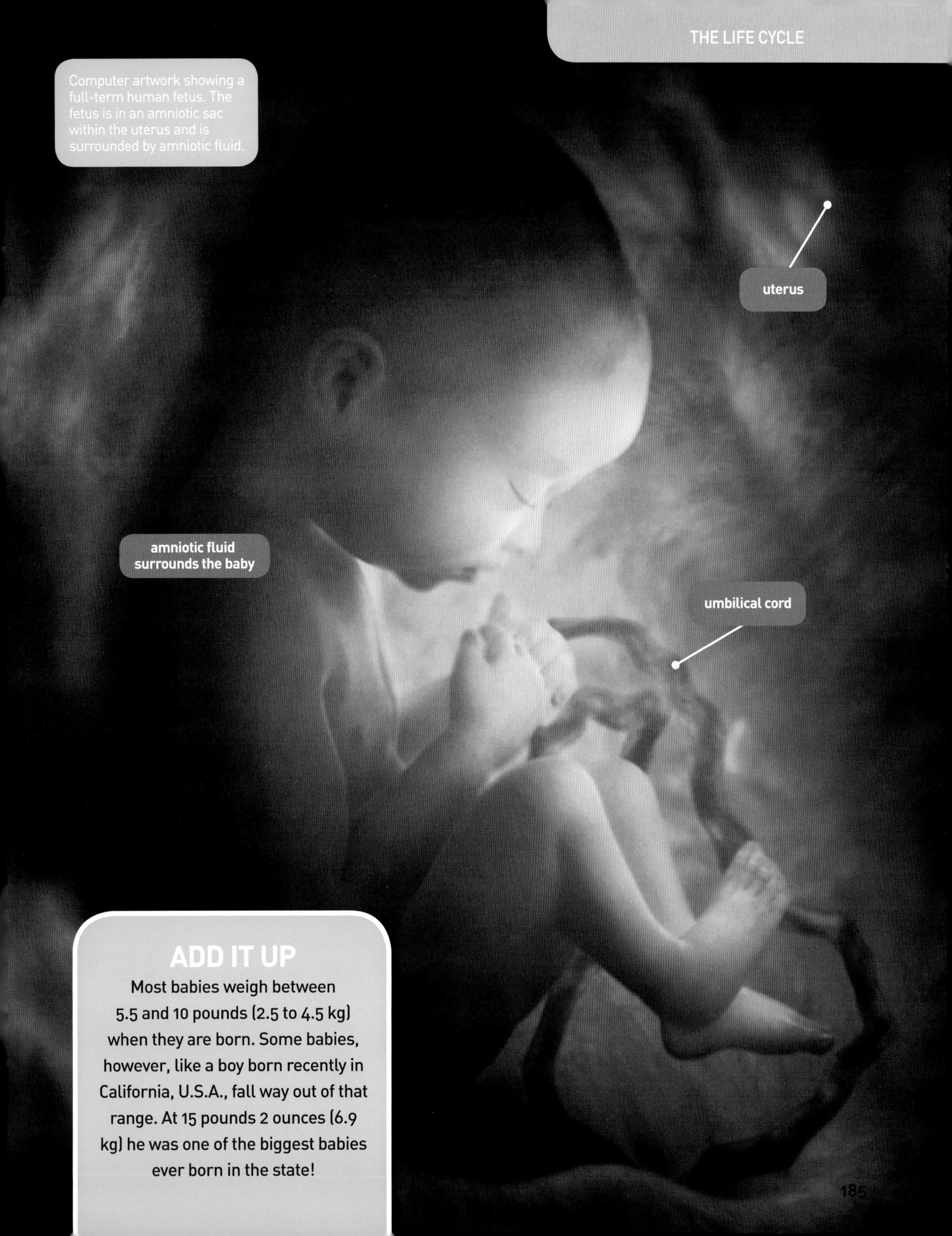

Computer artwork showing a full-term human fetus. The fetus is in an amniotic sac within the uterus and is surrounded by amniotic fluid.

uterus

amniotic fluid surrounds the baby

umbilical cord

ADD IT UP

Most babies weigh between 5.5 and 10 pounds (2.5 to 4.5 kg) when they are born. Some babies, however, like a boy born recently in California, U.S.A., fall way out of that range. At 15 pounds 2 ounces (6.9 kg) he was one of the biggest babies ever born in the state!

Babies have special "infant reflexes" when they are born and for a few months afterward. These reflexes tell doctors whether a baby is developing properly.

All About Me

BABYHOOD

Right after you were born, a doctor may have cut your umbilical cord, which connected you to your mom. (It was where your belly button is now.) As a newborn baby you ate often (either breast milk from your mother or formula milk made especially for babies) and probably slept a lot—up to 16 hours a day!

As you got a little bigger, you were awake more often. Between four and seven months, your neck, back, leg, and arm muscles got stronger, and you were likely able to roll over and to sit up. Eventually you could push yourself up on your arms and legs and almost "rock" back and forth—the first step to crawling. By about six months, you may have already weighed twice what you did when you were born!

Between seven and ten months, you may have crawled backward, or you may have "scooted" on your backside. But soon you were probably moving forward on all fours, then pulling yourself up, and then—around your first birthday—letting go and taking your first step.

And, amazingly, the whole first year of your life, while you were undertaking all these physical challenges and getting bigger and stronger, your brain was developing and taking in enormous amounts of information. By your first birthday, you may have been about ten inches (25.4 cm) longer and about three times your birth weight, and your head may have grown by about four inches (10.2 cm) around! You were learning so much about the world around you: getting to know the people (and maybe pets!) in your life, listening to language, and understanding a few words, including your own name. The first year of your life was a busy time, but your journey had just begun.

EYE-OPENER

Babies are born with blurry vision. Until they are a few months old, babies see best when objects are about 8 to 12 inches (20 to 30 cm) from their face.

Babies are not born with the ability to judge how near or far objects are from one another, called depth perception. It isn't until they are about five months old that their eyes are able to put together a 3-D view of the world.

And what about colors? A newborn's retina is not totally developed yet, so it can only "see" big differences between light and dark. Black and white make a big impression on a newborn's retina; high contrasts in a baby's environment help develop the visual part of its brain.

IT'S GREAT TO BE A KID

You started off your life after babyhood as a toddler. Around the age of one, you learned to walk, and then to run. You began to stand on your tiptoes, to jump, to climb, and to kick a ball. Between ages two and three, you probably started to notice other kids and share your toys. You began to play make-believe games and sort things by shape and by color. You knew a lot more words as a toddler and could understand nearly everything said to you.

When you got a little older and became a preschooler, around ages three and four, you might have been able to pedal a tricycle, and you could climb farther and run faster. You got better at taking turns, doing puzzles, and making mechanical toys work. You could talk in complete sentences and you might have begun to really express yourself and your opinions!

By the time you started elementary school, at around age five, you were facing lots of new challenges and getting more independent. You were learning not only how to read and do math but also the importance of eating healthy food and getting exercise. You made friends and learned how to be part of a larger group of kids.

Until about age four, girls tend to grow a little faster than boys. But from then on both boys and girls grow about two inches (5.1 cm) a year until the start of puberty, usually between ages eight and thirteen for girls and ages ten and fourteen for boys. Puberty generally lasts about three to four years and is a time when you will see a lot of changes in yourself and others.

CHEW ON THIS!

By now you've probably lost some of your "baby" teeth and had "adult" (permanent) teeth come in. Most of your adult teeth will be replacements for the baby ones that fall out—think of your top two and bottom two front teeth—but some are (and will be) in places where teeth hadn't poked through your gums before. "Six-year molars," which probably came in when you were about six years old, are teeth toward the back of your mouth that did not replace anything. This will also happen with your final teeth—"wisdom teeth"—which come in as you reach adulthood.

Bet you didn't know

By the time you were six years old, your brain was already 90 percent of the size it will be when you are an adult.

If you continued to grow as fast as an average baby, you'd weigh about **413,300 pounds (188,000 kg)** by age ten!

ADD IT UP
Weight, weight—there's more! During puberty, most boys will gain a total of about 45 to 50 pounds (20 to 23 kg) and most girls will gain between 35 and 55 pounds (16 to 25 kg).

THE TEEN YEARS

Becoming a teenager, or an adolescent, is filled with physical and emotional changes. Remember learning about hormones in Chapter 6? Hormones are responsible for a lot of the changes that will affect you during puberty. Located under your brain, your pituitary gland releases special hormones that act on the ovaries in girls and the testes in boys. These hormones begin to make changes happen in different parts of your body. Girls begin to develop a curvier shape that resembles that of a woman, and boys take on more of the broad-shouldered shape of a man. Boys' voices will also begin to sound deeper. Both boys and girls will grow more body hair, and each of their reproductive systems will begin changing to allow them to become parents, after they enter adulthood. Boys and girls may also notice a not-so-pleasant smell in their armpits. Hormones again! The hormones also stimulate the sweat glands under your arms and, when that sweat mixes with the bacteria (germs) that live on your skin, it can cause kind of an icky odor. Keeping good hygiene (showering daily) will help with this stinky situation.

SPURT ALERT!

Both boys and girls will get taller during puberty and hit a period of more rapid growth called a spurt. Girls hit their growth spurt about two years earlier than boys, at around age 10; most boys don't hit their spurts until ages 12 or 13. Even though boys start later, they soon catch up to girls and often grow even taller. As a kid enters puberty, he or she could experience a growth spurt of about three to five inches (7.6 to 12.7 cm) in one year! Height spurts can last a few years, with boys adding nine to eleven inches (23 to 28 cm) to their height and girls adding about nine inches.

How tall will you be? It's hard to say, because it depends a lot on your genes. If your parents are tall, there's a good chance you will be, too. If they're on the shorter side, you are more likely to be, too. You won't know until you stop growing!

BEING A
GROWN-UP

Once you become an adult, you are an independent person responsible for your own well-being. In your 20s and 30s, your body—by now finished developing—can be in great health if you take care of it through eating well and getting regular exercise.

When you reach your 40s and 50s, a time called middle age, the commitment you made to good health in your earlier years will keep your body working well. People start to notice more differences in their minds and bodies, such as lines (wrinkles) on their faces, thinner hair on their heads, and brown "age" spots on their hands; your memory, reasoning, and comprehension skills (your brain functions) may be less sharp than they used to be. The children you may have decided to have might now have achieved adulthood themselves, facing the life choices you did a couple of decades earlier. You may be thinking about retirement, or stopping work to do other things. On the horizon now is seniorhood.

ANIMALS GROW UP, TOO

Growing up isn't just for human beings. All animals go through life stages that include a beginning, a middle, and an end. Like us, some animals begin their lives as smaller versions of the similar-looking adults they later become (such as baby chicks becoming chickens). Other young creatures look very little like what they eventually turn out to be (such as tadpoles becoming frogs). Some insects, such as monarch butterflies, undergo four stages for a "complete metamorphosis" in a matter of weeks. They transform from an egg, into a larva (caterpillar), into a "pupa" (hard outer covering), and then emerge as fully grown adults.

Between the years 2000 and 2050, the percentage of the world's population age 60 and older will have **doubled,** from about 11 percent to 22 percent.

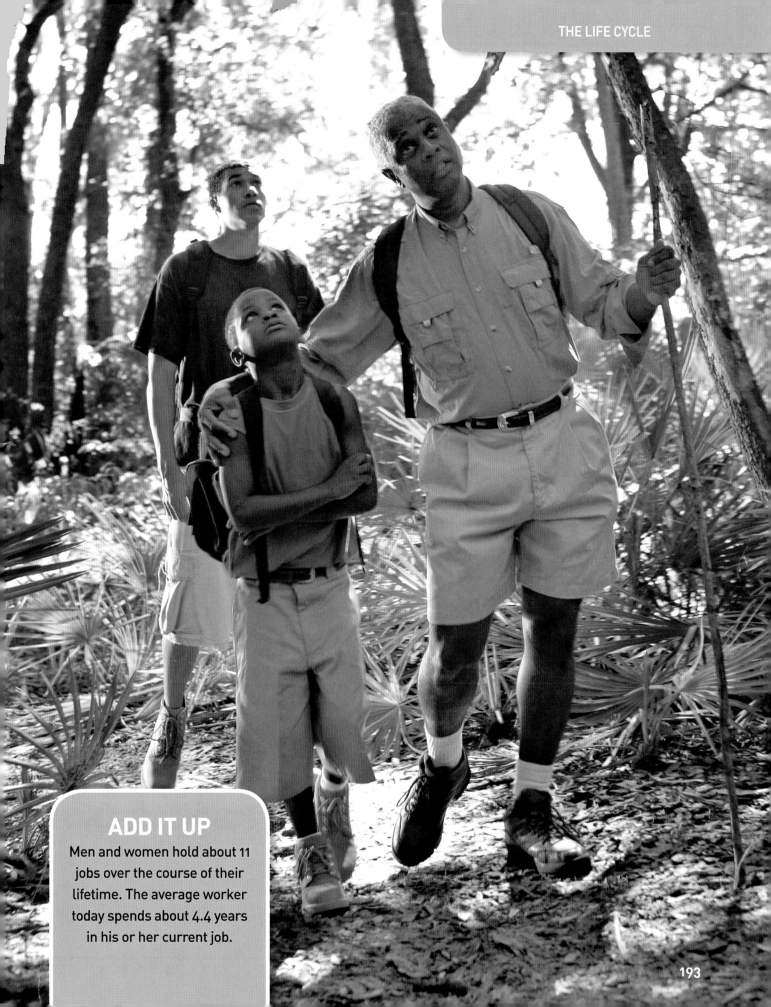

ADD IT UP

Men and women hold about 11 jobs over the course of their lifetime. The average worker today spends about 4.4 years in his or her current job.

ADD IT UP

Humans can live more than 100 years, but they are nowhere near the world's longest-living animals! Top contenders for this include the Galápagos tortoise, at 177 years; the red sea urchin, at 200 years; and the ocean quahog, at 400.

A **French** woman had the longest documented life span ever recorded. She lived for **122 years** and 164 days.

GETTING OLDER

You may be getting older, but staying committed to your health is still very important. Starting in their 60s, and continuing on into their 70s, 80s, and even 90s, people will notice more lines on their faces and other parts of their bodies, such as their neck and hands. Their hair might turn gray, or thin, or they might lose it altogether. They may have health problems they didn't before, such as something called arthritis, or pain and swelling in their joints, which might make moving around more difficult. Brain function—such as memory, reasoning, and comprehension skills—are in decline, and some people will even suffer from dementia, a loss of cognitive (brain) abilities such as memory and thinking that make taking care of themselves difficult.

Still, many seniors live active, healthy lives. Whatever seniors do, studies have shown that having a positive attitude can help them live longer. Other ways seniors can improve their quality of life are by being a loving pet owner, lowering stress through activities like meditation (relaxing the mind), eating foods with antioxidants (substances that can keep aging cells healthy), exercising (it increases heart health), and laughing (it reduces levels of stress hormones such as cortisol and adrenaline).

LIFE LESSONS

One National Geographic explorer found that people in Sardinia, Italy; Okinawa, Japan; and Loma Linda, California, U.S.A., live longer and healthier lives than almost anyone else in the world. These communities had larger numbers of people

who lived to be 100 and fewer people who suffer from diseases. What is their secret? They get regular exercise, stay active, and grow their own fruits and veggies. They also have a sense of purpose and live close to their families or within supportive communities.

COMING FULL CIRCLE

Time for a "self" exam! Test your knowledge about the human life cycle.

True or False?

1. Genes are instructions that make you uniquely "you."
2. Most boys hit their growth spurts about two years earlier than girls.
3. All adult teeth that grow in are replacements for baby teeth that have fallen out.
4. Hormones are responsible for many of the changes kids undergo during puberty.
5. Fraternal twins must always be the same gender.

Multiple Choice

6. Up to about how many hours per day does a newborn baby sleep?
   a. 8
   b. 16
   c. 4
   d. 24

7. How many chromosomes do human cells contain?
   a. 26, or 13 pairs
   b. 52, or 26 pairs
   c. 46, or 23 pairs
   d. 32, or 16 pairs

8. When do children often begin to walk?
   a. at 12 months
   b. at 6 months
   c. at 2 months
   d. at 4 months

9. Kids grow approximately how much per year from about age 4 until the start of puberty?
   a. 2 inches
   b. 5.1 centimeters
   c. 0.17 foot
   d. all of the above

Matching! Caption the photos at right.

10. "I may be a grown-up but I can still be one of the kids!"
11. "Longest . . . leap . . . ever."
12. "I hope my grandkids can keep up . . ."
13. "I'm new here. Can someone find me a sweater?"
14. "Thanks, growth spurt—I'm jumping way higher than last year!"
15. "Toddler versus slide . . . I win!"

Answers: 1) True; 2) False; 3) False; 4) True; 5) False; 6) b; 7) c; 8) a; 9) d; 10) e; 11) c; 12) f; 13) a; 14) d; 15) b

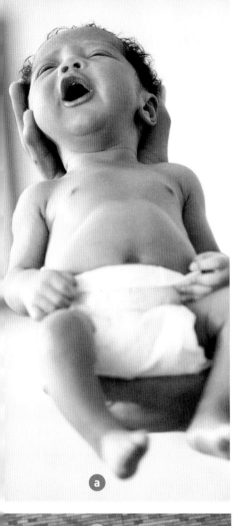

a

b

c

d

e

f

BEING STRONG, STAYING WELL

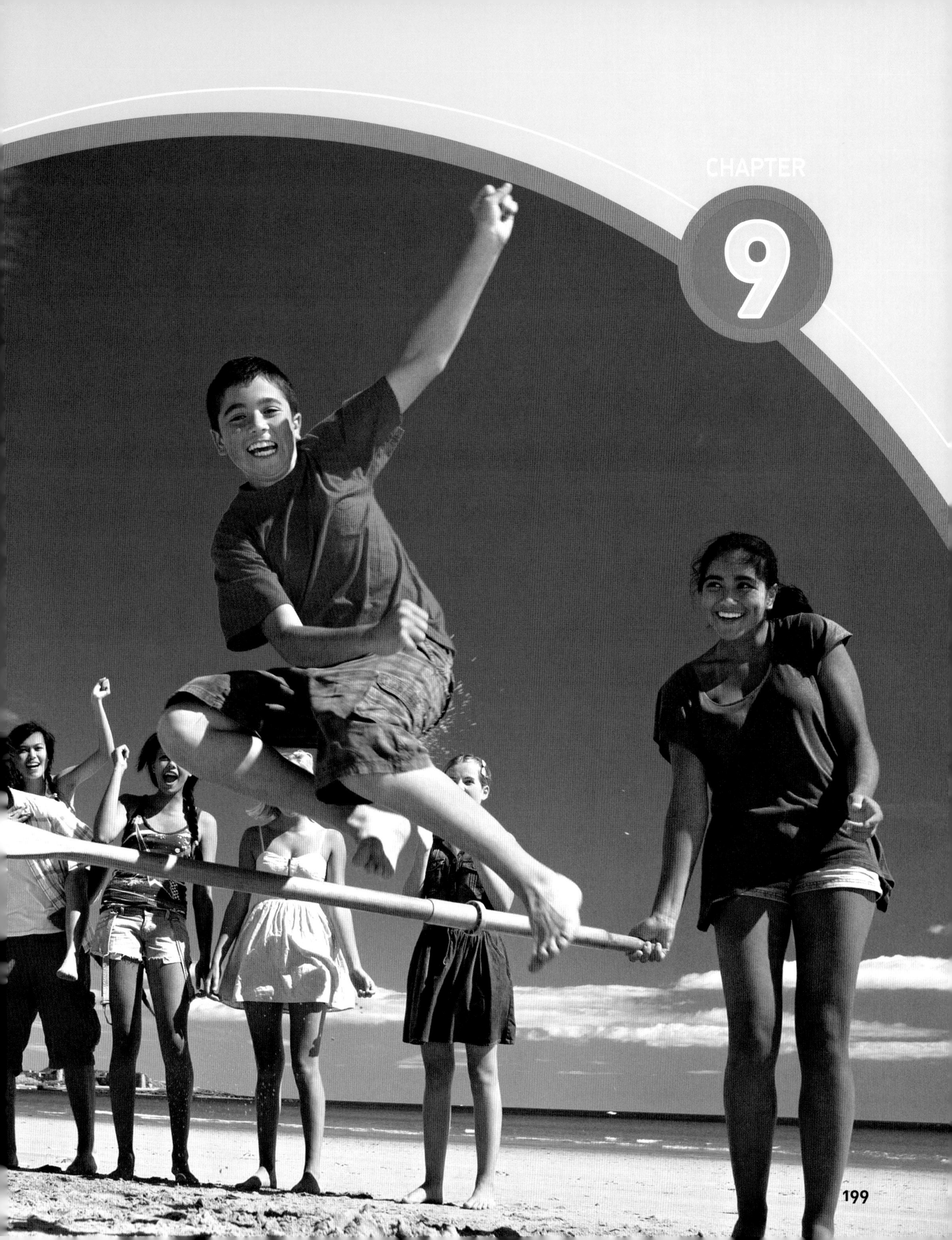

CHAPTER

9

YOUR IMMUNE ARMY

Your body has its own army. It's called your immune system, and it fights 24 hours a day, 7 days a week, 365 days a year to keep you healthy.

Your skin and organs and cells make up much of this protective army. The skin is like a wall, standing in the way of germs. Specialized cells and proteins are the second line of defense, filtering out attackers. White blood cells are the foot soldiers, marching through your bloodstream to find and battle invaders.

Your immune army is a superior fighting force, but you have a critical mission, too. You can be your immune system's ally in the fight to stay strong by doing a few simple things:

- Eating a balanced diet that includes fruits, vegetables, whole grains, and protein
- Keeping fit through sports and other fun physical activities
- Getting enough sleep
- Washing your hands, especially before you eat
- Getting regular checkups with your doctor
- Keeping your distance from people who have a contagious illness, such as a cold or the flu, until they are no longer contagious.

All this doesn't mean you'll never get sick, but it does mean you'll be doing all you can to fortify your defenses.

BREATHLESS!

Part of staying well is staying active. Physical activity can help you do better in school by improving your concentration and focus. But your mission to move can sometimes find you breathless! When you run, or play, or exercise a lot, you may start to breathe hard, or to pant. To keep up with all this extra activity, your body needs to provide more oxygen to your muscles so they have enough strength to keep you going. Your lungs and other parts of your respiratory system work to get more oxygen to your blood, which delivers it to your muscles. When this happens, you may feel like you need to take a little break before you rejoin the fun.

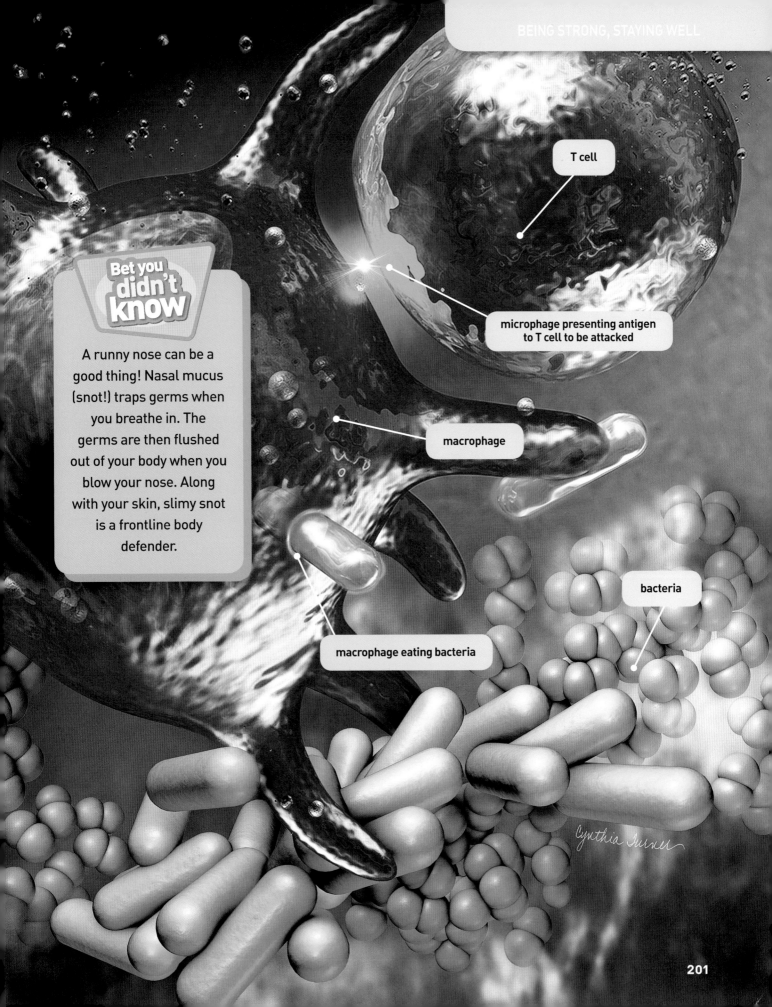

T cell

microphage presenting antigen to T cell to be attacked

macrophage

Bet you didn't know

A runny nose can be a good thing! Nasal mucus (snot!) traps germs when you breathe in. The germs are then flushed out of your body when you blow your nose. Along with your skin, slimy snot is a frontline body defender.

macrophage eating bacteria

bacteria

Cynthia Turner

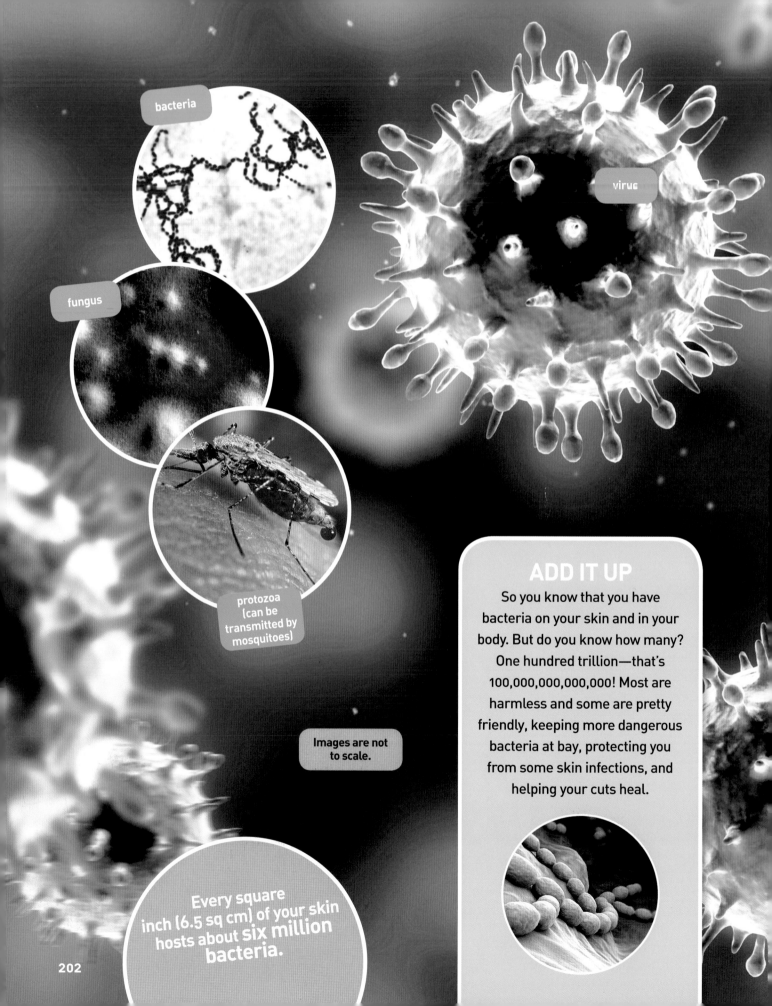

bacteria

virus

fungus

protozoa
(can be
transmitted by
mosquitoes)

Images are not
to scale.

ADD IT UP

So you know that you have bacteria on your skin and in your body. But do you know how many? One hundred trillion—that's 100,000,000,000,000! Most are harmless and some are pretty friendly, keeping more dangerous bacteria at bay, protecting you from some skin infections, and helping your cuts heal.

Every square inch (6.5 sq cm) of your skin hosts about six million bacteria.

THE INVADERS ARE COMING!

Some microorganisms (tiny living things) can make your body sick. They are too small to see with the naked eye. Scientists call them pathogens, but these tiny creatures—bacteria, viruses, fungi, and protozoa—are what you may know as germs.

Bacteria are microscopic organisms that live in nearly every habitat on Earth, including on and in the human body. Some are good for us, some make us sick, and some are generally harmless. "Good" bacteria that live inside us help our digestive systems work properly; "good" bacteria are even used in some medicines and foods. But harmful bacteria can cause ailments, including ear infections and strep throat.

Viruses need to live inside another living thing (a host) to survive; once a virus has found a host, it grows and multiplies throughout the host's body. Among the most common viruses that make us sick are cold and flu viruses.

Fungi get their food from the plants, animals, or people they live on. Some fungi can get on your body and cause skin diseases such as ringworm.

Protozoa are single-celled organisms that can spread disease to humans through contaminated water and dirty living conditions. Protozoa are also parasites that can cause infections such as malaria, which occurs when a person is bitten by an infected mosquito.

AMAZING DISCOVERY

Before scientists discovered germs, people had lots of different ideas about what caused illness. For many centuries people thought that gods or evil spirits made you sick. Then around 400 B.C., a Greek doctor named Hippocrates

(shown in the painting above on the right) told people that sickness was not caused by the gods. But it was another 2,000 years before the first germs were discovered and the connection was made between germs and disease.

GOING VIRAL

Ah-ah-choo! The kid at the next desk sneezes, then sneezes again, and doesn't cover his nose. A few days later, you're sniffling, coughing, and feeling icky. You've caught his cold! A few months later, a sick someone coughs into her hands, then touches a doorknob as she leaves a room—sure, she's left, but her germs stayed behind! Luckily, you know how germs are spread. You know that if you were to open that door, the germs could move from the doorknob to your hand. And then you could soon be sick, too.

Germs are spread many different ways: through direct contact with an infected person, such as sharing utensils or a water bottle, or by shaking hands with them and then rubbing your eyes; through the air, like when someone coughs near or on you without covering their mouth and nose; through food, if the food preparer has not washed his or her hands; through water, if the water source is contaminated; and from animal to person, such as when a person is bitten by malaria-infected mosquitoes.

AMAZING DISCOVERY

It took one persistent doctor, a map, and a pump handle to solve this germy mystery. In the 1850s, in a neighborhood near London, England, people began to get sick from cholera. This disease causes vomiting and diarrhea and can even kill. Most doctors thought cholera was spread through the air. But one doctor, John Snow (right), believed it spread through water.

In those days most people pumped water from public wells for drinking and washing. John Snow made a map of cholera cases around one pump. He showed that the people who had cholera all drank from this pump. His solution: Take the handle off the pump so people would no longer have access to the water. With the pump out of service, sure enough, people stopped getting sick! In time, Snow's discovery helped clean up water and sewer systems all over the world.

Bet you didn't know

A sneeze can fly across a room at 35 miles an hour (56 km/h) and land up to 17 feet (5 m) away!

Though it can feel pretty bad, a hacking cough is one way your body flushes out germs.

Colored scanning electron micrograph (SEM) of a type of bacteria called staphylococcus aureus. This bacteria can cause skin and respiratory infections as well as food poisoning.

staphylococcus aureus bacteria

mucus

hairlike cilia that protrude from epithelial cells to help move mucus

Bet you didn't know Your spleen works as part of your lymphatic system, helping to filter foreign substances from your blood and fight germs and infection. But did you know you can live without it? Yup, the spleen is an important, but not a vital, organ.

GERMS, STAY OUT!

Your skin is like a protective shield that blocks the germs charging to get in. If they try to enter through your eyes or mouth or nose, germs face other defenses. Tears and saliva (spit) foil them with the bacteria-killing enzyme lysozyme. So do the sticky mucous membranes that line your nose and throat and stomach. Backing them up are cilia, tiny hairs in your nose and lungs. Like little brooms, they sweep germs to the throat to be coughed or sneezed away.

Should the germs make it past this tough defensive line, powerful fluids produced in your stomach do their part, too, by neutralizing harmful, disease-causing bacteria. This mix of gastric juices contains hydrochloric acid, an acid so strong that even a drop of it could eat through a piece of wood! So, wait—why doesn't it eat right through your gut? Lucky for us, our stomach wall is protected by an acid-blocking mucus that lines it.

There are ten times more bacteria cells in your body than human cells.

SEE FOR YOURSELF

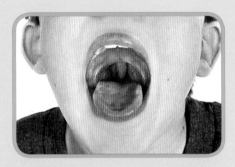

Sometimes sticking out your tongue is not only polite, it's also essential! When your doctor tells you to open up and say *aahhh*, it's for a really good reason: He or she can tell a lot about your health by looking in your mouth. For example, a healthy tongue is pinkish and moist; one that is pasty and white could mean you have an infection. A healthy tongue is slightly bumpy (that's the papillae, little hairs between your taste buds); one that's very smooth could mean a person is iron-deficient or not getting enough B vitamins. Take a look!

CELL BLOCK

Even with all the work your body does to keep germs out of your system, some still manage to get in. Germs may enter through a cut in your skin, or they may get past the defenses in your nose and your throat. But waiting to conquer them is another mean fighting force: your white blood cells.

Many kinds of white blood cells, or leukocytes, move through the blood so they can be ready to defend the body against a variety of germy invaders. Phagocytes kill unwanted organisms by surrounding and digesting them, and two types of lymphocytes (B and T) work together in a seek-and-destroy mission against infection. B lymphocytes (B cells) recognize that a particular kind of virus or bacteria is in your body and respond to the recognized threat by producing antibodies to get a "lock" on it. Your T lymphocytes (T cells) then finish off the offending invader. After destroying the invader, your body makes memory B and T cells so you are doubly ready the next time that same invader tries to attack. This is called immunity.

When many people in a community have been vaccinated against a contagious disease, it protects most of the population by lowering the chances of an **outbreak.**

VACCINES

You can become immune to a disease by getting sick from it or because your doctor gives you a vaccine to prevent you from getting sick in the first place. Most vaccines are given with a shot (as with the whooping cough vaccine, for example), but some vaccines are given orally (the rotavirus vaccine) or through a nasal spray (the inhaled flu vaccine). A vaccine works because it gives you a small weakened or dead amount of the disease it is designed to protect you against—not enough to make you sick but just enough to get your immune system to recognize the invaders and start making antibodies to kill them. The body "remembers" this particular enemy in case it ever encounters it again by making memory T and B cells.

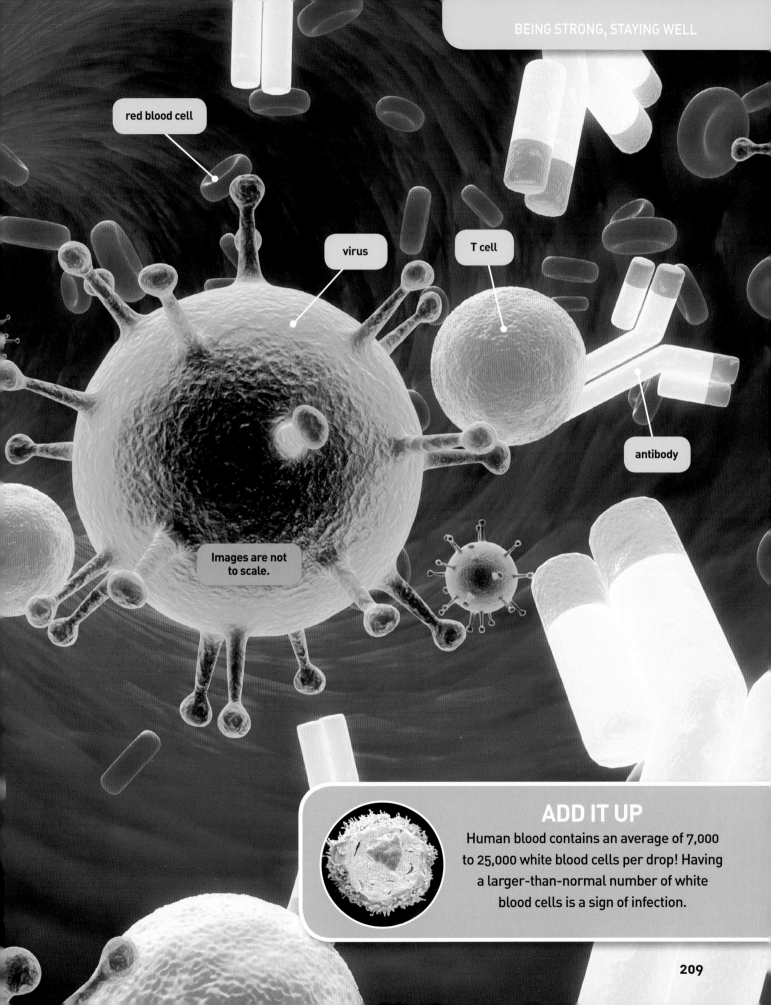

red blood cell

virus

T cell

antibody

Images are not to scale.

ADD IT UP

Human blood contains an average of 7,000 to 25,000 white blood cells per drop! Having a larger-than-normal number of white blood cells is a sign of infection.

skin prick test used for allergy testing

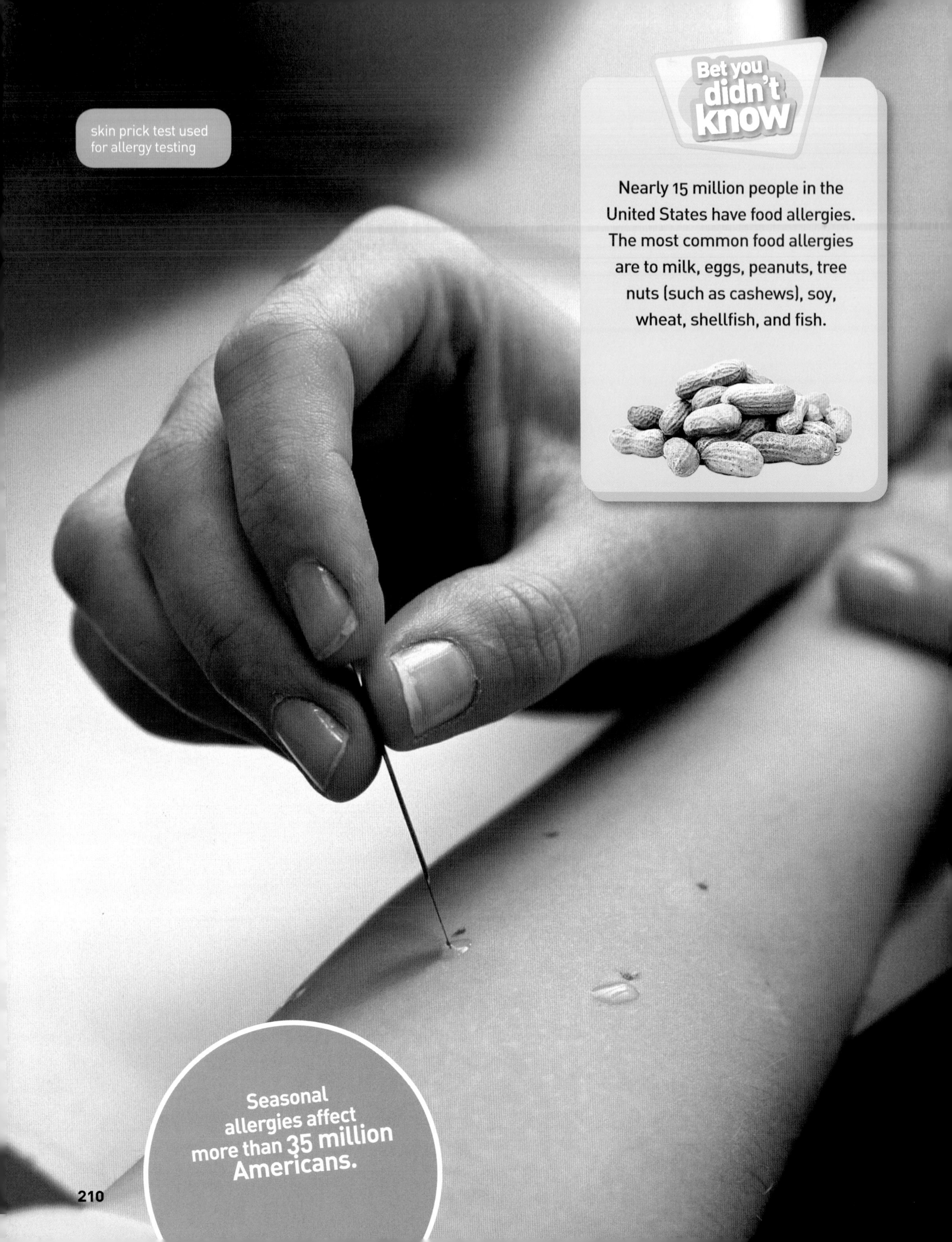

Bet you didn't know

Nearly 15 million people in the United States have food allergies. The most common food allergies are to milk, eggs, peanuts, tree nuts (such as cashews), soy, wheat, shellfish, and fish.

Seasonal allergies affect more than 35 million Americans.

ANNOYING ALLERGIES

Why do your eyes water when you smell flowers? Or pet your neighbor's cat? And why can't your best friend eat nuts? You know the answer: allergies. The same immune system that protects you from germs also "protects" you from things that are not usually considered harmful to people. Itchy eyes, runny nose, wheezing, and sneezing—each is a kind of allergic reaction your body might have to an allergen like pollen or pet dander. An allergic reaction to a type of food, such as nuts, might include hives, stomachache, or difficulty breathing. Some people prone to a serious or life-threatening reaction may carry around medicine with them at all times as a precaution. People with food allergies must always read food labels and be careful not to eat anything containing their allergen.

Why do we even have allergies? Maybe they run in our family and we are born with them; sometimes we develop allergies during the course of our lives. People can outgrow food allergies as they get older; other times, they stay allergic but can manage their allergies with different kinds of medicines. An allergist—a doctor who specializes in treating people with allergies—can help them find ways to feel better.

INTERESTING ALLERGIES

Pollen, mold, dust mites, animal dander, and food are among the more common allergens. Some people are allergic to insect bites, and some people are even allergic to medications. You may know someone allergic to one of those things or you may be allergic to one (or more) of them yourself. But can you imagine being allergic to sunlight? Some people are! It's rare, but those suffering from solar urticaria break out in hives when exposed to

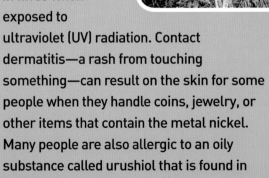

ultraviolet (UV) radiation. Contact dermatitis—a rash from touching something—can result on the skin for some people when they handle coins, jewelry, or other items that contain the metal nickel. Many people are also allergic to an oily substance called urushiol that is found in poison ivy.

HEROES IN GERM HISTORY

We didn't always know what we know today about pathogens and disease.

Through the hard work and tireless inquiry of scientists, inventors, and pioneers—some of whom you'll meet here—our understanding has awakened, deepened, and broadened—and made us a lot healthier.

1796: DR. EDWARD JENNER discovers vaccination by experimenting with the idea that people who caught "cowpox" from their livestock seemed to avoid getting smallpox, the deadliest and most feared disease of his time. His deliberate infection of a young boy with cowpox made the child immune to smallpox.

1600　　　**1700**　　　**1800**

1670s–80s: Dutch scientist and microscopist **ANTON VAN LEEUWENHOEK,** using a microscope he made (left), is the first person to observe the existence of bacteria. He also discovers parasitic protozoa by studying his own feces and observes different kinds of bacteria in his saliva and poop. The "father of microbiology" also discovers bacteria in dental tartar.

1860s–80s: French chemist and microbiologist **LOUIS PASTEUR** discovers that microbes cause contamination of wine (and other beverages) and determines that he can prevent this by heating the liquid to a high temperature. This process—known as pasteurization—eliminates potential pathogens (disease-carrying bacteria and viruses) in a variety of foods and drinks. His work contributes to the idea that infectious diseases can be caused by microorganisms entering the body. Pasteur also develops the first vaccines to fight anthrax and rabies.

1915: Physician **JOSEPH GOLDBERGER** declares that neither bacteria nor viruses cause pellagra, a disease that causes rashes, diarrhea, and brain disease. His research on people suffering from the disease leads him to conclude that it is related to its victims' diets. But at this time the world is so convinced that disease is spread through germs that Goldberger has a hard time convincing people that poor nutrition can also cause sickness.

1870s: Scottish-born scientist **PATRICK MANSON** realizes that elephantiasis is transmitted by mosquitoes carrying a parasitic worm. This leads scientists to discover that insects also carry other diseases, such as malaria.

1870s–80s: German doctor and microbiologist **ROBERT KOCH** proves that the bacterium *Bacillus anthracis* is the cause of anthrax. He studies diseases caused by bacteria and develops a method of staining bacteria to make them easier to see under a microscope. By growing bacteria in his lab, Koch determines which bacteria cause which diseases, including tuberculosis and cholera.

1928: Scottish doctor and bacteriologist **SIR ALEXANDER FLEMING** notices that the mold he finds growing on a dish of bacteria is surrounded by an area that is bacteria-free. He experiments with the mold—called penicillium—and publishes reports on its potential uses. It isn't until the Second World War that penicillin—one of the world's first antibiotics—is mass-produced for the first time.

1900

1884: CHARLES CHAMBERLAND, a French bacteriologist, develops a porcelain filter that traps bacteria in water. This invention improves the sanitation of drinking water by removing microscopic germs, including those causing diseases such as typhoid, cholera, and diphtheria.

1955: JONAS SALK (below) develops a vaccine for polio, a communicable disease that could cause paralysis and death and whose victims were often children. Salk had realized that a vaccine of inactivated (killed) viruses would work to protect people from a disease, a major breakthrough. The vaccine was a success in helping to end a significant public health crisis and save many lives.

CORREOS CUBA
1993
JOSEPH
LISTER
1827 - 1912
CELEBRIDADES
DE LA CIENCIA

1865: English surgeon **SIR JOSEPH LISTER** (left) begins covering wounds with dressings soaked in a cleaner called carbolic acid, reducing infections and introducing the concept of antiseptic surgery. He also starts the practice of washing hands and sterilizing instruments.

You're used to seeing bugs in your garden, but how about on your plate? Nutritious, edible insects including grasshoppers, beetles, wasps, worms, cicadas, and caterpillars are packed with vitamins and minerals and are eaten by people around the globe! Visiting China or Thailand? Stop for a deep-fried cicada on a stick! Next stop the Netherlands? Grab a grasshopper spring roll!

ADD IT UP

This food plate helps you remember what to eat. Fruits and vegetables take up half the plate, meaning half the food you eat each day should be fruits and veggies. The other side of the plate is made up of grains and proteins, and the circle that looks like an outline of a glass of milk reminds you to have some dairy (which is also a protein) every day.

Fruits
Grains
Dairy
Vegetables
Protein

FUEL YOUR BODY

Food is like fuel for your body. It's what gets you up and keeps you moving. Your body turns the food you eat into chemicals called nutrients, which it needs for, well, everything. Food keeps your bones healthy and strong. It maintains and repairs your tissues. It gives you energy. It powers your body and it powers your brain.

Your body turns the food you eat into fuel in a process called digestion. Imagine biting into a fresh and delicious apple. First your teeth chop up the apple and break it into little pieces. The apple chunks go down a tube (your esophagus) into your stomach, where they are mashed and smashed and further broken down by gastric juices. Then the tiny apple pieces enter your small intestine, where they are broken down even further so your body can absorb their nutrients—the fuel. This fuel travels through your blood to all parts of your body. (See Chapter 4 for more on digestion.)

Some foods are better for you than others. Healthful foods keep you in shape and give you the best kind of energy. How do you know what kinds of food you should eat to stay healthy? Back when your parents were growing up, food scientists, called nutritionists, used a food pyramid to show the healthiest foods. Now nutritionists use a food plate (at left) to help you remember the foods that are best to eat.

FUN FOODS!

Try these fun recipes (with an adult's help) and find out how yummy healthy eating can be.

Smooth Smoothies: Blend plain yogurt, your choice of fruit (old bananas work well), ice (you can use frozen fruit instead of adding ice), and a little juice or milk.

Personal Pizzas: Toast an English muffin, bagel, or pita bread. Add tomato sauce, cheese, and your choice of veggie toppings. Bake in the toaster oven with the help of an adult.

Poppy Pops: Pour juice into ice trays, put the trays in the freezer, and insert wooden sticks as the juice starts to freeze. Or push a stick into a peeled banana and pop it in the freezer.

FIT AND FUN!

What does it mean to be physically "fit"?

Maybe you think being "fit" is a goal only grown-ups or athletes strive for. It's not! Being fit is about making good choices—choices that you can make for yourself every day. Eating healthy foods and staying active are ways to be fit. Fitness experts recommend that kids get at least one hour of physical activity a day and that they not stay inactive for more than two hours at a time.

Kids who are fit have stronger heart muscles, fewer breathing problems, and less body fat. Studies show that healthier kids are absent from school less often, are more focused on learning, get better grades, and report liking school more. Also, kids who are physically fit tend to be less stressed out, feel better about themselves, and be all-around happier!

Though you are born with a genetic makeup that may affect your overall health, it's how you live each day that counts the most.

Being **active** makes you feel good. When you exercise, your body releases endorphins, which can make you feel **happier.**

FUNKY FITNESS!

Want to shake up your approach to exercise? "Working out" does not have to feel like work! Here are some activities that will help you let go and have a good time.

Hula-Hooping: Strengthen your tummy muscles and get your heart pumping! Be sure to keep shifting your weight back and forth to keep that circle spinning.

Jumping Rope: You can do this one solo anytime or with a few pals on the playground. Swing that string, strengthen your muscles, and hop your way to good health!

Roller, Ice, or Inline Skating: Low-impact and high fun! Be sure to always wear your protective gear (including helmet and pads) and choose skates that are a good fit.

Yoga: Not just for grown-ups! Yoga gives you energy and helps you stay balanced and healthy. Bend, stretch, and breathe your way to a healthier you.

Skipping: Maybe you haven't skipped since you were a little kid, or you think you might look silly. So what? Grab a friend and give it a try!

Bet you didn't know

How do people in cities around the world keep fit? Many go outdoors! People in Bangkok, Thailand, head to Lumphini Park to run or do tai chi. Residents of San Francisco, California, U.S.A., windsurf, skateboard, or hike their way to fitness at Golden Gate National Recreation Area.

OUR FUTURE BODIES

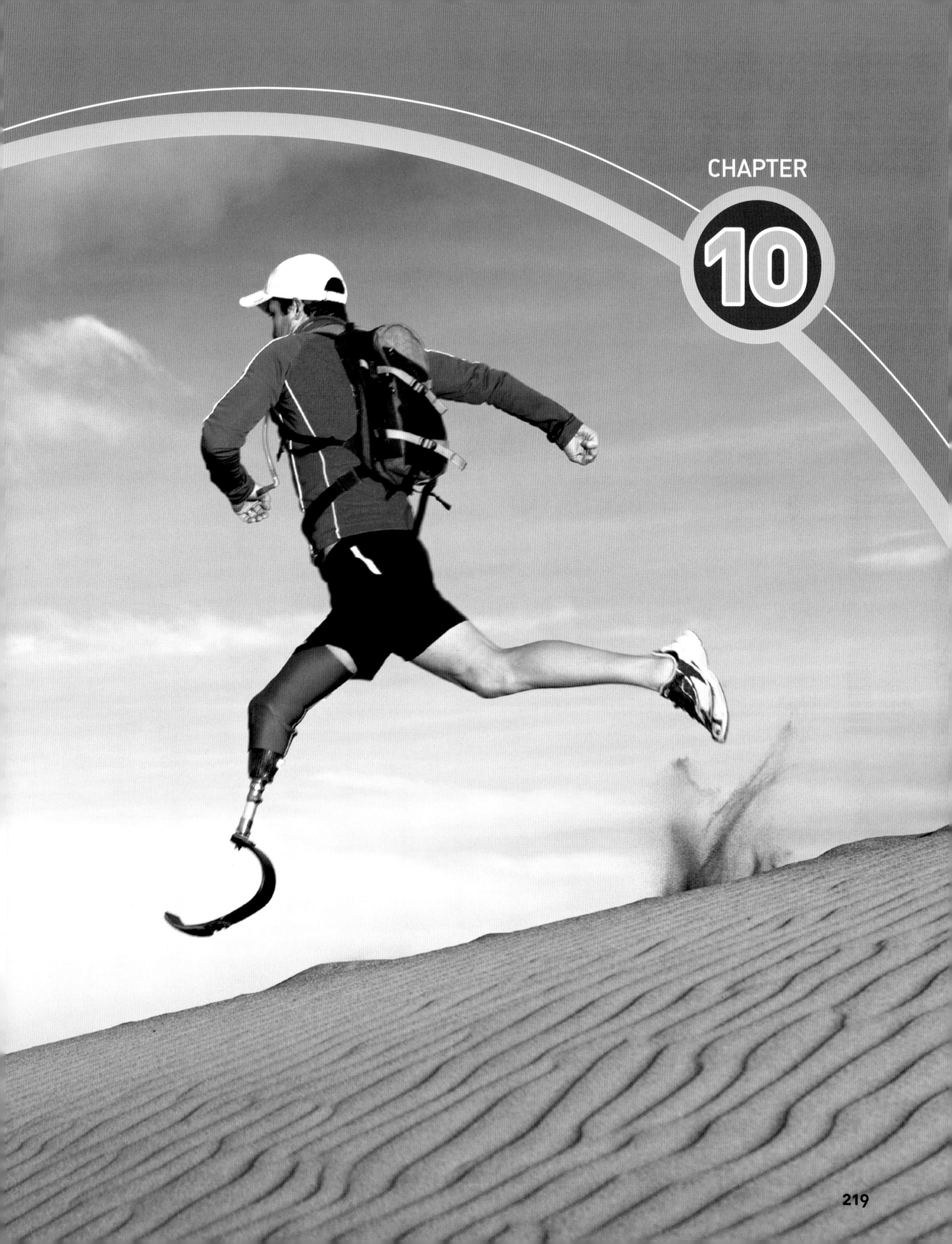

CHAPTER 10

WHAT'S NEXT?

With so much already known about the human body, how much is there left to discover? Plenty! In this chapter you'll find out how doctors and researchers are solving more and more of the body's mysteries. They're developing technologies to create prostheses (artificial devices that replace missing or injured body parts) and repair old ones. They're exploring how and why people get certain diseases, in the hopes of preventing those diseases or treating them more effectively. And they're undertaking exciting brain research, including investigating how our brains can talk directly to computers. The deeper science goes "into" the human brain, the more it can unlock the brain's power and potential to help us live longer, healthier lives.

Kids are helping to solve these mysteries, too, in an effort to make the world a happier, healthier place.

Learning all the secrets of the human body may be many years off, but the process of getting there is pretty exciting!

SECOND SIGHT

A "bionic retina" is giving new hope to some people who have lost their sight slowly over time. The Argus II is a "retinal prosthesis" that can restore some vision to people with a variety of inherited eye diseases. These diseases affect approximately 1 in every 4,000 people.

The Argus II uses a video camera attached to a pair of sunglasses. The camera sends images to a surgical implant on a patient's retina. Those images are then changed into electrical signals that the optic nerve sends to the brain (see Chapter 7). Patients see patterns of light, and the brain learns to interpret these patterns as vision. Blind patients have been able to see shapes and recognize large letters.

The Argus II has been approved for use in patients in Europe and in the United States.

Bet you didn't know

The parietal lobes in genius Albert Einstein's brain (the parts that deal with math, visual, and spatial understanding) were 15 percent wider than the average person's!

In 1904, George Eyser, who had a **wooden leg,** won three Olympic **gold medals** in gymnastics.

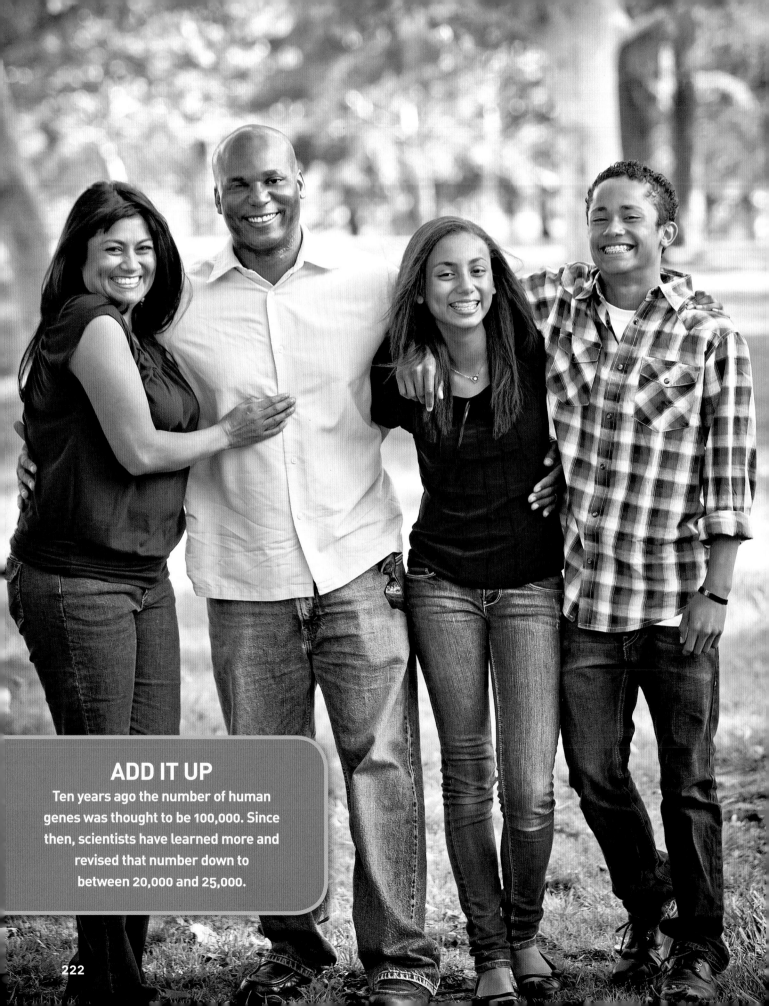

ADD IT UP

Ten years ago the number of human genes was thought to be 100,000. Since then, scientists have learned more and revised that number down to between 20,000 and 25,000.

THE GENE SCENE

Genetics is the study of heredity, or how traits from parents are passed along to their children. And genes are the elements we inherit from each of our parents that combine to make us the individuals we are. By studying genes, scientists have been able to learn not only what makes us similar to and different from one another, but also the causes of certain diseases that are inherited (passed down) from one generation to another.

Amazingly, advances in research have helped scientists discover that there are "disease genes"—genes that indicate that a person who is carrying them may be more likely to get a specific disease. Researchers are also developing ways to test people to see if they have these genes. They are digging deeper into the genetics behind more and more diseases, such as cancer and heart disease, to see which healthy patients could be at risk in the future. Doctors are now even able to know in advance whether a patient will respond well to a particular treatment (medicine) based on their genetic code! Going forward, researchers are working to make genome sequencing (studying a person's unique genetic makeup) more widely available so many people can have access to this amazing medical care. One day we may be able to fix these broken genes.

NATURE'S BLUEPRINT

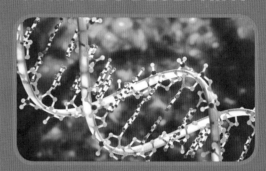

In 2003, after more than a decade of hard work, scientists completed a very ambitious task called the Human Genome Project. They mapped the entire "sequence" of human DNA—our hereditary "code" containing tens of thousands of genes. DNA is nature's blueprint for human beings, and it makes up the building blocks of life.

Would it surprise you to know that, despite how different individual people seem from one another, more than 99 percent of DNA is the same in all people? It's true! Though there are definite physical and other differences we can identify—such as eye color, hair color, height, and skin color—humans are genetically mostly the same.

BUILDING NEW PARTS

Sometimes an organ, such as a heart, liver, or kidney, isn't working the way it's supposed to; it needs repairing—maybe it even needs replacing. You've probably heard of an organ transplant, in which a person receives a new organ from an organ donor. But finding a donor often isn't easy and can take a lot of time. Wouldn't it be amazing if we could grow these parts back, sort of the way we grow back our hair, or our nails, or our skin?

Someday maybe we'll be able to, through a growing field of research called regenerative medicine. Scientists are learning how to build organs and tissues in the laboratory using stem cells. These cells do not have a specialized job like other cells do, so they can be made into the type of cell needed to grow a certain tissue or organ. Most of these lab-made organs have not been used in humans yet, though a lab-grown trachea (windpipe) was recently successfully implanted into a patient whose own trachea had been damaged by illness.

Researchers all over the world are working on many exciting projects using stem cells in the laboratory, to grow new bones, bladders, and kidneys and to repair failing livers.

Routine regrowing or repairing of organs for human bodies may be years away, but the promise of this gives hope to many people.

AMAZING ANIMALS

As humans, we may not be able to regrow most body parts on our own, but some animals can! If only we were more like the salamander (below). These little amphibians regrow arms and legs all the time. And sharks? Their mouths never stop growing new teeth. Some sharks go through 30,000 teeth in a lifetime!

The planarian is a worm that really knows how to keep its head: If you chop its head off, the head grows back. Cut off its tail, and that grows back, too! And the detached head and tail will *each* generate a new full-size worm!

The worm has powerful stem cells that restore its body parts—making new parts grow—throughout its life. This little worm could give scientists big answers to questions about how humans can repair their own bodies.

Bet you didn't know

A group of scientists used cells, gel, and a 3-D printer to create a kind of "bionic" ear, complete with a coiled antenna that can pick up radio signals and "hear" them as sound.

a researcher's work with stem cells in the lab

If you donate part of your **liver** to someone sick who needs it, your missing piece will **grow back.**

225

A Canadian filmmaker—who lost his vision in one eye as a boy—developed a replacement eye that is also a battery-powered wireless video camera.

When you—*ouch!*—hit your "funny bone," it hurts because it's really your ulnar nerve (which runs down the inside part of your elbow) being bumped against your humerus (the bone of your upper arm that runs from your elbow to your shoulder).

Lindsay Block demonstrates her i-LIMB (bionic) hand. She was born without the lower part of her arm.

SMART PARTS

Sometimes, if someone has a body part that is very, very seriously injured or ill, doctors need to remove the sick or hurt body part to help the patient stay healthy. This is often a patient's limb, such as an arm or a leg.

An option for amputees (people who have had a limb removed) is to be fitted with an artificial, or substitute, part, called a prosthesis. Prostheses have been around for a long, long time, but these days they're pretty high-tech. Today's prosthetic parts are made from springy, lightweight metal and plastic and have movable joints. Many have robotic parts and are powered by electricity.

A goal of new research and technology is to have a prosthesis work together with the rest of an amputee's natural body as smoothly as possible—including having their brain communicate directly with their mechanical limbs. Prosthetic legs currently being developed and tested, for example, allow amputees to create different kinds of movements, such as rotating their ankles and walking up stairs, by just *thinking* about rotating their ankles and walking up stairs. Their brains send messages to the nerves about what they want to do; the nerves communicate with a computer in their artificial limb. The computer then turns those thoughts *about* actions *into* actual actions. Now that is technology moving forward!

A DOLPHIN'S TALE

Maja Kazazic had become used to living with pain—and feeling different. As a teen, Maja lost her leg after she was badly injured in the Bosnian civil war. And an uncomfortable prosthesis made every movement painful.

Maja's life changed when she met Winter, a dolphin at Clearwater Marine Aquarium in Florida (above). Winter had lost her tail in a crab trap as a baby. When Winter got a high-tech tail to help her swim, Maja wondered if a similar device could help her be pain free. The aquarium put Maja in touch with the company that made Winter's prosthesis. Maja received a new leg out of the same materials that helped Winter. Soon the pair were swimming together—one with a new leg, the other with a new tail.

LIMBS FROM LIMBS

You've learned about organ transplants, in which a person receives a new organ, such as a heart or a liver, on the inside of their body. But did you know that people can sometimes receive transplants on the *outside* of their bodies, too?

It hasn't happened very often but, instead of prosthetic parts, some patients can get new human limbs through transplant surgery. This complicated procedure involves surgeons attaching the limbs of a donor to the body of the person who is receiving them.

Up to now, people have had limbs, including hands and arms, transplanted—some successfully and some not. Now, a hospital in Boston, Massachusetts, is working toward successfully performing leg transplant surgery on amputee patients. This kind of operation is very new and has not yet been performed in the United States.

The hospital began looking for patients in 2013, but it's not certain when it will begin attempting this groundbreaking surgery. One thing is certain, however: This incredible development could one day change the lives of countless people who have lost their legs.

ARMED AND BRAVE

In 2012 a U.S. Army soldier who had lost all four limbs after being injured by a roadside bomb in 2009 received a rare double-arm transplant—one of only a small number of people to successfully undergo this risky surgery. In a 13-hour operation, a team of

16 surgeons joined bone, muscles, blood vessels, nerves, and skin of donor arms with those of former sergeant Brendan Marrocco's. In his right arm, they transplanted the arm from his donor above the elbow; in his left arm, to preserve his remaining elbow joint, they took the entire forearm from the donor and transplanted it on top of his existing forearm bone. With time and physical therapy, these replacement arms have helped Marrocco do many of the things he did before, such as drive a car.

Bet you didn't know

The oldest known prosthetic body part is more than 2,500 years old. It's a wood-and-leather toe that archaeologists found attached to an Egyptian mummy!

A young Malaysian girl named Chong Lih Ying received an arm transplant as a baby.

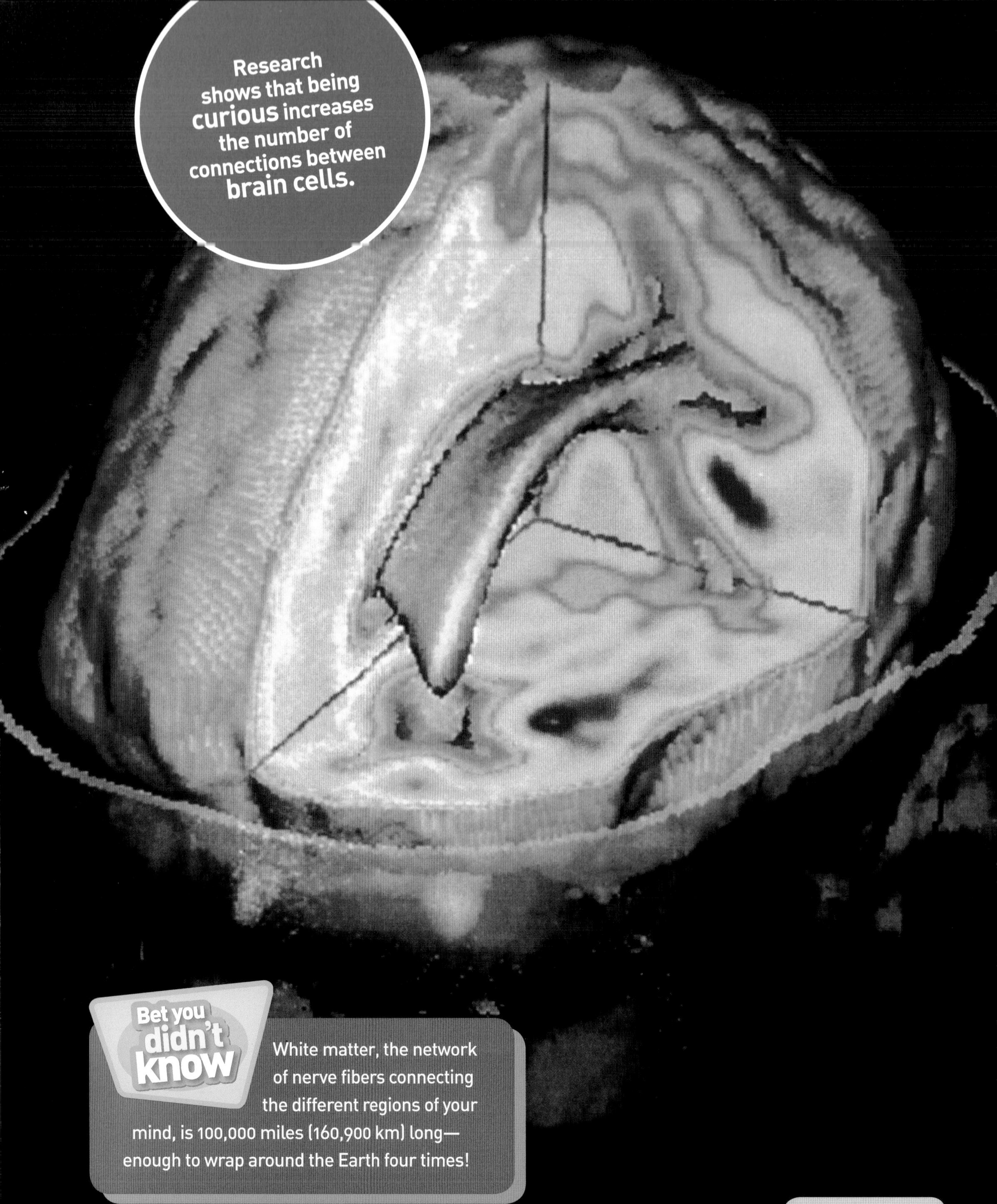

Research shows that being **curious** increases the number of connections between **brain cells.**

Bet you didn't know

White matter, the network of nerve fibers connecting the different regions of your mind, is 100,000 miles (160,900 km) long— enough to wrap around the Earth four times!

EXPLORING THE BRAIN

Many of the most exciting advances in science have to do with the human brain. In Chapter 6, you learned a lot about how our brains work, including some ways that scientists have been able to "map" the brain. This mapping has taught scientists an amazing amount about how we understand and relate to the world around us.

Do you remember something called functional magnetic resonance imaging, or fMRI (see page 141)? For 20 years, fMRIs have helped scientists learn more about which parts of our brains are involved in different mental processes and tasks. Now scientists would like to know not only what parts of the brain are working when we do or think something, but also how the different parts are connected to each other—how they "network" to process information. Researchers have begun to investigate new possibilities for mapping the actions of the brain more precisely—specifically, what our neurons (nerve cells) are doing. The goal for this and future research is to have a complete picture of how the brain works. We already know so much, but there is so much more to discover!

WEIGHT A MINUTE!

Different kinds of animals have different-size brains. Scientists generally believe that human beings are the smartest creatures on Earth, so you might think that humans have the biggest brains in the animal kingdom, right? A human brain weighs about 3 pounds (1.4 kg). In contrast, an elephant has a brain that weighs around 11 pounds (5 kg)! Elephants  are pretty smart animals, but is an elephant more than three times smarter than a person?

It's actually not the size of the brain that is a factor in intelligence but more the size of the brain in relationship to the size of the entire body. A brain in a 150-pound (68-kg) person accounts for about 2 percent of total body weight. In a 6,000-pound (2,271-kg) elephant, the brain accounts for less than 0.2 percent of body weight. The brain makes up more of a human's total weight than it does in other animals. Now that's big!

BRAIN, MEET COMPUTER

New understanding of the power of our brains and progress in the power of computers leads to an important question: How can scientists get these two powerful forces to work together? The answer lies in something called brain-computer interface (BCI), an exciting field scientists have been researching for decades (see demonstration in photo, right). Investigating how the brain turns thoughts into actions has helped scientists develop this incredible technology.

In BCI, sensors either on the surface of the scalp or on the surface of the brain itself measure the electrical signals that are fired off between neurons (nerve cells). These signals are then sent to a computer, which converts the thoughts into actions. This amazing technology has already helped people who are paralyzed—people who cannot move their arms or legs or both—do everyday things like use a computer or use a robotic arm to feed themselves. Recently researchers in Rhode Island created the first wireless (and rechargeable) BCI, which would allow its users to move around more freely and allow scientists to gather even more data about what is happening in their brains and when.

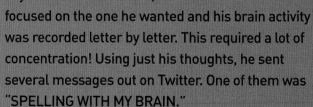

NETWORK CONNECTION

If you could work a computer with your mind, what would you tell it to do? How about send a tweet?

That's what Adam Wilson did in 2009. The University of Wisconsin biomedical engineering student wore a special cap with electrodes that sensed changes in his brain activity and sent that information to his computer.

Wearing the cap, he looked at a keyboard on his computer monitor. As the keyboard flashed letters, he focused on the one he wanted and his brain activity was recorded letter by letter. This required a lot of concentration! Using just his thoughts, he sent several messages out on Twitter. One of them was "SPELLING WITH MY BRAIN."

This amazing technology could be used to help people whose bodies aren't working due to a condition or injury—a spinal cord injury, for example—but whose brains are working normally.

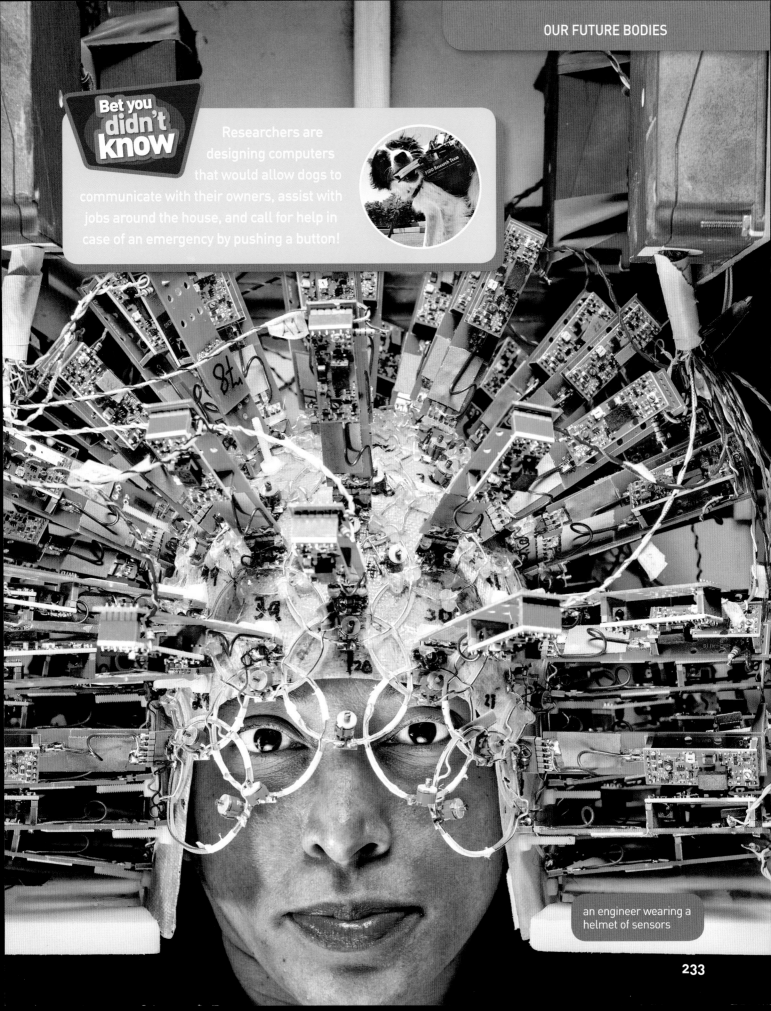

Bet you didn't know

Researchers are designing computers that would allow dogs to communicate with their owners, assist with jobs around the house, and call for help in case of an emergency by pushing a button!

FIDO Research Team

an engineer wearing a helmet of sensors

One of the coolest developments in medicine over the past few decades has been the use of robots during surgery. Robots help to make surgeries more precise and safer for patients.

A team of Swiss researchers built a **robot** small enough to swim through **human arteries.**

an example of a robotic device used by doctors that allows them to see patients remotely

Double

THE DOCTOR IS IN THE COMPUTER?

Did you know doctors can now diagnose patients without being in the same room with them?

They don't even have to be in the same country! "Remote devices" from small handheld machines to five-foot (1.5-m)-tall robots on wheels have a camera, speakers, and a microphone so patients can communicate with doctors in much the same way they would if they were right next to each other. (Except the doctor's face is on a screen!) The doctor can see readings from medical equipment and check out the patient's speech, eyes, and skin. Some hospitals are now also using this amazing technology in intensive-care units and emergency rooms to give patients access to specialists, such as neurologists (brain doctors) and cardiologists (heart doctors). This kind of long-distance medical care can also help patients in hard-to-reach places to receive treatment.

APP-LY YOURSELF

You are the boss of your body and the master of your muscles! You know you should eat healthy foods and get lots of exercise—but do you also know that there are some fun apps that can help you stay on top of your game?

To get the whole "picture," try an animated and interactive app that shows you the different parts of your body, what they look like, and what they do. The Human Body by Tinybop is one and Discover Your Body HD is another. To stay in shape, check out an app like FitnessKids that shows you lots of different exercises you can try and allows you to keep track of your progress.

And what about nutrition? Learn about fruits and veggies and sort them from a conveyor belt into baskets with Awesome Eats from the Whole Kids Foundation. You'll rack up points and learn cool food facts, too!

UNSTOPPABLE STUDENTS

Every year Google holds an online worldwide contest for the next generation of scientists. Through the Google Science Fair, students ages 13 to 18 can create a science or engineering project and share their amazing inventions and discoveries.

The kids who have won prizes in this cool contest took on some serious challenges and invented some amazing stuff. Fifteen-year-old Canadian student Ann Makosinski (see opposite page) invented a flashlight powered by the heat given off by a human hand. Sixteen-year-old Elif Bilgin, from Turkey, used banana peels to make a bioplastic (a plastic made from renewable materials) that could be used to insulate cables and make cosmetic prostheses (such as replacement fingers or toes). Fourteen-year-old Australian Viney Kumar created a system using Internet and smartphone tools that alerts drivers to an approaching emergency vehicle. And for his work researching new medicines to combat the sometimes deadly flu virus, 17-year-old Eric Chen of San Diego, California, was the 2013 Grand Prize winner.

Other kids have researched or created an eco-friendly way to clean polluted water, a way to detect skin cancer early, a treatment for liver inflammation, and a method to improve the way people with hearing loss can experience music.

These kids had an idea for a way to make the world a better place—and they made their ideas come true. As you get older, study hard, and learn more, see if you can turn your ideas into reality, too!

NETWORK FOR SUCCESS

Brittany Wenger (above with President Obama) was 17 when she won the 2012 Google Science Fair's Grand Prize by writing a computer program that could help doctors better diagnose breast cancer. A test that doctors use to look for breast cancer in a patient is called fine-needle aspiration, in which they remove some body tissue and look for cancer cells. This test can sometimes produce results that may not show for sure whether a patient has a cancer. However, Brittany's amazing program—a network designed to act like a human brain—was able to detect patterns in tissue sample data and make diagnoses, correctly identifying more than 99 percent of cancerous tumors.

Bet you didn't know

The National Gallery for America's Young Inventors is a hall of fame specifically for amazing student achievers! Recent inductees have created such incredible inventions as a low-cost device for detecting breathing disorders and a quick and inexpensive paper sensor to screen patients for pancreatic cancer.

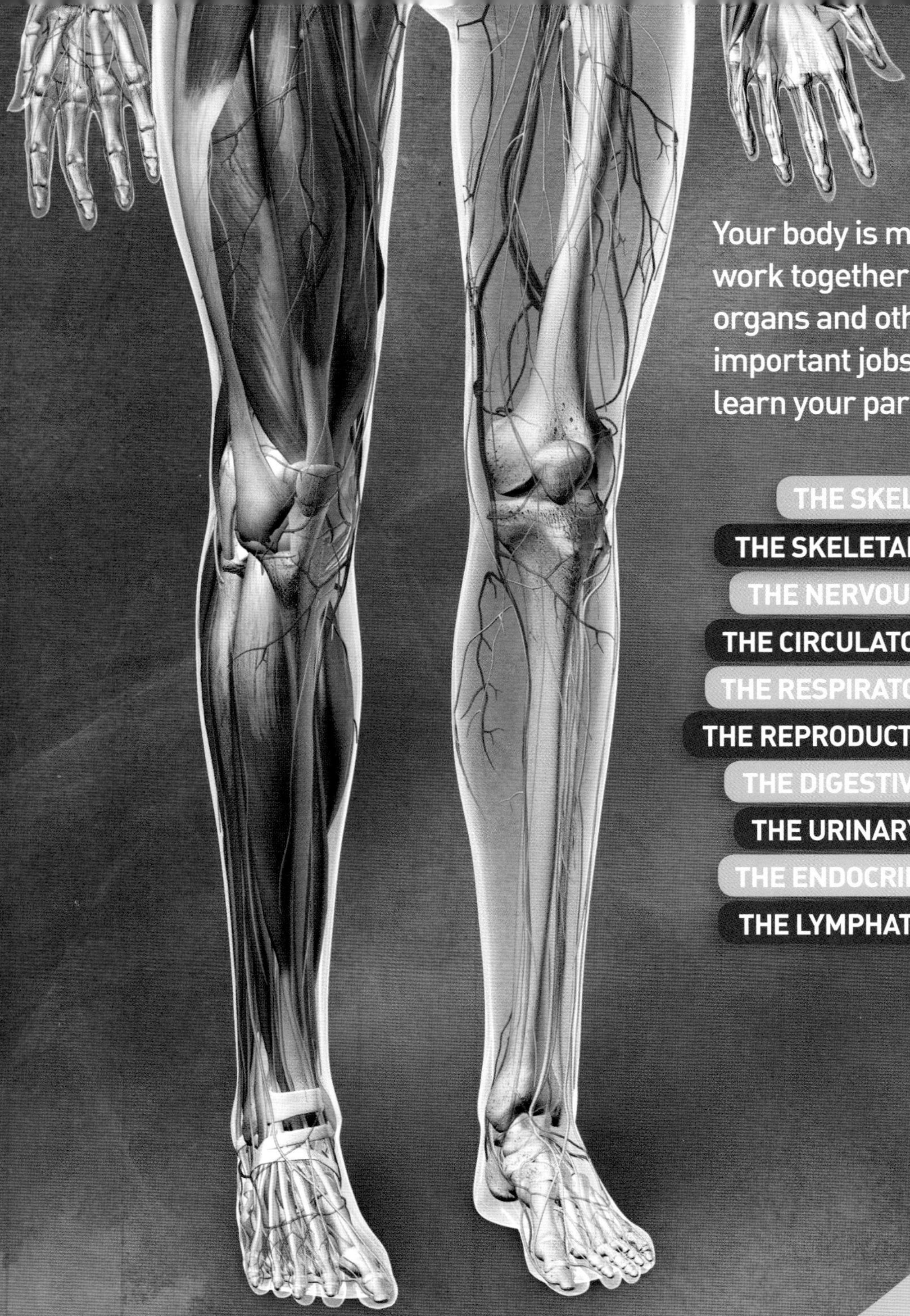

Your body is made up of different systems that work together to keep you running well. Each has organs and other essential elements that have important jobs to do. Use this detailed Body Atlas to learn your parts, their place, and their purpose!

THE SKELETON

1

A

B

C

D

E

Г

G

H

2

3

4

5

6

8

7

9

10

11

14

12

13

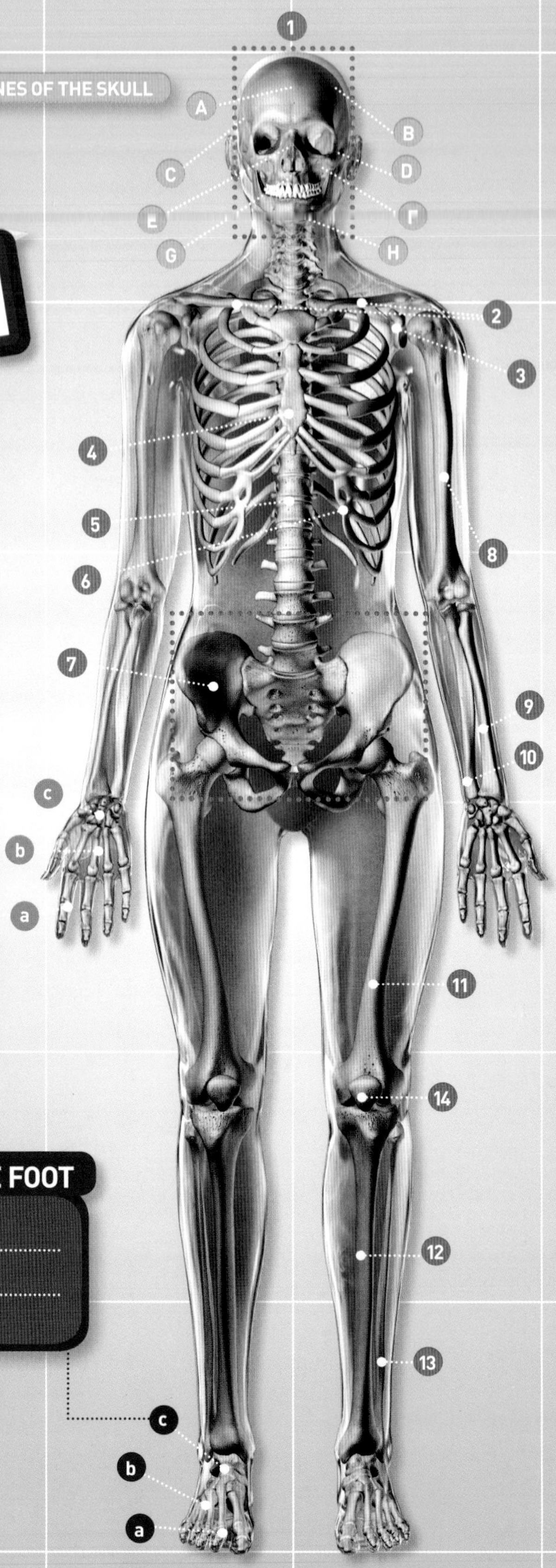

BONES OF THE HAND

a	**PHALANGES** Bones of the fingers and thumb
b	**METACARPALS** Bones of the palm
c	**CARPALS** Wrist bones

BONES OF THE FOOT

a	**PHALANGES** Toe bones
b	**METATARSALS** Bones of the sole
c	**TARSALS** Ankle bones

c

b

a

0 1 square = 1 foot (0.3 m) **1'**

6-FOOT (1.8-m)-TALL PERSON

The **skeleton** is a structure that **supports** and **protects** our organs and tissues. **Two hundred and six bones** make up the adult body's framework, the skeleton. A springy spine and swinging joints let it bend and fold. Here are some of the most important bones of the main **skeleton, the skull,** and the **hands and feet.** (See pages 52–69 for more on bones and the skeleton.)

MAIN BONES OF THE SKELETON

1. **SKULL** (Cranium) Protects the brain
2. **COLLARBONE** (Clavicle) Connects the shoulder to the sternum
3. **SHOULDER BLADE SCAPULA** (Scapula) Connects to the top of the arm
4. **BREASTBONE** (Sternum) Helps hold the ribs together
5. **BACKBONE** (Vertebrae) Protects the spinal nerves; keeps the body upright
6. **RIBS** Protect the heart and lungs
7. **HIP BONES** (Pelvis) Anchor the hips and the legs
8. **UPPER ARM BONE** (Humerus) Extends from the shoulder to the elbow
9. **LOWER ARM BONE** (Radius) Extends from the elbow to the wrist
10. **LOWER ARM BONE** (Ulna) Extends from the elbow to the wrist
11. **THIGHBONE** (Femur) Connects the hip to the knee
12. **SHINBONE** (Tibia) Main bone of the lower leg
13. **FIBULA** Twists around the tibia
14. **KNEECAP** (Patella) Protects the knee

MAIN BONES OF THE SKULL

A. **FRONTAL BONE** Forms the forehead
B. **PARIETAL BONE** Top and side of the skull
C. **TEMPORAL BONE** Side of the skull
D. **SPHENOID BONE** Forms part of the base of the skull and part of the eye sockets
E. **NASAL BONES** Form the bridge of the nose
F. **CHEEKBONE** Forms arch of the cheek
G. **MAXILLA** Forms upper jaw
H. **JAWBONE** (mandible) Forms movable lower jaw

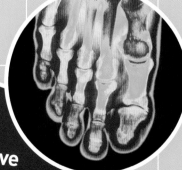

Twenty-five percent of your bones are in your feet.

THE SKELETAL MUSCLES

Of the body's many muscles, the **gluteus maximus** (or butt muscle) is the largest.

0 ⊢ 1 square = 1 foot (0.3 m) ⊣ **1**

242

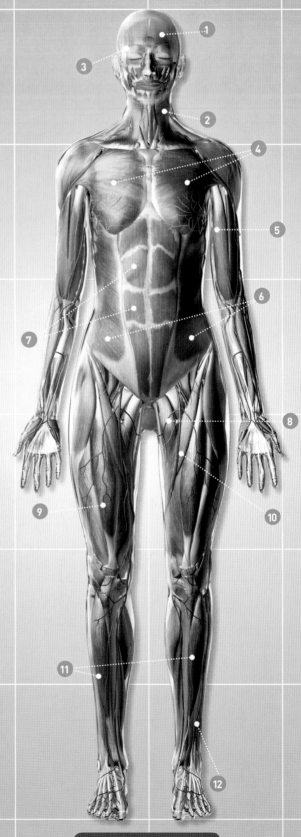

1
3
2
4
5
6
7
8
9
10
11
12

6-FOOT-TALL PERSON

The **skeletal muscles** are forces that contract and extend to help your bones move. You have **muscles** all over your body. Your intestines have muscles. Your heart is a muscle. But the muscles we think of first are the **skeletal muscles.** These are usually attached to bones and tendons. Your muscles contract to make your body bend and stretch and **move around.** There are **650 muscles inside** the body. Here are some of the **biggest ones,** as well as one important **tendon.** (See pages 70–77 for more on muscles and tendons.)

MUSCLES: FRONT OF THE BODY

1. FRONTALIS MUSCLE Wrinkles the forehead
2. STERNOCLEIDOMASTOID MUSCLE Turns the head
3. ORBICULARIS OCULI Blinks the eyelids
4. PECTORAL MUSCLES Pull on the arm and shoulder
5. BICEPS Bend the arm
6. OBLIQUE MUSCLES Twist the body
7. ABDOMINAL MUSCLES Bend the body forward
8. ADDUCTOR LONGUS Pulls the leg inward
9. QUADRICEPS Four muscles that straighten the knee
10. SARTORIUS Bends and twists the leg
11. TIBIALIS MUSCLES Bend the ankle
12. EXTENSOR DIGITORUM LONGUS Bends the toes upward

MUSCLES AND TENDON: BACK OF THE BODY

A. SPLENIUS CAPITIS MUSCLE Tips the head back
B. TRAPEZIUS MUSCLE Pulls head and shoulders back
C. DELTOID MUSCLE Raises the arm
D. LATISSIMUS DORSI MUSCLE Pulls the arm down or back
E. EXTENSOR DIGITORUM MUSCLE Straightens the fingers
F. GLUTEUS MAXIMUS MUSCLE Moves the thigh
G. HAMSTRING MUSCLE Bends the knee
H. CALF MUSCLE Flexes the foot and the ankle and flexes the leg at the knee
I. ACHILLES TENDON Connects the calf to the heel bone

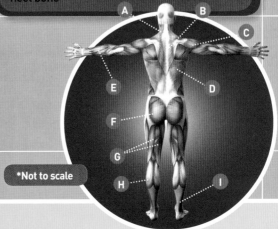

*Not to scale

THE NERVOUS SYSTEM

MAJOR NERVES

1. **BRAIN** Central control
2. **FACIAL NERVES** Control facial expressions
3. **PHRENIC NERVE** Controls the diaphragm
4. **VAGUS NERVE** Helps control the heart rate
5. **SPINAL CORD** A thick bundle of nerves that connects the brain and the body
6. **LUMBAR NERVES** Carry signals to the abdominal and leg muscles
7. **MEDIAN, RADIAL, AND ULNAR NERVES** Carry signals to and from the hands
8. **SCIATIC NERVE** Controls the thigh muscles
9. **TIBIAL NERVE** Controls the calf muscles
10. **PERONEAL NERVE** Controls the muscles that lift the foot upward
11. **PLANTAR NERVES** Carry signals from the bottom of foot

0 — 1 square = 1 foot (0.3 m) — 1

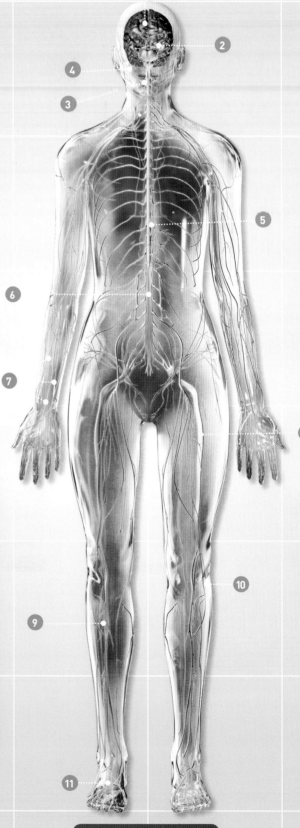

6-FOOT-TALL PERSON

The **nervous system** is a system of "wiring" that directs and controls your body's functions. Your brain and your nerves are your **body's message** and **control system.** The brain is the body's headquarters. The nerves are like roads on which it sends its signals. The **spinal cord** is the main nerve highway. Branching off from it are **31 pairs of nerves,** which run to the torso, arms, and legs. The head is controlled by another **12 pairs of nerves,** which branch out from underneath the brain. (See pages 142–145 for more information about nerves.)

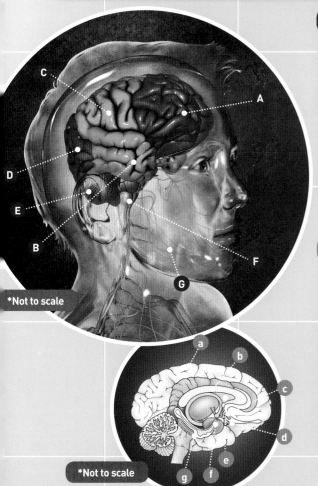

*Not to scale

*Not to scale

OUTSIDE OF THE BRAIN

A **FRONTAL LOBE** Handles decision-making, speech, skilled movements, learning

B **TEMPORAL LOBE** Recognizes sounds, stores some memory

C **PARIETAL LOBE** Receives sensations such as touch or pain

D **OCCIPITAL LOBE** Handles vision

E **CEREBELLUM** Coordinates movement and balance

F **BRAIN STEM** Controls heartbeat, breathing, swallowing

G **NERVES** Control heartbeat, breathing, swallowing

INSIDE OF THE BRAIN

a **CEREBRAL CORTEX** The outside of the brain, which handles thought, sensation, memory

b **CORPUS CALLOSUM** Nerves connecting the two halves of the brain

c **HYPOTHALAMUS** Controls basic body functions such as hunger, handles emotions

d **PITUITARY GLAND** Controls other endocrine glands

e **THALAMUS** Carries signals about touch or pain

f **HIPPOCAMPUS** Helps form memories

g **AMYGDALA** Triggers fear

THE CIRCULATORY SYSTEM

ARTERIES AND VEINS

1. **CAROTID ARTERIES** Carry blood to the head
2. **JUGULAR VEINS** Drain blood from the head
3. **SUPERIOR VENA CAVA** Brings blood from the upper body to the heart
4. **AORTA** Main artery carrying blood away from the heart
5. **HEART** pumps blood
6. **INFERIOR VENA CAVA** Carries blood from the lower body to the heart
7. **ABDOMINAL AORTA** Provides blood to the lower half of the body
8. **RADIAL AND ULNAR ARTERIES** Carry blood to the forearm and the hand
9. **FEMORAL ARTERY** Carries blood to the thigh
10. **FEMORAL VEIN** Carries blood away from the thigh

0 | 1 square = 1 foot (0.3 m) | 1

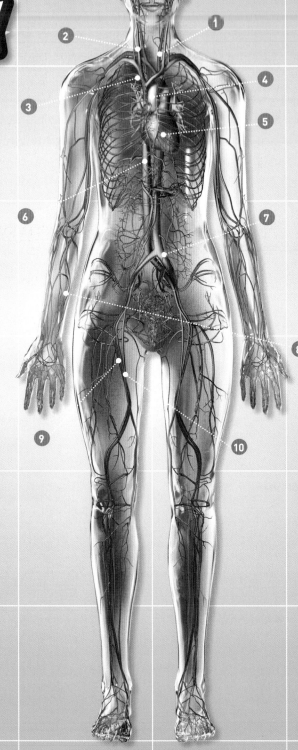

6-FOOT-TALL PERSON

The **circulatory system** is a network that moves blood around the body to supply cells with nutrients, oxygen, and more. Carrying the fuel and oxygen your body needs, your blood swishes through your body with every heartbeat. **Arteries** carry blood away from the heart. **Veins** carry it back. Tiny blood vessels called capillaries (not shown here) connect the arteries and veins.

The central pump, **the heart,** has four main chambers. **Valves** keep the blood flowing in the right direction through the chambers. The blood leaves the heart through the **aorta** or **pulmonary artery.** (See pages 108–121 for more about the circulatory system.)

THE HEART

A **SUPERIOR VENA CAVA** Brings blood from the upper body to the heart

B **AORTA** Carries blood to the body

C **PULMONARY ARTERY** Carries oxygen-poor blood to the lungs

D **PULMONARY VEINS** Carry oxygen-rich blood from the lungs

E **BICUSPID (MITRAL) VALVE** Stops blood from flowing backward up into the left atrium

F **PULMONARY VALVE** Stops blood from flowing backward up into the right ventricle

G **LEFT VENTRICLE** Receives blood from the left atrium

H **RIGHT VENTRICLE** Receives blood from the right atrium

I **TRICUSPID VALVE** Stops blood from flowing backward up into the right atrium

J **RIGHT ATRIUM** Receives blood from the vena cava

K **LEFT ATRIUM** Receives blood from the pulmonary vein

L **AORTIC VALVE** Stops blood from flowing backward up into the left ventricle

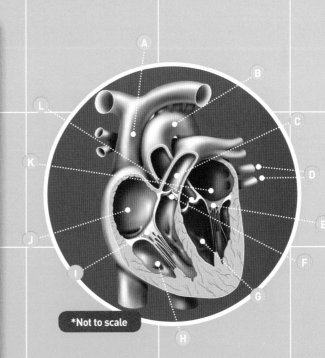

*Not to scale

THE RESPIRATORY SYSTEM

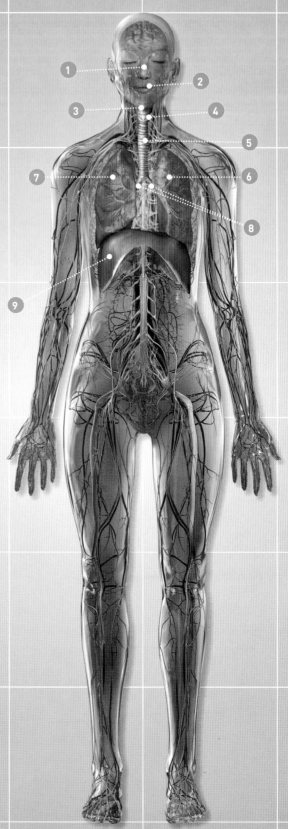

AIRWAYS

1 **NOSE** Pulls in air, traps dust

2 **MOUTH** Pulls in air

3 **THROAT** (Pharynx) Connects the nose and the mouth to the trachea

4 **VOICE BOX** (Larynx) Makes sounds when air passes through

5 **WINDPIPE** (Trachea) Carries air to the lungs

6 **LEFT LUNG** Has two lobes

7 **RIGHT LUNG** Has three lobes

8 **BRONCHI** Bring air from the trachea to the left lung

9 **DIAPHRAGM** Moves up and down to help pull air into the lungs

0 ⟷ 1   1 square = 1 foot (0.3 m)

6-FOOT-TALL PERSON

The **respiratory system** brings oxygen into the body and rids it of carbon dioxide. "Respiration" means breathing. It also means the process of **getting oxygen in** and **out of your bloodstream.** Your respiratory system keeps air flowing, in and out of your lungs. And it moves oxygen from your lungs into your blood vessels, to be carried throughout your body.

Your head holds your **upper** respiratory system—your nose, mouth, and throat. Your chest holds the **lower** respiratory system—your lungs and the diaphragm. (See pages 122–129 for more about the respiratory system.)

LUNGS

A WINDPIPE (Trachea) Carries air to the lungs

B LEFT PRIMARY BRONCHUS Brings air from the trachea to the left lung

C RIGHT PRIMARY BRONCHUS Brings air from the trachea to the right lung

D LEFT SECONDARY BRONCHUS Brings air from the primary bronchus to one lobe of the lung

E LEFT TERTIARY BRONCHUS Branches out from the secondary bronchus

F LEFT BRONCHIOLES Small airways that branch out from each tertiary bronchus

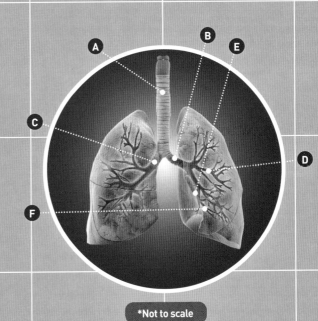

*Not to scale

THE FEMALE REPRODUCTIVE SYSTEM

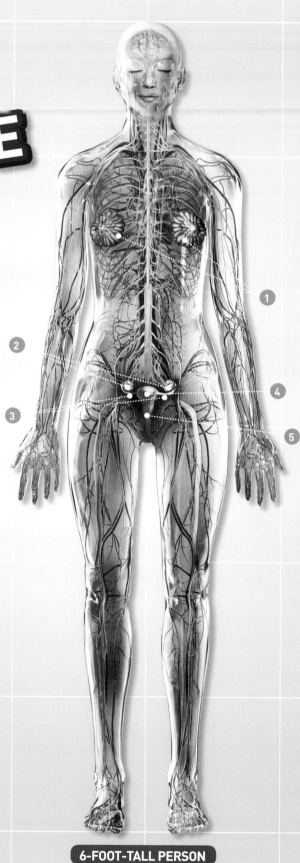

1

2

3

4

5

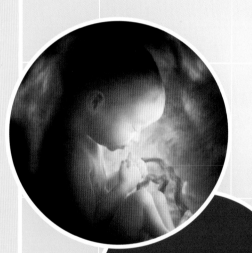

Babies **yawn** even before they are born, in their **mother's womb.**

0   1 square = 1 foot (0.3 m)   1'

6-FOOT-TALL PERSON

The **reproductive system** is made up of external and internal organs that produce **sex cells** and allow for the creation of new human beings. After undergoing the changes of **puberty,** male and female bodies are able to make babies together. Men and women have different organs for this. Men's bodies make male sex cells, called **sperm,** which swim around like little tadpoles. Women's bodies make female sex cells, called **ova or eggs.** Women also have a **uterus,** or womb, that will hold a growing fetus before it's born. (See pages 180–185 for more about reproduction.)

FEMALE REPRODUCTIVE SYSTEM

1 MAMMARY GLANDS Produce milk

2 OVARIES Hold female sex cells (eggs)

3 FALLOPIAN TUBES Carry eggs from the ovaries to the uterus

4 UTERUS (womb) Holds the growing fetus when a woman is pregnant

5 VAGINA Tube leading out of the uterus

AN EGG'S JOURNEY

Every month in a woman's body, an egg leaves one ovary and travels to the uterus. If a man's sperm swims up to the woman's egg at just the right time to fertilize it, the egg starts growing into a human body. The dividing cells travel on to find a home in the uterus, where the fetus will grow.

IMPLANTATION The growing ball of cells settles in the uterus

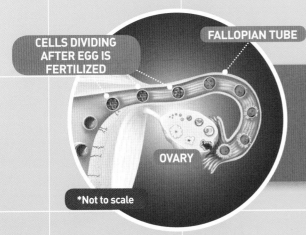

CELLS DIVIDING AFTER EGG IS FERTILIZED

FALLOPIAN TUBE

OVARY

*Not to scale

A cutaway view of the ovulation cycle showing an egg making its way from the ovary into the fallopian tube where it has been fertilized. Cells inside the fertilized egg are dividing. The egg will then turn into an embryo.

THE MALE REPRODUCTIVE SYSTEM

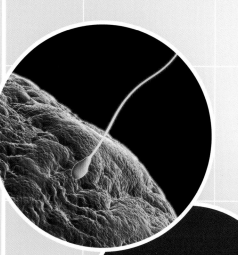

Sperm cells are the smallest in the body. They measure only .002 inches (.005 cm).

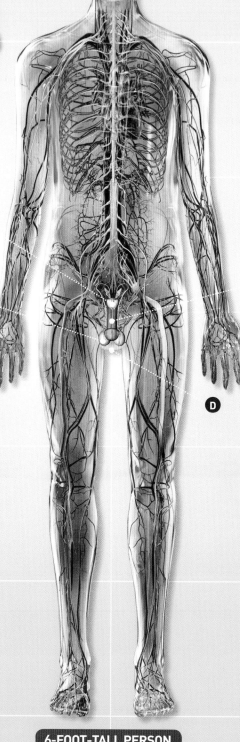

A

B

C

D

0   1 square = 1 foot (0.3 m)   1'

6-FOOT-TALL PERSON

The organs of the **male** reproductive system are found both inside and outside the body. The **penis, scrotum,** and **testes** are located on the exterior, while the accessory glands (including the **prostate**) are on the interior. Male sex cells, called **sperm,** are produced and stored in the testes and transported to the penis, which releases them. If a released sperm meets a woman's egg and fertilizes it, this **fertilized egg** can settle into the lining of the uterus and begin to grow into a baby. (See pages 180–185 for more about reproduction.)

MALE REPRODUCTIVE SYSTEM

A PROSTATE GLAND releases fluid that protect sperm

B PENIS Carries sperm

C TESTES Make sperm (male sex cells)

D SCROTUM Sac that holds the two testes

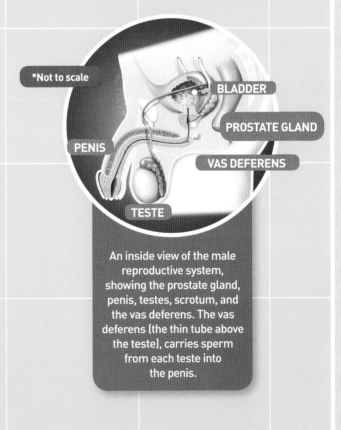

*Not to scale

BLADDER

PROSTATE GLAND

PENIS

VAS DEFERENS

TESTE

An inside view of the male reproductive system, showing the prostate gland, penis, testes, scrotum, and the vas deferens. The vas deferens (the thin tube above the teste), carries sperm from each teste into the penis.

253

THE DIGESTIVE SYSTEM

Americans eat about 100,000 pounds (45,400 kg) of food in a lifetime.

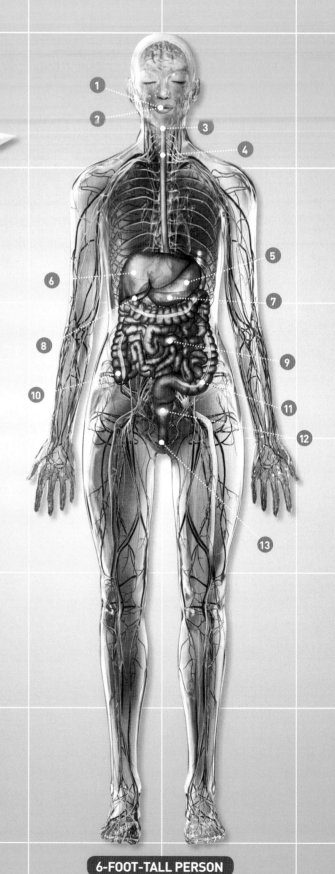

0   1 square = 1 foot (0.3 m)   1

6-FOOT-TALL PERSON

The **digestive system** breaks down food and converts it into energy and essential nutrients. If you could stretch it out, the adult digestive tract would be one **30-foot (9.1-m)-long tube.** Food enters the top of the tube at your mouth. As it passes through the digestive system, it is chewed, squished, and dissolved. Organs such as the **pancreas** add digestive chemicals. The parts of food your body can't use leave your body at the other end of the tube, at your **anus.** As food is pushed through your system, your body pulls out the nutrients that it needs to power its way through daily life. (See chapter 4 for more about the digestive system.)

DIGESTION, TOP TO BOTTOM

1. **TEETH** Chew up food
2. **TONGUE** Tastes and moves food around
3. **PHARYNX** (throat) Carries food from the mouth to the esophagus
4. **ESOPHAGUS** Pushes food toward the stomach
5. **STOMACH** Holds, sanitizes, and breaks down food
6. **LIVER** Handles and stores nutrients from food
7. **PANCREAS** Makes chemicals that help digest food
8. **GALLBLADDER** Holds bile, which helps to digest fat
9. **SMALL INTESTINE** Absorbs nutrients from digested food
10. **LARGE INTESTINE** Absorbs water and nutrients
11. **COLON** Part of the large intestine; pulls water and minerals back into the body
12. **RECTUM** Part of the large intestine; makes leftover food into feces
13. **ANUS** Last part of the large intestine; opens to get rid of feces

THE STOMACH

A. **LONGITUDINAL MUSCLE** Runs the length of the stomach

B. **CIRCULAR MUSCLE** Runs horizontally around the stomach

C. **OBLIQUE MUSCLE** Runs diagonally around the stomach

D. **STOMACH WALL** Holds glands that make digestive juices

E. **PYLORIC SPHINCTER** Opens and closes to allow food slowly into the small intestine

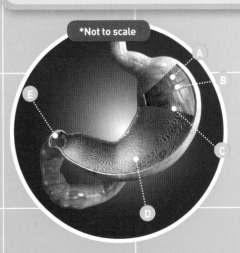

*Not to scale

THE URINARY SYSTEM

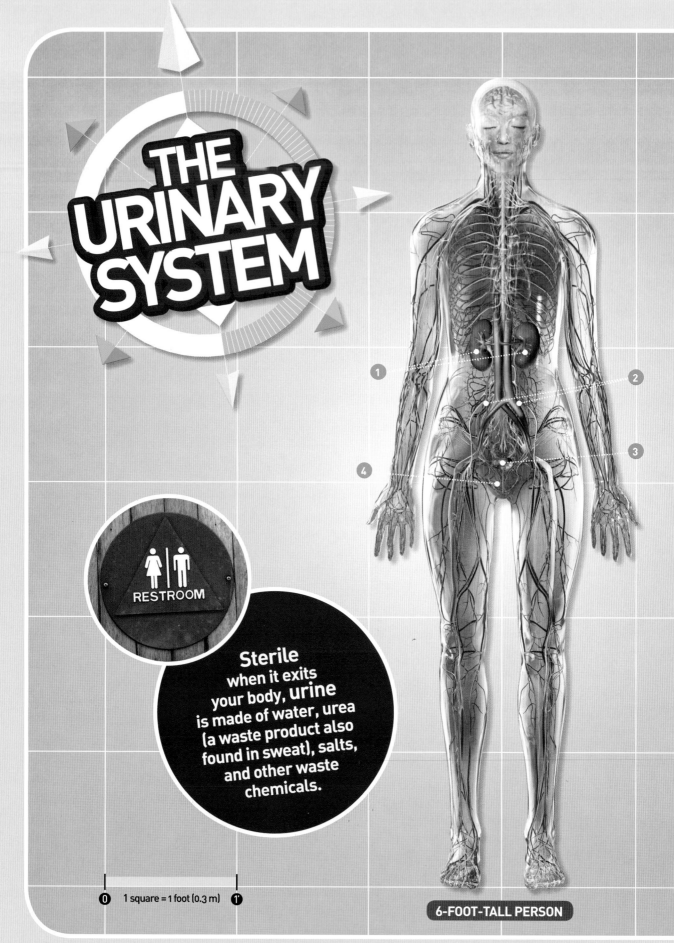

1

2

3

4

Sterile when it exits your body, **urine** is made of water, urea (a waste product also found in sweat), salts, and other waste chemicals.

RESTROOM

1 square = 1 foot (0.3 m)

0
1'

6-FOOT-TALL PERSON

The **urinary system** produces, stores, and eliminates urine from the body. This is the body's cleaning team. Lots of blood flows through the two kidneys every day. Out of the blood, the **kidneys** filter waste, extra water, and salt. The **bladder** stores this watery fluid as **urine.** Many times a day, it flushes the fluid out of the body through the **urethra.** This regular cycle keeps the body in **balance.** (See pages 130–131 for more about the urinary system.)

CLEANING THE BLOOD

1 **KIDNEYS** Filter waste from the blood and make urine

2 **URETERS** Carry urine from the kidney to the bladder

3 **BLADDER** Holds urine

4 **URETHRA** Carries urine from the bladder and out of the body

THE KIDNEY

A **RENAL CAPSULE** Outer protective layer

B **CORTEX** Filters fluid out of the blood

C **MEDULLA** Absorbs needed nutrients back into the blood

D **RENAL PELVIS** Sends urine into the ureter

E **RENAL VEIN** Takes blood away from the kidney

F **RENAL ARTERY** Carries blood to the kidney

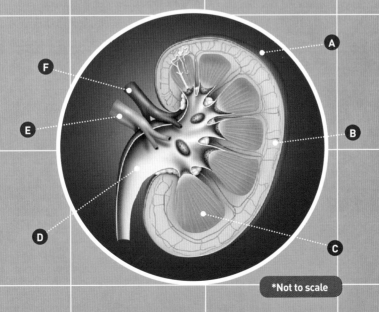

*Not to scale

THE ENDOCRINE SYSTEM

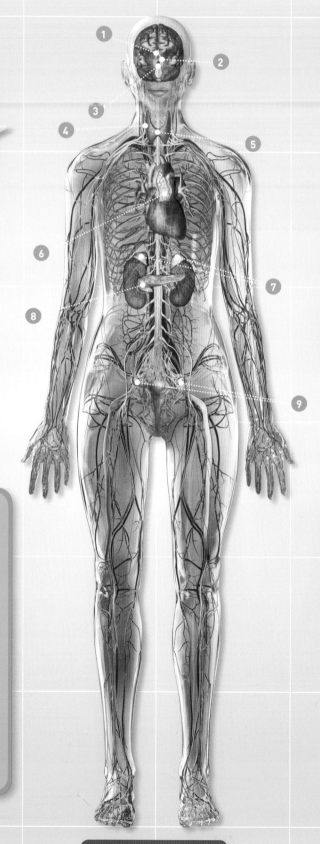

6-FOOT-TALL PERSON

ENDOCRINE GLANDS

1. **PINEAL GLAND** Controls body rhythms

2. **HYPOTHALAMUS** Connects the nervous system and the endocrine system

3. **PITUITARY GLAND** Controls growth and commands other glands

4. **PARATHYROID GLANDS** Control calcium in the blood; another pair of these are located on the back of the thyroid gland

5. **THYROID GLAND** Controls metabolism—how your cells burn fuel

6. **THYMUS GLAND** Helps direct the immune system in younger people

7. **ADRENAL GLANDS** Make adrenaline (epinephrine), which prepares the body for action

8. **PANCREAS** Controls the level of sugar in the blood

9. **OVARIES** (found only in women) Help control reproduction

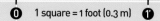

0   1 square = 1 foot (0.3 m)   1

258

The **endocrine system** releases hormones regulating many functions including **sleep, metabolism, growth,** and **mood.** Along with your nervous system, the endocrine system controls your body. It doesn't send electrical signals, like nerves. Instead, small glands and special cells all over your body release hormones into your bloodstream. These **chemicals** deliver messages. They tell the body to grow and stop growing. They control how much sugar is in your blood. They get the female body ready to have a baby.

The most important endocrine gland might be the **pituitary.** Small but powerful, it sends out ten major hormones that control the body's growth, repair, reproduction, water balance, and more. (See pages 146–147 for more about the endocrine system.)

PITUITARY, THE MASTER GLAND

A **HYPOTHALAMUS** Region of the brain that keeps track of body functions such as hunger and sleep; controls some glands

B **PITUITARY STALK** Connects the pituitary to the hypothalamus

C **ANTERIOR LOBE** Lobe in front, which contains gland tissue

D **BLOOD VESSELS** Carry hormones to the rest of body

E **POSTERIOR LOBE** Lobe in back, which contains nerve tissue

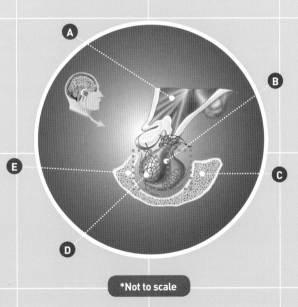

*Not to scale

THE LYMPHATIC SYSTEM

VESSELS, ORGANS, AND NODES

1. **TONSILS** Trap germs

2. **LEFT LYMPHATIC DUCT** Moves lymph from most of the body into the bloodstream

3. **RIGHT LYMPHATIC DUCT** Moves lymph from the upper right side of the body into the bloodstream

4. **THYMUS GLAND** Handles white blood cells

5. **SPLEEN** Filters and recycles blood

6. **LYMPH NODE** One of many nodes that filter out germs

7. **LYMPH VESSELS** Carry lymph throughout the body

0 1 square = 1 foot (0.3 m) **1**

6-FOOT-TALL PERSON

The **lymphatic system** collects, filters, and transports fluid (lymph) from tissues to the bloodstream. Your body doesn't just have blood vessels. It also has **lymph vessels.** These are spread throughout your body and are connected to your blood vessels. Lymph vessels carry lymph—a clear fluid that seeps out of your blood. Lymph holds **white blood cells** that fight infections. It also picks up germs.

Lymph fluid gets pushed through lymph vessels when your muscles contract. As lymph flows around the body, it passes through little bean-shaped glands called **lymph nodes.** These filter out germs. Sometimes, when you're sick, these glands swell up. The lymphatic system is also connected to a few larger organs, such as the **spleen,** which help clean up the blood and store white blood cells. (See page 115 for more about the lymphatic system.)

LYMPH NODE

A CAPSULE Tough covering for the node

B LYMPH VESSEL Carries lymph in and out of the node

C CORTEX Outer part of the node

D MEDULLA Inner part of the node

E FOLLICLES Help support the node and store white blood cells

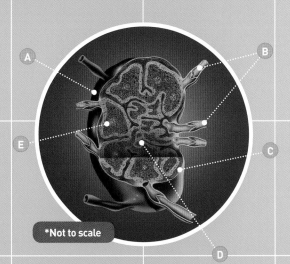

*Not to scale

GLOSSARY

ALVEOLI thin-walled sacs in the lungs where oxygen molecules enter and carbon dioxide molecules leave the blood

ANTIBODY a substance, made by cells in blood plasma, that defends the body against specific invaders

ANTIGEN a substance your immune system sees as "foreign" and produces antibodies against, such as a bacteria or a virus

ARTERY a blood vessel that carries blood away from the heart

BACTERIA microscopic one-celled organisms

BILE a yellow-green liquid made by the liver that helps the body digest fats. It is stored in the gallbladder, which sits below the liver. It flows into the small intestine during digestion.

BRAIN STEM connects the brain to the spinal cord; controls basic body functions such as breathing and heart rate

CANCER a disease in which cells that are not normal multiply very quickly and invade organs and other parts of the body

CAPILLARY a very fine blood vessel that links an artery and a vein. The blood picks up waste and drops off oxygen and nutrients in capillaries.

CARDIAC MUSCLE muscle found only in the heart that contracts automatically, causing the heart to pump blood

CARTILAGE a strong, flexible, fiber-filled tissue. It is found in joints and also forms the outer ears and the nose.

CELL the basic unit of a living thing. Cells divide to make new cells, which in turn build new tissues, repair injuries, and cause growth.

CEREBELLUM the part of the brain primarily responsible for movement and balance

CEREBRAL CORTEX the outer layer of the brain, responsible for language, planning, and perception

CEREBRUM the biggest part of the brain, it's divided into two halves (or hemispheres); controls voluntary actions, stores memories, and helps reason thoughts

CHROMOSOME a threadlike structure made up of DNA and proteins; located in the nucleus of the cell

CILIA tiny hairlike structures attached to cells

COLLAGEN a fiber-rich, strong, flexible protein found in bones, cartilage, tendons, and other tissues that connect body parts

CONCEPTION the act of making a new life

CONCUSSION an injury that occurs when the brain bounces off the inside of the skull; like a brain bruise

CONSCIOUS aware or alert. Conscious movements are ones that you know you are controlling.

CORNEA the clear covering of the eyeball

CORPUS COLLOSUM a thick band of millions of nerve fibers that divides your brain into two hemispheres and allows them to communicate with each other

CORTEX the outer layer of the brain, where most conscious thought happens

DERMIS the second-deepest layer of the skin. It lies under the epidermis and above the subcutaneous tissue.

DIENCEPHALON located between the two hemispheres of the brain and comprising the thalamus (relays and processes sensory information), the hypothalamus (controls the automatic nervous system), and the epithalamus (includes the pineal gland; helps regulate sleep and wakefulness)

DNA a substance found in the center of cells that contains genes, the basic units of inheritance. The initials DNA stand for deoxyribonucleic acid.

EGG female reproductive cell containing 23 chromosomes

EMBRYO what a baby growing in a uterus is called up until the end of eight weeks

ENZYME a substance produced by the body that helps make different processes take place. Enzymes produced by the small intestine, for example, digest food.

EPIDERMIS the outermost layer of the skin

ESOPHAGUS the tube that runs from the mouth to the stomach

FERTILIZATION the moment when a male reproductive cell (sperm) joins with a female reproductive cell (egg), creating a new cell that will develop into a baby

FETUS what a baby growing in a uterus is called after it is about eight weeks old

"FLIGHT OR FIGHT" an automatic response of the body—such as changes in heart rate, blood pressure, and muscle tension—that prepares a person to either fight or run for his or her life when faced with danger

FOLLICLE a tiny pocket in the skin from which a hair grows

FRONTAL LOBE part of the cerebrum that controls problem-solving, decision-making, reasoning, and emotions

GASTRIC something relating to the stomach, such as the "gastric juices" that help break down food

GENE a piece of DNA that tells cells how to make proteins. Those proteins control or influence the traits you inherit from your parents.

GERM a tiny living thing, too small to see, that can cause disease

GLAND a body part that makes substances used in the body or excreted from it. Glands in the stomach, for example, make substances that break down food. Sweat glands in the skin produce sweat, which flows out of the skin.

HEMOGLOBIN a substance in blood that carries oxygen and gives the blood its red color

HIPPOCAMPUS a part of the brain involved in forming and storing memories

HORMONE a chemical messenger that flows through the bloodstream and has an effect on cells or organs

IMMUNE being very resistant to a disease

INFECTIOUS able to pass a germ or disease to another person

INHERIT to receive a genetic trait. For example, a blue-eyed person might have inherited blue eye color from a parent.

JOINT the flexible meeting points of bones, which allow the skeleton to bend and move. Your hips, ankles, knees, and elbows are examples of joints.

KERATIN a tough protein that forms hair and nails and the dead cells forming the outermost layer of the skin

LIGAMENT a band of tissue that connects one bone to another bone or holds an organ in place

LYMPH a watery fluid that carries infection-fighting white blood cells throughout the body

MARROW the jellylike substance inside bones that makes red blood cells for the body

MEDULLA OBLONGATA the section of the brain stem that controls some of the body's most important functions, such as breathing and heart rate. It also contains the body's motor and sensory nerves and is where nerves from the left and right sides of the body cross each other on their journey toward the cerebrum.

MELANIN a pigment made by the body that gives skin and hair their color. Melanin comes in two forms: brown-black and red-yellow.

MELANOCYTE skin cells that produce melanin

MEMBRANE a thin layer, such as the outer border of a cell

MICROORGANISM an organism (living thing) that is so small it is invisible to the naked eye and can only be seen with a microscope

MOLECULE the smallest part of a substance that has all the features of that substance

MOTOR something that causes motion. Motor neurons are cells that start muscles moving.

MUCUS a slimy, thick fluid made by the nose, the esophagus, and other parts of the body. Mucus forms a protective lining that coats the stomach's wall. In the nose, it helps capture substances such as dust.

NERVES thin, threadlike bundles of neurons that carry messages between your brain and the rest of your body, in both directions

NEUROLOGIST a doctor who specializes in the human brain

NEURON a "nerve cell" that carries signals between different parts of the body

NUCLEUS a key part of almost all living cells which holds the genes that control a cell's activities

NUTRIENT a substance in food that provides nutrition. Fats, proteins, and carbohydrates are examples of nutrients.

OCCIPITAL LOBE part of the cerebrum that processes the information coming in from your eyes

ORGAN a group of tissues that perform a job in the body. The skin, for example, is an organ that covers the body, protecting it and helping to maintain its temperature. The heart is an organ that pumps blood.

OVARIES the pair of almond-size female reproductive organs that produce a woman's eggs

OXYGEN an odorless gas that the body needs to sustain life. Oxygen forms a part of the air breathed in by the lungs. It is then picked up by the blood and distributed to the body's cells.

PARIETAL LOBE part of the cerebrum that processes sensory information

PATHOGEN something that causes illness or disease in its host

PINEAL GLAND located in the middle of the brain, it sends out chemicals that aid in sleeping and staying awake. In some religions, the pineal gland is thought to be the "third" or "all-seeing" eye.

PITUITARY GLAND located under the brain, it is often called the "master gland" because it's in charge of many functions, including the growth of bones and tissues. It also sends out chemicals that can reduce pain and increase feelings of happiness.

PUBERTY period of a few years in adolescence when a boy's or a girl's body grows considerably in height and weight and begins to look more like an adult's. It's also when the reproductive system begins changing to allow boys and girls to become parents when they are adults.

RADIATION energy that moves in waves or particles

RECEPTOR a special cell or part of a cell that reacts to outside sensations

RED BLOOD CELL blood cells that transport oxygen to the body's cells

REPRODUCTION the process by which parents create babies; when a male reproductive cell (sperm) fertilizes a female reproductive cell (egg), creating a new cell that develops into a baby

SALIVA a fluid produced in the mouth that softens food and makes it easier to swallow. It also contains enzymes that start digesting the food.

SKELETAL MUSCLE a muscle that makes a body part, such as the tongue, an eye, or an arm, move

SKELETON the bones that form the body's framework

SMOOTH MUSCLE a muscle found in body parts such as blood vessels, the stomach, and the intestines. Smooth muscles work automatically, for example, to push food through the digestive system.

SPERM male reproductive cell containing 23 chromosomes

SUBCUTANEOUS TISSUE the third-deepest layer of the skin. It lies beneath the dermis.

SYSTEM a collection of linked body parts that work together to carry out a function, such as digestion or reproduction

TASTE BUD taste receptors (of sweet, sour, salty, bitter, and umami), mostly on the tongue, with some at the back of the throat and on the palate

TEMPORAL LOBE the part of the cerebrum that handles hearing, language, memory, emotions, and learning

TENDON a tough cord that links a muscle to a bone

TISSUE a material formed by cells of the same type. Muscle tissue, for example, is made up of muscle cells.

TRAIT an inherited characteristic that sets one person apart from another. Curly hair is an inherited trait.

URINE a waste product made up of water, salt, and other substances filtered from the blood by the kidneys. Urine is stored in the bladder before being released from the body.

UTERUS muscular organ in the female reproductive system where a fertilized egg implants and is nourished and protected as a developing embryo and fetus

VACCINE a substance that can be given a person to protect against a particular disease

VEIN a blood vessel that carries blood back to the heart

VERTEBRA a bone that forms part of the backbone

VIRUS a very tiny microbe that can cause an infectious disease

WHITE BLOOD CELL a blood cell that fights disease by destroying bacteria, viruses, or other disease organisms

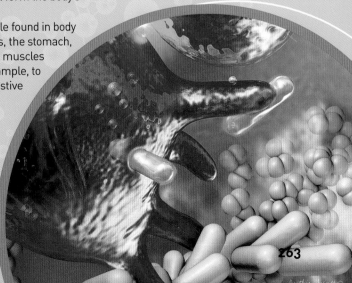

263

FIND OUT MORE

Great Websites, Movies, and Places to Visit

Want to find out even more about how the body works? Check out these sites, movies, and places to visit.

Websites

Find tons of information about the human body and human health at National Geographic's "Explore the Human Body" website: science.nationalgeographic.com/science/health-and-human-body/human-body.

Learn about the human body systems while enjoying activities, puzzles, and more at the Discovery Kids' website: kids.discovery.com/tell-me/science/body-systems.

Explore the human body including your brain and senses at the Children's University of Manchester's science website: childrensuniversity.manchester.ac.uk/interactives/science.

Get interactive with the human anatomy, system by system, at the website "Inner Body": innerbody.com.

Discover more about the human body, health, and safety when you visit the Centers for Disease Control's "BAM! Body and Mind" website: cdc.gov/bam.

Play games, take quizzes, watch short movies, and read lots about how the human body works at the KidsHealth website: kidshealth.org/kid/htbw.

Learn about the Google Science Fair and how you can change the world at googlesciencefair.com/en.

Take an amazing 3-D tour of the human brain at PBS's "The Secret Life of the Brain": pbs.org/wnet/brain/3d.

Investigate more about your incredible brain at "Neuroscience for Kids": faculty.washington.edu/chudler/neurok.html.

Films

Inside the Human Body [2004]: This collection of NOVA films about the human body explores genetics, the development of a baby, and the world inside you.

Inside the Living Body [2007]: This National Geographic film uses high-tech devices to show what goes on inside a person's body.

Inside the Human Body [2011]: This multipart BBC series explores the inner and outer workings of the human body.

Places to Visit

U.S.A.:

The Amazing You, Museum of Science and Industry, Tampa, Florida

Being Human Hall, Perot Museum, Dallas, Texas

The Body Human, Science Museum of Virginia, Richmond, Virginia

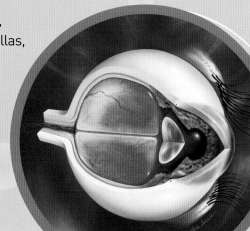

Explore You, Buffalo Museum of Science, Buffalo, New York

The Giant Heart exhibit, Franklin Institute, Philadelphia, Pennsylvania

Hall of Human Life, Museum of Science, Boston, Massachusetts

The Health Museum, Texas Medical Center, Houston, Texas

Human Adventure, St. Louis Science Center, St. Louis, Missouri

Human Phenomena, Exploratorium, San Francisco, California

The Lab, Museum of Life and Science, Durham, North Carolina

Professor Wellbody's Academy of Health & Wellness, Pacific Science Center, Seattle, Washington

World of Life, California Science Center, Los Angeles, California

You! The Experience, Museum of Science and Industry, Chicago, Illinois

Your Body: The Inside Story, Maryland Science Center, Baltimore, Maryland

Canada

The AstraZeneca Human Edge, Ontario Science Centre, Toronto, Ontario

Bodyworks, Science World at Telus World of Science, Vancouver, British Columbia, Canada

South/Central America

Museum of Science and Technology, Porto Alegra, Brazil

Universum, el Museo de las Ciencias de la Universidad Nacional Autónoma de México, Mexico City, Mexico

Europe

Corpus Museum, Oegstgeest, the Netherlands

German Hygiene Museum, Dresden, Germany

Human Biology Gallery, Natural History Museum, London, England

Man and His Genes, Citi des Sciences et de l'Industrie, Paris, France

National Museum of Science, Technology, and Medicine, Oslo, Norway

Pharmaceutics exhibit, Deutsches Museum, Munich, Germany

Who Am I? exhibit and The Science and Art of Medicine, Science Museum, London, England

Asia

Health Education Exhibition & Resource Centre, Kowloon, Hong Kong, China

Human and Health exhibit, Shanghai Science and Technology Museum, Shanghai, China

Human Body exhibit, Nagoya City Science Museum, Nagoya, Japan

Australia

The Human Body, Melbourne Museum, Victoria, Melbourne, Australia

Sportsworks, Scienceworks, Victoria, Melbourne, Australia

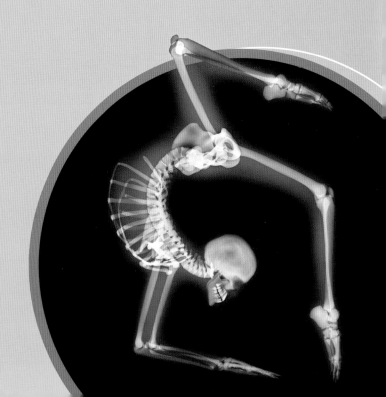

INDEX

Boldface indicates illustrations.

PHOTO AND ILLUSTRATION CREDITS

Cover: (heart), AnnaSumska/iS; (DNA), doomu/SS; (girl), FoodPix/Jupiterimages/GI; (eyeball), Markus Gann/SS; (boy), Juanmonino/iS/GI; (x-ray glasses), Wendy Idele/Hulton Archive Creative/GI; (x-ray), Anja Weber-Decker/plainpicture; (foot skeleton), Allison Achauer/SS; (brain), Sebastian Kaulitzki/SS; (blue cells), Henrik5000/iS; (molecules background), djem/SS; (green texture), majcot/123RF.com; **back cover,** (background), Henrik5000/iStockphoto; (UP), Nerthuz/Shutterstock; (LO), Roger Harris/Science Source; front flap (UP), Markus Gann/Shutterstock; (CTR), doomu/Shutterstock; (LO), Allison Achauer/Shutterstock; **spine,** (UP), Henrik5000/iStockphoto; (LO), Sebastian Kaulitzki/Shutterstock; back flap (UP), courtesy Christina Wilsdon; (CTR), courtesy Patricia Daniels, (LO), courtesy Jen Agresta, (bottom), courtesy Cynthia Turner. **UK edition:** Cover: (background), CLIPAREA l Custom media/SS; (blood cells), Bart Sadowski/iS; (germs), Cynthia Turner; (heart) SS; **front matter:** 1 (UP), Nerthuz/SS; (CTR), Allison Achauer/SS; (LO), AnnaSumska/iS; (Background), djem/SS; 2-3, Henrik5000/iS; 3 (UP), Markus Gann/SS; (LO), Sebastian Kaulitzki/SS; 4 (UP), Paul Kennedy/Lonely Planet Images/GI; (LO), Roger Harris/SCS; 4-5, David Marchal/SCS; 5 (Background), Scott Camazine/SCS; (LO), Cynthia Turner; 6 (UPRT), doomu/SS; (UPLE), courtesy Christina Wilsdon; (CTR), Du Cane Medical Imaging Ltd./SCS; (LO), AnnaSumska/iS; 7 (LO), Markus Gann/SS; (UPLE), Eraxion/iS; (UPRT), Allison Achauer/SS; (UP CTR), courtesy Tammatha O'Brien; (LOCTR), Maya2008/SS; 8 (UPLE), janulla/iS; (UPRT), Mehau Kulyk/SCS; (boy), iS/GI; (glasses), Wendy Idele/Hulton Archive Creative/GI; (x-ray), Anja Weber-Decker/plainpicture; (LORT), Cynthia Turner; 9 (UPLE), Zeljko Santrac/E+/GI; (UPRT), Nerthuz/SS; (LO), Claus Lunau/SCS; **Chapter 1:** 10-11, David Young-Wolff/Alamy; 12, Jak Wonderly; 13 (INSET left), Patrick Rolands/SS; 13, Michael Krasowitz/The Image Bank/GI; (INSET right), R. Gino Santa Maria/SS; 14, Adrian Sherratt/Alamy; 15, Morris MacMatzen/Reuters; 16, Katsumi Kasahara/AP Images; 17, itsmejust/SS; 17 (INSET), Daily Mail/Rex/Alamy; 18, Carol and Mike Werner/SCS; (INSET), Dasha Petrenko/SS; 19, Oleg Mikhaylov/SS; 20, powerofforever/iS; 21, Peshkova/SS; (INSET), Martin Harvey/Photolibrary RM/GI; 22, Brand X/GI; (INSET), Africa Studio/SS; 23, SSPL/Science Museum/GI; 24, Nathan Devery/SCS; 25, Cynthia Turner. **Chapter 2:** 26-27, Sean Justice/Photonica/GI; 28, DRB Images, LLC/iS; 29, Aldo Murillo/E+/GI; 29 (INSET), evemilla/iS; 30, Cynthia Turner; (INSET), shutterup/SS; 31, Africa Studio/SS; 32, Barry Willis/Photographer's Choice/GI; 33, Michael Krinke/E+/GI; 33 (INSET), Biophoto Associates/SCS; (INSET up), Nyvlt-art/iS; 34, RonGreer.Com/SS; (INSET), Michel Gilles/SCS; 35, INTERFOTO/Alamy; 36, NinaMalyna/SS; 37, Rido/SS; 37, Biophoto Associates/SCS; 38, Paul Kennedy/Lonely Planet Images/GI; (INSET), Gubin Yury/SS; (INSET A), Yu Lan/SS; (INSET B), jcarillet/iS; (INSET C), Suzanne Tucker/SS; 39 (LO), val lawless/SS; (UP), Roman Sigaev/SS; 40, Jason Stitt/SS; 41, Garry DeLong/SCS; (INSET lo), Bele Olmez/Imagebroker RF/GI; (INSET up), BSIP/SCS; 42, Image Source/GI; (INSET), Archive Photos/GI; 43, Winnie Au/fStop/GI; 44, Chen kang/AP Images; 45, Elizabeth Livermore/Flickr Open/GI; (INSET), Biophoto Associates/SCS; 46, BSIP SA/Alamy; 46 (INSET), Robert Harding Picture Library Ltd/Alamy; 47, 3445128471/SS; 48, Andrew Syred/SCS; 49, Eye of Science/SCS; (INSET), Cheryl Power/SCS; **Chapter 3:** 50-51, Andres Rodriguez/Alamy; 52, Digital Vision/Photodisc/GI; 53, Gelpi JM/SS; 54, Gunilla Elam/SCS; 55, Cynthia Turner; (INSET), DNY59/E+//GI; 56, Anatomical Travelogue/SCS; (INSET), Carl Roessler/Digital Vision; 57, Lindsay France/Cornell/Corbis; 58, simplytheyu/iS; 59, Du Cane Medical Imaging Ltd./SCS; (INSET), Winston Link/SS; 60, Radius Images/Alamy; 60 (INSET), Laguna Design/SCS; 61, oksana2010/SS; 62, Christian Aslund/Photographer's Choice/GI; 63, Gusto Productions/SCS; (INSET), Image Source/GI; 64, spepple22/iS; 64 (INSET), Marco Prati/SS; 65, SoRad/SS; 66, Ted Kinsman/SCS; 67, Alfred Pasieka/SCS; (INSET), Classic Image/Alamy; 68, Anatomical Travelogue/SCS; (INSET), Eric Isselee/SS; 69 (INSET), Springer Medizin/SCS; 70, Shaber/SS; 71, Roger Harris/SCS; (INSET), rubberball/GI; 72, David Deas/DK Stock/GI; (INSET), Pavel Hlystov/SS; 73, wrangel/iS; 74, Mary Evans Picture Library/Alamy; 75, Roger Harris/SCS; (INSET), 3D4Medical/SCS; 76, Jonathan Larsen/Diadem Images/Alamy; 77, MyLoupe/UIG Via GI; **Chapter 4:** 78-79, Kondoros Eva Katalin/E+/GI; 80, XiXinXing/GI; 81, Evgeny Tomeev/SS; (INSET), locke_rd/iS; 82, PhotoAlto/Laurence Mouton/GI; (INSET), Stefano Paterna/Alamy; 83, oksana2010/SS; 84, Dianne McFadden/SS; 85, Anatomical Travelogue/SCS; (INSET), Steve Cukrov/SS; 86, George Doyle/Stockbyte//GI; 87 (LE), Gwen Shockey/SCS; (CTR), Gwen Shockey/SCS; (RT), Gwen Shockey/SCS; 88, Ken Cavanagh/SCS; 89, Cynthia Turner; 90, Alfred Pasieka/SCS; (INSET), Eric Isselee/SS; 91, Bettmann/Corbis; 92, Aaron Haupt/Photo Researchers RM/GI; 93, Springer Medizin/SCS; 94, Springer Medizin/SCS; (INSET), galdzer/iS; 95, Mary Evans Picture Library/Alamy; 96, portishead1/iS; 97, 3D4Medical/SCS; 98, DNA Illustrations/SCS; (INSET), Andrey Nosik/SS; 99, SPL/SCS; 100, Eric Isselee/SS; 101, Scimat/SCS; (INSET), Milkovasa/SS; 102, Biophoto Associates/SCS; (INSET), Revel Pix LLC/SS; 103, Mega Pixel/SS; 104, Olga Popova/SS; 105, Laguna Design/SCS; (INSET), claffra/SS; **Chapter 5:** 106-107, MamiGibbs/Flickr RF/GI; 108, Jan Wolak/iS; 109, Scott Camazine/SCS; (INSET), nex999/SS; 110, Roger Harris/SCS; 111, NYPL/SCS/Photo Researchers RM/GI; 112, Ken Welsh/*/Design Pics/Corbis; 113, Steve Gschmeissner/SCS; (INSET), B Calkins/SS; 114, Quest/SCS; (INSET), percom/SS; 115, 3D4Medical/SCS; 116, piotr_pabijan/SS; 117, Cynthia Turner; 118, Zephyr/SCS; (INSET), Jorge Nunes/SS.com; 119, Andrew Rich/iS; 120, Carol and Mike Werner/SCS; 121, Susumu Nishinaga/SCS; (INSET), Gelpi JM/SS; 122, Jupiterimages/Photolibrary RM/GI; 123, Susumu Nishinaga/SCS; 124, eldemir/iS; 125, Cynthia Turner; 126, David Marchal/SCS; 127, maximino/SS; 128, Eye of Science/SCS; 129, Dorling Kindersley/Vetta/GI; 130, Warrick G./SCS; 131, Jovanka Novakovic/iS; **Chapter 6:** 132-133, Image Source/Alamy; 134, Zephyr/SPL//SCS; 135, Viktoriya/SS; 136, pixologicstudio/iS; (INSET), Dorling Kindersley/GI; 138, Wikipedia; 139, Cynthia Turner; 140, Maya2008/SS; 141, Kondor83/SS; 142, martan/SS; 143, Mike Agliolo/SCS; 144, Spencer Sutton/SCS; 145, Tim Vernon/SPL//SCS; 146, NYPL/SCS/Photo Researchers RM/GI; 147, Sebastian Kaulitzki/SS; (INSET), Evan Oto/SCS; 148, (INSET), Sebalos/iS; 149, Wolfgang Lienbacher/iS; 150, Fredrik Nyman/Johner Images/GI; 151, Jennifer Boggs/Amy Paliwoda/Blend Images RM/GI; 152, Niels Laan/E+/GI; (INSET), vitalytitov/iS; 153, Petra Wegner/Alamy; 154, Mark Harmel/SCS; 155, Image Source/Digital Vision/GI; 156, Tom Merton/OJO Images RF/GI; 157, MarkSwallow/iS; **Chapter 7:** 158-159, Holger Leue/Lonely Planet Images/GI; 160, Fort Worth Star-Telegram/MCT via GI; 161, Cimmerian/Vetta/GI; (INSET), irfanazam/SS; 162, Cynthia Turner; (INSET), samer chand/iS; 163 (INSET), cobalt88/SS; 164, MedicalRF/SCS; 165, John Scott/E+/GI; (INSET), Gaertner/Alamy; 166 (UP), Rachael Hamm; (LO), Public Domain; 167, bgblue/iS/GI; (LO), Heritage Image Partnership Ltd/Alamy; 168, Steve Gschmeissner/SCS; 169, Cynthia Turner; 170, J. Bavosi/SCS; 171, Louie Psihoyos/Corbis; 172, keith morris/Alamy; 173, SPL/SCS; (INSET), Olaf Speier/SS; 174, Holly Wilmeth/GI; 175, s7chvetik/SS; 176 (UP), reptiles4all/SS; (LO), Brian J. Skerry/National Geographic Creative; 177 (UP), Brian J. Skerry/National Geographic Creative; (LO), Kichigin/SS; **Chapter 8:** 178-179, Leren Lu/Taxi Japan/GI; 180, somersault1824/SS; 181, vitstudio/SS; 182, Christian Darkin/SCS; 183, Christine Caldwell/Photolibrary RM/GI; 184, Marcos Paternoster/E+/GI; 185, Jellyfish Pictures/SCS; 186, Matthew Rakola; 187, Gosia Biernikiewicz/iS; 188, andipantz/iS; 189, Darryl Vest/SS; 190, AE Pictures Inc./Photodisc/GI; 191, Sonja Foos/SS; 192, Cristian Baitg/iS; 193, Purestock/GI; 194, Sappington Todd/BloomImage RF/GI; (INSET), Sebastian Radu/iS; 195, nycshooter/E+/GI; 197 (UPLE), Mike Kemp/Blend Images/GI; (UP CTR), Regina Belen; (UPRT), Alina Solovyova-Vincent/E+/GI; (LOLE), Design Pics Inc./Alamy; (LOCTR), Spike Mafford/Photodisc Red/GI; (LORT), Kali Nine LLC/GI; **Chapter 9:** 198-197, StockbrokerXtra/Alamy; 200, josef volavka/E+/GI; 201, Cynthia Turner; 202, Eraxion/iS; 202 (INSET A), Dimarion/SS; (INSET B), Wikipedia; (INSET C), Wikipedia; (INSET), iLexx/iS; 203, Nina Aldin Thune/Wikipedia; 204, Wikipedia; 205, Chris Cooper-Smith/Alamy; 206, Juergen Berger/SCS; (INSET), Dr. Jack Bostrack/Visuals Unlimited/Corbis; 207, Suzanne Tucker/SS; 208, Alexander Raths/SS; 209, Eraxion/iS; (INSET), Steve Gschmeissner/SCS; 210, James King-Holmes/SCS; (INSET), Hong Vo/SS; 211, NatalieJean/SS; 212 (LE), SPL/SCS; (RT), Bettmann/Corbis; 213 (UPLE), Michal Kowalski/SS; (UPRT), CDC/Wikipedia; (LOLE), catwalker/SS; (LORT), Everett Collection Inc/Alamy; 214, Ilene MacDonald/Alamy; (INSET), USDA; 215, Michael Piazza; 216, Henry Westheim Photography/Alamy; 217, David Deas/DK Stock/GI; (INSET), Christopher Futcher/GI; **Chapter 10:** 218-219, Michael Svoboda/iS; 220, Martin Cleaver/AP Images; 221, Eric_Schroeder/iS; 222, Adam Kazmierski/GI; 223, 4X-image/iS; 224, Jason Patrick Ross/iS; 225, Noah Berger/Bloomberg via GI; 226 (INSET), Kenneth Garrett/National Geographic Creative; 226, Brandi Simons/GI; 227, Digital Beach Media/Rex/REX USA; 228, Jose Luis Magana/Reuters; 229, Reuters Photographer/Reuters; (INSET), aastock/SS; 230, Stegerphoto/Photolibrary RM/GI; 231, Lori Epstein/National Geographic Creative; 232, Frank Augstein/AP Images; 233, Robert Clark/National Geographic Creative; (INSET), Adil Delawalla; 234, doublerobotics.com; (INSET), Helen Neafsey/Greenwich Time/AP Images; 235, courtesy howwemontessori.com; 236, Andrew Federman; 237, Aude Guerrucci-Pool//GI; **Body Atlas:** 238-239, Cynthia Turner; 240, Cynthia Turner; 241, Mehau Kulyk/SCS; 242 (LE), Brand X/GI; 242 (RT), Cynthia Turner; 243, Roger Harris/SCS; 244, Cynthia Turner; 245 (UP), Cynthia Turner; (LO), Dorling Kindersley/GI; 246, Cynthia Turner; 247, BSIP/SCS; 248, Cynthia Turner; 249, Springer Medizin/SCS; 250 (RT), Cynthia Turner; (LE), Jellyfish Pictures/SCS; 251, BSIP/SCS; 252 (RT), Cynthia Turner; (LE), David Mack/SCS; 253, BSIP/SCS; 254 (RT), Cynthia Turner; (LE), Ilene MacDonald/Alamy; 255, MedicalRF/SCS; 256 (RT), Cynthia Turner; (LE), joebelanger/iS; 257, BSIP/SCS; 258, Cynthia Turner; 259, Stocktrek Images/GI; 260, Cynthia Turner; 261, J. Bavosi/SCS; **End matter:** 262 (UP), Brand X/GI; (LO), Markus Gann/SS; 263 (UP), Sebastian Kaulitzki/SS; (LOLE), Nerthuz/SS; (LORT), Cynthia Turner; 264 (UP), Friedrich Saurer/SCS; (LO), Cynthia Turner; 265, Gustoimages/SCS

CREDITS

The Publisher would like to thank Tammatha O'Brien at the University of Maryland, College Park's College of Computer, Mathematical, and Natural Sciences for generously taking the time to review this book from start to finish. The publisher would also like to thank Reid Compton, director of the University of Maryland's College of Computer, Mathematical, and Natural Sciences, and Raymond St. Leger, professor of molecular and cellular biology at the University of Maryland, College Park, for their generous input.

For my husband, Tony, who provides endless support. Thanks for all the salads. —CW

My profound thanks to Priyanka Lamichhane Sherman and Susan Bishansky for their essential guidance and support. —JA

I would like to thank Yasir Al-Hassani for his gracious assistance. —TO

The National Geographic Society is one of the world's largest nonprofit scientific and educational organizations. Founded in 1888 to "increase and diffuse geographic knowledge," the Society's mission is to inspire people to care about the planet. It reaches more than 400 million people worldwide each month through its official journal, *National Geographic,* and other magazines; National Geographic Channel; television documentaries; music; radio; films; books; DVDs; maps; exhibitions; live events; school publishing programs; interactive media; and merchandise. National Geographic has funded more than 10,000 scientific research, conservation, and exploration projects and supports an education program promoting geographic literacy.

For more information, please visit nationalgeographic.com, call 1-800-NGS LINE (647-5463), or write to the following address:
National Geographic Society
1145 17th Street N.W.
Washington, D.C. 20036-4688 U.S.A.

Visit us online at nationalgeographic.com/books

For librarians and teachers: ngchildrensbooks.org

More for kids from National Geographic:
kids.nationalgeographic.com

For information about special discounts for bulk purchases, please contact National Geographic Books Special Sales:
ngspecsales@ngs.org

For rights or permissions inquiries, please contact National Geographic Books Subsidiary Rights: ngbookrights@ngs.org

Hardcover ISBN: 978-1-4263-1721-7
Reinforced library edition ISBN: 978-1-4263-1722-4
UK ISBN: 978-1-4263-2013-2

Printed in China
14/RRDHN/1

EVER HEARD THE EXPRESSION "WALKING ON EGGSHELLS"? C'MON, TRY THIS!

Eggshells are specially made to protect what's inside—and so are egg cartons. See how much they can take!

REACTIONS

WALKING ON EGGS

Distribute your weight evenly ... then wait.

CONCEPTS
WEIGHT DISTRIBUTION AND DYNAMICS, PACKAGING, CUSHIONING

HOW LONG IT TAKES
one hour

WHAT YOU NEED
at least four one-dozen cartons of eggs (the cartons preferably made of varied materials: cardboard, plastic, Styrofoam)
a curb or low stool
your bare feet
optional: crutches, a cane, a railing, a staircase with a banister

Do you feel like you're walking on eggshells around us? You could be. Eggshells are specially made to protect what's inside—and so are egg cartons. See how much pressure they can take.

98 TRY THIS!

WHAT TO DO

1 HERE'S THE IDEAL setup; try to replicate it or to create a similar situation.

A porch stoop with a railing on each side. Place the open egg carton on the sidewalk and stand on the lowest step. Holding the railings, gently place your bare feet atop the eggs. Carefully shift your weight until you are standing squarely on top of the eggs, then let go of the railings.

2 REPEAT WITH the other two boxes of eggs, being careful to do it the same way each time.

WHAT TO EXPECT You are highly likely to break or crack some eggs, but one package type may triumph over the others in terms of cushioning effect.

WHAT'S HAPPENING? Different materials respond in various degrees to the weight of your body atop the eggs.

QUESTION THIS!

• What would happen if you closed the cover of the egg carton before standing on it?

• How well would the box cushion the eggs if you just jumped on them or stood on them without taking the trouble to distribute your weight evenly?

• Does it make a difference whether the smaller ends of the eggs are turned up or down?

• How would you design an egg box that would do a better job of cushioning the eggs?

"Cracks are forming!"
—Dylan

TRY THIS! 99

© 2014 National Geographic Society

WARNING
Better check with mom or dad before raiding the fridge! And if you need some recipes for any broken eggs, find them in the *National Geographic Kids Cookbook!*

From toothbrush robots to exploding soda bottles, *Try This!* is packed with 50 cool science experiments that will knock your socks off, using materials you probably have at home! TRY them all—you'll have a BLAST!